Analogy and Philosophical Language

Analogy and Philosophical Language

by David Burrell, C.S.C.

New Haven and London   Yale University Press

1973

Published with assistance from

Designed by John O. C. McCrillis
and set in Times Roman type.
Printed in the United States of America by
Vail-Ballou Press, Inc. Binghamton, N.Y.

Published in Great Britain, Europe, and Africa by
Yale University Press, Ltd., London.
Distributed in Canada by McGill-Queen's University
Press, Montreal; in Latin America by Kaiman & Polon,
Inc., New York City; in Australasia and Southeast
Asia by John Wiley & Sons Australasia Pty. Ltd.,
Sydney; in India by UBS Publishers' Distributors Pvt.,
Ltd., Delhi; in Japan by John Weatherhill, Inc., Tokyo.

To my parents

Contents

Preface ix

Introduction 1

Part One: From Counterclaims to a Position 7
   1. What Analogy Is and Why 9
   2. What Analogy Might Be 21

Part Two: Origins of the Question in Classical
           Philosophy 35
   3. Plato: Inquiry as Dialectic 37
   4. Aristotle: Inquiry and Its Method 68

Part Three: Contrasting Medieval Positions 93
   5. John Duns Scotus: The Univocity of Analogous
      Terms 95
   6. Thomas Aquinas: Analogical Usage and
      Judgment 119
   7. Contrasting Aquinas and Scotus 171
   8. Review of Philosophical Usage 194

Part Four: A Proposed Account 213
   9. A Proposed Account 215
   10. Analogy, Metaphor, and Models 252
   11. Conclusion: Analogies in Use 264

Index 269

Preface

The most useful and available key to someone's position lies in the expressions he is prepared to make his own. Language clearly reflects the bearings we have taken as well as it reveals how aware we are that we have taken them. The language he uses not only shows us where someone stands but also lets us in on the extent to which he understands where he stands. The difference between a high or low degree of self-awareness can be measured rather accurately by the amount of jargon or cliché a man allows himself.

And if the expressions we are prepared to utter are so revealing about our position in the world, perhaps the language we use can also reveal some basic facts about the world itself—or the world-as-we-most-basically-see-it. Language would then prove a valuable key to that style of question long called metaphysical. In fact, the very structure of our language—the way we say whatever it is we say—has long been recognized to be the most available if not the only way of adjudicating questions in metaphysics. Another look at Aristotle with this in mind shows how thoroughly he relied upon a native feel for language, and how much he based upon it.

This book is an attempt to follow out some of the clues that language gives us about the world, specifically those offered by a privileged set of expressions: analogous terms. In following the argument we are led through the ways in which four eminent figures tried to explain or explain away the fact that we need to have recourse to expressions like 'simple', 'order', 'good', 'fruitful', and countless others. What sets these expressions apart is their resistance to any single formula to convey their meaning, combined with our penchant to use them in diverse situations to serve our shared purposes.

Aristotle publicized the usage by giving it a name: analogous. But Plato had already provided the basis for Aristotle's logical analysis by isolating certain expressions as worthy of a special type of inquiry called *dialectic*. The expressions Plato examined were invariably linked to common and critical human concerns —the sorts of things Socrates cared about. Aristotle went further to link this sort of expression with everything that is by noting how 'to be' functions analogously in its various forms.

Aquinas put the semantics of Aristotle which he had at his disposal to quite sophisticated use in trying to explain how it is that man can speak intelligently of his God. John Duns Scotus, however, found this enterprise too sophisticated. In the interest of common sense and a simplified semantics, he elaborated a way of explaining how it is that we talk the way we must about God, the world, and many things important to us, without giving any lasting credit to analogous expression.

So Scotus enters as an antiwitness, to show the results of an operating method which denies that language really functions in any revelatory way. The way we speak is one thing, but the way things are is another. The clash between Scotus and Aquinas dramatizes what happens when two thinkers are at odds on basic ways of proceedings. By bringing the conflict into the light, how-ever, many implications of my original suspicion come more clearly into focus. The role of language and especially of anal-logous language in shaping and giving voice to our basic view of the world becomes more and more explicit. The precise roles analogous language plays are elucidated by the tools of con-temporary logic and semantics. The result, I hope, will be a firmer trust in the ability we have to use our language, and the power as well as the limitations of using in a discriminating fashion the language we cannot help but employ.

So the results are quite far-reaching yet surprisingly simple. And they have the advantage of helping us to see something of the same power and simplicity in the language which responsible philosophers are wont to use. In this respect the conclusion con-trasts with the somewhat technical opening chapters where re-cent as well as venerable theories about analogy are examined, then in part discarded and in part put to use, so that we can go on with the historical study and the systematic analysis. The conclusion culminates both historical study and systematic analysis, and that is the key to its power as well as its simplicity. For the great minds of the past can unravel many a knot for us today, provided we are willing to read them with sensitivity to their concerns and are yet unafraid to submit them to whatever critical skills we possess.

My gratitudes extend over time and space. They focus first on the teachers who provided models of a life of inquiry, notably R. Catesby Taliaferro and Bernard J. F. Lonergan. The first opened my eyes to the discipline of mathematics and the world of Plato, the second to the logical acumen of Thomas Aquinas and to a more ample vision of the role of intelligence in the world. This particular work owes its earliest form to Rulon Wells, whose experienced hand and firm mind helped to shape it.

Subsequently my own reflection on these topics has been nurtured and challenged by the community of inquirers gathered at Notre Dame, notably by Kenneth Sayre, Frederick Crosson, and Vaughn McKim. I am grateful to the University and to the philosophy faculty for a year's leave in 1968–69, when this version began to take its present form. The reader will join me in thanking Sister Elena Malits for the care with which she unscrambled many a tortuous expression. Without the encouragement of her painstaking work, these pages would probably not have become a book. To my friends who have sustained me so often, especially Michael Novak and David Tracy, as well as to my religious community which provides support in so many unobtrusive ways, I offer this small recompense.

In the final stages it was Mrs. Jane Isay who received the manuscript for the Yale University Press and proved generous in offering the editorial assistance I needed. And Mrs. Anne Wilde executed the detailed work of copyediting. Any remaining errors will be mine.

Chapter 5 is reprinted here, with the kind permission of the publisher, from *The Monist, 49,* no. 4, 1965.

D. B.

Notre Dame, Indiana
1972

Introduction

Being attentive to what we say becomes, before long, an unrelenting ideal. It is difficult to say what it exacts from us, for there seem to be no set tasks involved. What must I do to ensure that I say what I mean? What sort of an accomplishment is it to mean what I say? Questions like these bring the intractable faces of teaching and learning into relief and compose the relationship by calling our attention to its frustrating and mysterious features. It is something of a revelation to realize that all our dealings take place in a language.

It is startling enough to appreciate how much we rely on words—to reflect, for example, how much more handicapped are the deaf than the blind. But it becomes unnerving to realize that our nonverbal transactions become more comprehensible as we cast them in terms introduced to explain the working of words. That is, the more we become aware of language, the more we realize that it comprises both verbal and nonverbal behavior. In fact, we cannot understand the workings of one without the other. What they share is what 'language' comes to mean: a structured form of communicating. Structure becomes the key, then—as paying attention to language demands that we take more and more notice of form.

Philosophy as Apprenticeship

Recommendations like these resonate with classical overtones: "attention to form" is a fair capsule formulation of the philosophic attitude held by Socrates and shared by both Aristotle and Plato. Yet one must know their writings himself to taste the salt that is philosophy, for it quickly loses its savor when we are told about it. This very observation is but a variant on the original theme: there is no substitute for the original expression, so pay attention to it.

A gifted reporter may be able to render quite accurately what was said, so we may not be misinformed if we rely on reports but we shall most certainly be misled. For paying attention to what is said carries with it a sensitivity to how it is said and urges us to discern those clues that indicate what someone is up to. And to be up to philosophy is one thing while reporting on it is quite another. At least, that is what paying attention to philosophers' language brings home to us.

The difference between doing philosophy and telling about it provided the impetus for this study of philosophical language. A privileged set of expressions—so-called analogous ones—provides the material. The approach involves a sensitive yet analytic reading of certain key figures, as an exercise in recognizing when one is doing philosophy.

The more we become aware of the gap between doing philosophy and telling about it, the more studying philosophy takes on the character of an apprenticeship: learning how to do it. A simple enough approach, certainly, yet executing it leaves one quite vulnerable to criticism. For recovering philosophical figures as one's own demands that we recognize the work of the master and also exhibit a capacity to work in his spirit. We have not only to be able to read him in his terms but also to hear him in ours. And with centuries dividing us, this project becomes something of a hermeneutical feat.

The early steps in this inquiry had to be guided carefully by critical-historical studies lest I be tempted to read others merely in support of my own views. In fact, I consistently found historical and linguistic studies to be of more assistance than philosophical constructions. In fidelity to that indebtedness, I have tried to let the chosen philosopher's work display those features of reflective critical consciousness which might lead others to undertake a similar work. To the extent that this study also does philosophy in attempting to lay bare what it is to do it, I have systematically avoided construction in favor of critical reflection. This reflection has certain characteristics, it is true, which presumably could be gathered up and reported as my philosophical position. But certainly no philosophical reporter could be that interested in a handbook for apprentices.

If historical-critical studies provided the indispensable groundwork, it is the conviction of philosophy as doing philosophy and of studying philosophy as an apprenticeship that inspired me to use these studies and the men studied as I have. What Plato said was said many centuries ago, but to take up his writings as a way of learning how to deal with questions as alive today as then deliberately effects a certain contemporaneity by initiating a conversation with him. More is required, certainly, than the will to converse. But if historical and linguistic studies have accomplished their purpose, have they not effected in us a hermeneutical sense both wary enough and appreciative enough to learn from Plato, Aristotle, Aquinas, and Scotus in the ways I have suggested? Is not this quality of understanding precisely what scholarship of the historical-critical sort hopes to effect? The question, then, is not whether it is possible to apprentice oneself to Plato but whether this handbook helps or hinders the process.

THE GUIDANCE OF HEIDEGGER AND WITTGENSTEIN

If the extensive critical-historical work of the last half-century has brought figures out of the past to make them accessible, the questions I have put to them are inspired by the presence of two contemporary persons: Heidegger and Wittgenstein. The witness of these men has given me the courage to enter into dialogue with the past, for their lives of reflective inquiring testify that philosophy is an activity and that the skills required to do it and displayed in the doing of it seem little affected by time or the passage of time. In fact, the more we understand the activity of philosophy as a discipline, the less are we held by the prevailing picture of something past as passé.

If learning philosophy consists primarily in assuming viewpoints rather than accumulating them, then it becomes more a matter of recovering past figures than of building upon their results. To conceive of philosophical inquiry as yielding results seems, in fact, to convict oneself nicely of Heidegger's charge that philosophy has grown fat and "forgetful of being." In the measure that a philosophic tradition allowed itself to be conceived as a gradual accumulation of established positions, philosophy became something to be acquired. Acquiring it demanded some skills, certainly, but the discipline involved was subordinated to assimilating what one philosopher after another had said.

Working in quite different ways, Heidegger and Wittgenstein have shown that this model of progressive, accumulating knowledge betrays the very genius of philosophy and subverts its peculiar contribution. Socrates emerges as the prototype, yet the tradition continues to restage his trial. The fact that philosophers are well versed in terms borrowed from Socrates' own writings simply muddies the situation even more than it was for Athenians of his day. Philosophy has become, then, one of the major obstacles to philosophical reflection. By uttering the right words but failing to use them in *propria persona,* philosophy induces a kind of soporific amnesia bewitching us into forgetting our God-given task. That task is, of course, to do what Socrates did and to live as he lived. Beyond this dramatic ikon, Wittgenstein and Heidegger part company, but their aim is remarkably similar: to return language to its ordinary uses, to think being by allowing it room to speak.

What comes through more clearly in Wittgenstein is the discipline, the self-discipline, required to release ourselves from the pervasive bewitchment that language infected by academic philosophical concerns can work upon us. The frugal structure of the *Tractatus* bespeaks a discipline, and everything Wittgenstein undertook after returning to philosophy displayed that discipline by its relentless questioning form. This makes him much more useful to guide us than the enigmatic dark-saying manner of Heidegger.

In fact, one suspects that Heidegger is far less consistent than Wittgenstein, and that he tends toward espousing a posture that gives access to what he is—a position precariously close to a philosophy with results. All this is hard to assess, of course, and largely because of the dark-saying manner. Yet it is the manner which troubles one, for the consistency that his assertions exact is one reflected in the manner of doing what he says. In this respect I find Wittgenstein more often doing what Heidegger says one ought to be doing. Yet Heidegger's sayings can illuminate along the way, and they have quite unexpectedly illuminated me. So I wish to speak my gratitude to him now, though this may well be the final reference. For the guide throughout will be Wittgenstein, whose manner requires us to become more and more aware of what it is we are after, of how we are undertaking it, and of how little we can say of what it accomplishes for us and in us.

SHAPE OF THE ARGUMENT

By selecting a specific way of using language—analogously—I have inevitably associated myself with that philosophic tradition beholden to Aristotle. Yet by focusing attention on the uses of language, I have managed to avoid aligning myself with that tradition conceived as a body of doctrine. In fact, what turns up is more a way of doing philosophy than a set of conclusions, and the exercise of turning it up offers a way of getting at what any philosopher is doing. So this exercise itself is a bit of philosophy.

It must begin by examining certain attempts, classical and contemporary, to collate the ways we use analogical expressions into one theoretical mold. To examine these theories is to clear them out of the way so that we can learn to respect the different needs we have for employing expressions analogously. Is there anything, however, that allows us to single out analogous usage? The answer turns out to be yes and no. No one has succeeded in uniquely characterizing the many uses of language we can recognize to be analogous. Nor does it appear possible to formulate this usage in an algorithmic way. Yet we can be sensitized to recognize it.

Here we stumble over the inner connection between analogous use of language and doing philosophy. The fact that philosophers tend to have recourse to certain terms whose logic is clearly analogous, or to press less accepted expressions into analogous roles, is more than coincidental. The practice testifies to that feature which distinguished philosophy from theory construction, and links learning philosophy firmly with doing it. For theory construction demands that its key terms remain unambiguous. The formulation must stand still if it is to admit of multiple application. But analogous terms may usefully be described as "systematically ambiguous." It is as though one can never let them out of sight; one must always be molding them to serve one's purpose.

Attention to analogous usage, then, and the subsequent effort to pin it down, makes us more conscious of philosophy as an art than a science. Reading the works of classical philosophers with an eye and an ear for their ways of using language reveals their efforts in a new light. In this way an inquiry designed to analyze and to clarify analogical usage in philosophical writing became itself a philosophical exercise. Its aim: to free philosophy from certain theoretical pretensions to the yet higher role of a discipline and a way of life.

Part One

From Counterclaims to a Position

1. What Analogy Is and Why

Moving into the arena of analogous discourse is perilous because it admits of nearly universal interest yet has been especially claimed by a particular school. Generations of Thomists have subjected analogous usage to a painstaking analysis, but their collective impact has been unduly restricted by an excessively intramural cast. To quarrel with the detailed formulations of one or another Thomist would undermine my explicit intent: to liberate the entire discussion from the confinement of a particular school and articulate a more catholic interest. Yet the sheer body of Thomist writing demands attention. Fortunately, the received doctrine of analogy is fairly settled and can be roughly divided into formal analysis and metaphysical claims. I shall address both aspects of the doctrine in discussing what analogy is not, leaving the more subtle and engaging questions of Aquinas' own usage to the chapter devoted to him. (The hiatus between Thomistic doctrine and Aquinas' usage has been the subject of a number of recent monographs which I shall also review at that time.) This strategy will permit me to introduce and to examine other formal accounts of the way analogies function. For while these attempts bear little relation to Thomistic concerns, they share the Thomistic aspiration for a quasi-mathematical articulation of analogous usage.

A Formal Paradigm

The most common picture we have of the structure of analogous predication is the mathematical proportion, $a:b::c:d$. It was suggested by Aristotle (for the term he adopted, 'analogous', means 'proportional'), often used as an illustration by Aquinas, and erected into a quite canonical form by Aquinas' voluminous commentator, Cajetan. Before considering Cajetan's presentation, however, the most obvious fact about this schema is that it won't work. And since this is a common critique, it would seem politic to register my agreement with it from the outset.

9

Those who insist that analogy will not work are presumably directing their remarks against the schema of proportionality employed as a device for normalizing otherwise ambiguous usage. For unless there were question of a device, a kind of algorithm, it would be difficult to understand the claim that it does work. Various feats are claimed for this device. The most notable one makes it an engine of transcendent predication sensitive enough to maneuver between the twin threats of univocity and equivocity. The mathematical form of the account promises clarity, yet an accompanying commentary guides and tempers this expectation. Often enough the commentary asks what no schema can provide: insight. The resulting conflict upsets the original algorithmic expectations.

Thus 'good' said of a citizen and a train robbery is justified by recourse to the paradigm $a:b::c:d$—'good:citizen::good:robbery'—which reminds us strongly of $2:4::3:6$. Now the mathematical example is useful to clarify what language leaves ambiguous: $good_1$,—said of a citizen, must be distinguished from $good_2$, said of the robbery. For generally, if b differs from d, so must a from c if we are to preserve a proportion. Yet from this point on mathematical proportion ceases to be useful and becomes misleading. For ordered couples can be unequivocally expressed—in our case as $1:2$—and so form equalities: $2:4 = 3:6$. But all attempt to find an element (like the $1:2$) common to the ratios 'good:citizen' and 'good:robbery' have failed. Such efforts must fail since the very search for a schema to regularize the usage of terms like good sprang initially from want of a formula to express the conditions for their use. This failure to conform to an account which will not vary from one context to another is precisely what merits such terms being classified "systematically ambiguous" or "analogous." So the commentary must point out that the '::' relating $a:b$ with $c:d$ may not be interpreted as '=', and this discrepancy signals the limits of any promise of systematic clarity. Since we know how to operate with = but have no idea what to do with ::, the schema $a:b::c:d$ becomes itself an analogy, at once useful and misleading, for analogous usage.

The circularity, nevertheless, is vitiating only for those who make formal or systematic claims for the schema. In such cases "analogy" *will not work*. But once having made it, we see the limits of this retort. It is directed against a doctrine of analogy which courts systematic promise and offers the proportionality as a paradigm or normal form of analogous discourse. Should we, however, consider the schema rather as a model, looking to it more for illustration and understanding than for justification, we will no longer expect it to work in a systematic way. Yet it might nonetheless prove useful.

Of course, by invoking the schema as a model, we also open the way to different styles of "analogy." While a canonical form is by definition unique and looks quite definitive, we think more easily of alternative models. The project itself of putting ambiguities to work, however, seems to merit a single name. And 'analogy' has certainly come to be used in just this way: to refer to a project rather than a doctrine or canonized set of procedures. Harnessing ambiguities to systematic service requires a skill and a know-how that can be acquired only within a particular domain of discourse. Yet the very fruitfulness of the enterprise invites an investigation sensitive to the myriad ways we shape and use our language, while on the lookout for enough similarity to warrant the common name.

Cajetan: The Received Account

The theory I shall reject both as misleading and inadequate to its task dates from Cajetan's *De Nominum Analogia* (1498).[1] The aim of his monograph was to sort out from the writings of the master, Thomas Aquinas, the form of analogous usage proper to metaphysics and theology—a form that would allow us to justify the assertions made in these exalted domains. Cajetan found three styles of analogous usage which he dubbed "analogy of inequality, attribution, and proportionality" (*De Nominum,* n. 3). Proportionality he divides into *improper:* "when the common term has absolutely one formal meaning

1. Cajetan, *Scripta Philosophica: De Analogia Nominum,* ed. P. N. Zammit (Rome, 1952), n. 3.

which is realized in one of the analogates and predicated of the other by metaphor," and *proper:* "when the common term is predicated of both analogates . . . proportionately" (n. 25). In the first case, we might speak of fortune smiling upon us, quite conscious that 'smiling' has a proper usage which is here being extended to convey a particular point. In the second, we might call the heart the principle of life in an animal and the furnace the principle of heat in a house, for 'principle' is no more properly employed in one context than another. (The fact that neither phrase seems very appropriate is not particularly relevant here. The examples are Cajetan's, slightly modified to make the English somewhat less implausible.) An expression like principle, then, is properly metaphysical since it knows no privileged use and can be employed in contexts related proportionately one to another.

As an observation about usage and a criterion distinguishing certain expressions, Cajetan's remarks will prove most useful. But he claimed to have discovered in "proper proportionality" an instrument whereby "we might know the intrinsic entity, goodness, truth, etc. of things, which are not known from the other analogies" (n. 26). On the strength of this exclusive recommendation, proper proportionality has more recently been adopted as the normal form of metaphysical discourse about the "analogy of being" (Maritain, Anderson) and of statements about God (Penido). Indeed, even the writers dissenting from Cajetan have tended to assume his divisions, though perhaps only for purposes of discussion (Sylvester of Ferarra, Blanche, Simon), and most writing in the field concurs with his evaluations.

Recent critics, it is true, have challenged Cajetan's interpretation of Aquinas and his relative evaluation of the kinds of analogy. I shall call upon them in the discussion of Aquinas. Cajetan interests us here rather because of the dominant role he has played in philosophical and theological discussion of analogous usage, and for the type of claims he makes for properly proportional usage. For him and for the school he has inspired, this usage not only supplies a criterion for admissible expressions but also provides a method which the metaphysician and theologian might employ to justify their exalted use of quite ordinary expressions. Thus the universe and a substance may be said to be *one,* or God and Socrates *just.* To be sure, both types of statement call for a good deal of commentary. Most Thomist commentators, for example, feel that statements relying on an implicit comparison of God with man require an added premise explicitly avowing participation via creation.[2] The form of the added premise involves "analogy of attribution" in Cajetan's list. But it is still proportionality that apparently turns the trick and certifies certain expressions for responsible transempirical use.[3]

Yet proportionality is itself a bag of tricks. We have already glimpsed some of them in exposing the *a:b::c:d* scheme. A close scrutiny of Cajetan reveals a host more. Analogous terms are set off from univocal by the peculiar unity they exhibit. Categories like quantity and substance, for example, sort out predicates expressing quite distinct facts about things—'*x* is vast and sprawling', '*x* is a ranch house'. "Nevertheless," Cajetan will say, "they are the same in nature, not absolutely but proportionally, for the notion of one is proportionally the same as that of the other" (n. 65). They are "proportionally the same . . . in this that substance or quantity is apprehended as having a certain relationship to its own 'to be' (for it is in this that proportional similitude is found)" (n. 46).

Even categories so diverse and irreducible as substance and quantity then, can be considered as having something in common, if that something is not a thing but a proportion. "The very same thing which the analogous term predicates, say, what 'being' predicates of quantity, it also predicates proportionally of substance, and vice versa. For it is proportionally the selfsame thing which it posits in substance, and vice versa" (n. 66). Being, then, does not represent a single viewpoint; it does not con-

2. Hampus Lyttkens, *The Analogy between God and the World* (Uppsala, 1952), pp. 196, 254; Battista Mondin, *Principle of Analogy in Protestant and Catholic Theology* (The Hague, 1963), p. 70.

3. J. F. Anderson, *Bond of Being* (St. Louis, 1949).

vey a common concept, in Cajetan's terms, but rather many "significations in one word." Depending on the type, the "analogous term signifies the primary analogate distinctly and the others confusedly (attribution)" or is permitted to be "related indistinctly to all its significations (proportionality)" (n. 54). Yet even though "it is impossible to abstract from these many something which is absolutely one," even if we cannot pretend to a common concept, we still can and do use a single term like being (or principle). Cajetan allows us to do so on the strength of a similitude, but the "very similitude itself is only proportional, and its foundation is only proportionally one"; in this way "proportional similitude in its very nature includes . . . diversity" (nn. 48, 49).

Something is very wrong here, of course. Language is taking a holiday. If one needs to speak of a similitude, it had best be a single one and not a proportional one. For whether we think of a similitude as a kind of template or prefer to be guided by a careful use of language, the upshot will have to be something invariant, else why invoke the expression? Careful attention to language would note that 'x is similar to y' is an ellipsis which must furnish 'in respect z' on demand. Now the precise respect in which substantial and quantitative predicates are similar defies expression. This is indeed the entire thrust of Cajetan's work: they are similar in so far as each is related to its *to be* (*esse*).

But we possess no characterization of to be independent of relations such as these, distinct from ways of being. To say that the respect in which they are similar is itself proportional, where this cannot be specified, introduces an irremediable circularity into the use of 'similar'. What is really being said here is that two or more things are similar in similar respects; and when one asks how the respects are similar, one is told that such a question cannot be asked in this case. This is not an ordinary similarity but a proportional one, and irreducibly proportional so that the proportion cannot even be granted the relative invariance of a mathematical function, for that would introduce a sameness. But can we ask 'similar' or 'similitude' to be ready at our call when we have cut their moorings? Can we honestly invite a term like proportional to carry the burden of a new and unique usage when we have severed its mathematical spine? The respect in which one thing is similar to another may not always be specifiable, but this fact must be squarely faced. If it is glossed over, the role of a term like similitude becomes utterly gratuitous, and a term like proportional loses in the end that very specification which it promised at the outset.

Limits of Formal Analysis

To expose Cajetan's formal analysis in this way does not pretend, of course, to shatter the metaphysical pretensions of analogy. There are other and subtler ways than his of looking at these uses of language. The insistence that certain ways of speaking are peculiarly apt for metaphysics harkens back to Aquinas and is embedded in the Western philosophical tradition. If we are to take that tradition seriously, we must trace the preoccupation with language and expression from Plato through Aristotle to the medieval idiom. That will be the burden of the chapters following. At this point, however, it may prove useful to examine two recent attempts to salvage Cajetan's formal analysis, along with an independent formal account offered in the context of scientific theories. After we have seen the limits of formal analysis in treating analogous uses of language, we can consider in Chapter 2 certain contemporary styles of thought that suggest an advantageous viewpoint from which to consider more traditional accounts.

A formal account of Aquinas' usage, following the accepted interpretation of Cajetan, has been offered by I. M. Bochenski and elaborated by James Ross.[4] I have already questioned the plausibility of Catejan's interpretation of Aquinas, but suppressing these doubts for the moment, I may ask what Bochenski

---

4. I. M. Bochenski, "On Analogy," *Thomist* 11 (1948) 424–47, reprinted and corrected in A. Menne (ed.), *Logico-Philosophical Studies* (Dordrecht, 1962); James F. Ross, "Analogy as a Rule of Meaning for Religious Language," *Inter. Phil. Quar.* 1 (1961) 468–502, and "Logic of Analogy," ibid., 2 (1962) 633–42, 658–62.

and Ross contribute to an ongoing inquiry. Bochenski's proposal turns on the fact that any definition of properly analogous terms must be schematic. We say that x is good when it fulfills its nature, achieves its purpose. Hence there can be no "content" common to the various uses because any phrase that might substitute for 'good' contains analogous terms itself. What is common then can only be the *schema,* and schemata are designedly "empty of content," reflecting only what can remain invariant from one context to another, the formal properties of logic.[5] We know certain of these properties for relations: thus '. . . precedes . . .' is assymmetrical, transitive, and nonreflexive, while '. . . is identical with . . .' is symmetrical, transitive, and reflexive. But even if 'good' be construed as a relational predicate, '. . . is good for . . .'—which cannot reflect the total range of our usage, as anti-utilitarian arguments have shown—the most we could know would be that none of the three properties necessary holds for it. (For grass is not always good for grass [reflexive], and if grass is good for cows, cows need not be said to be good for grass [symmetrical], and finally there might well be certain flora good for cows which would not be good for men, though cows be good for men [transitive].) This fact has elicited the criticism that Bochenski's ingenious scheme does not tell us very much and hardly explains our usage, even though it comprehends clearly the terms of the problem: analogous usage can presume no "common content."

In the face of such a critique, Ross amended Bochenski's proposal to read: "the common formal properties with respect to a formal or *merely linguistic* set of axioms." The notion of formal property then opens to embrace "semantical" as well as syntactical properties.[6] What are these properties, these axioms? Ross admits that he is not "really sure what [they] would be like," and further concedes (p. 497) that

the proposal that relations have common properties with respect to linguistic axioms which are presupposed by im-

5. Bochenski, pp. 442–44.
6. Ross, "Analogy," p. 495, emphasis added.

plicit language rules governing the employment of the analogous term, is very similar to St. Thomas' assumption that if the relations are sufficiently similar we will recognize that fact and use the same term to signify two relations. One need not formulate a satisfactory criterion of similarity of relations in order to *employ* the rule of analogy (but only to explain them fully); one need only recognize such similarities when confronted with them or with evidence for them.[7]

This concession moves Ross mightily toward the style of account I shall be promoting, a style strongly reminiscent of Wittgenstein. But what happened to the "common formal properties"? They seem to have been quietly eliminated by concession and qualification and, if I would reintroduce them, it must be done deliberately by way of "presupposition." Thus the ability to recognize similarities presupposes common formal properties. But if the most one can say of such properties is that they amount to "recognizing similarities when [we are] confronted with them," one has simply rephrased the problem. Bochenski cannot be improved in this direction without losing the force of his proposal. For its force derived from formal logic, which promised an unequivocal criterion of similar usage devoid of representational content. When the axiom base is broadened from "formal" to "merely linguistic," the common properties fan out from the syntactical ones we know to semantic ones we do not, and the clarity promised by the "common formal property" solution is quite effectively sacrificed.

It was this very clarity of course that made Bochenski's proposal inadequate to its task, but if one seeks to modify it in the direction of linguistic adequacy, one can no longer trade on the promise of formal clarity. (I would suspect, as well, that the set of linguistic axioms of which Ross speaks would have to include some on usage, the most conspicuous dividing line between artificial, or formal, and natural languages. And such axioms, incorporating point and purpose, would need others to

7. Ross, "Logic," p. 660.

account for adjudicating between purposes. The formulation of such axioms would presumably contain the appraisal terms I have singled out as paradigms of "analogy." But it is not necessary to discover circularity in so telling a form: the weakness indicated above will suffice.) This critique gains strength as soon as Ross begins to speak of a criterion of *similarity*. Bochenski spoke of *isomorphy*, which implies "the identity of a series of formal properties of the relations involved".[8] Isomorphy is clearly a formal notion, and attempts to explain similarity therefrom have proved abortive.[9]

Mary Hesse [10] has turned to higher algebra to give an account of "degrees of analogy." She proposes an ingenious employment of lattice theory to discover an algorithm to yield a fourth term in the presence of three (pp. 79–100). Her concern to systematize analogy springs from a well-documented conviction of the role that models and analogies play in scientific theory, coupled with the desire to grant them a more trustworthy status than the "psychology of discovery" (p. 79). Hesse applies lattice theory to cross-generic classification (as Aristotle suggested in *Parts of Animals*, 645b6 sq) and to tracing analogies among words—in fact, nouns. The analysis is structural, with no mention of purpose, though the difference of degrees of analogy makes use of *"relevant* joins" among the qualities that form the sets (p. 89). This suggests a degree of circularity in the account, since the number of terms possessed in common tells no more about *relevance* than the number of words under an item in Roget measures its generality (p. 99). Thus if one is told how to calculate the "dimension interval," this may well not suffice to reckon the "degree of analogy," which is said to vary with the dimension interval between terms and their relevant joins (pp. 86, 89). This weakness appears to endanger even Hesse's use of analogy, for nothing in her program is able to

---

8. Ross, Analogy," p. 497; "Logic," p. 660; Bochenski, p. 444.
9. Cf. L. Wittgenstein, *Philosophical Investigations* (Oxford, 1953), ##66–67; W. V. O. Quine, *From a Logical Point of View* (Cambridge, Mass., 1953), pp. 60–64.
10. "On Defining Analogy," *Proc. Aris. Soc.* 60 (1959–60).

predict which analogies will prove suggestive and fruitful, the very functions thought integral to their role in science.[11]

But a stipulation made early in her paper concerns me more. Hesse considers it to be "possible without serious loss of generality to suppose that all the classes defined . . . have one property in common." She recognizes that this assumption is equivalent to requiring the initial individuals to be chosen out of the world in virtue of some common property, noting that "we are not usually in practice interested in classifications where this is not the case" (p. 84). No doubt it is true of analogical classifying, but traditionally this function has represented only a small segment of the uses of analogy. Yet it is evident that this stipulation is central to the lattice-theory proposal. Indeed without such a stipulation we would be deprived of the additive property for any two sets, since classes are so defined that "the sum of two classes is not a class unless their intersection is non-empty" (p. 83). We have seen, however, that the most promising of the traditional statements on "analogy" emphatically deny the presence of a single common property, for the usage they sought to explain could not be restricted by a "something common" clause. We need not imply that God and Socrates share any features when we call them both just. If we could find anything identifiably common, analogy would prove superfluous. So the terms of Hesse's proposal, while ingenious, make it impossible for it to come to grips with traditional demands on analogy and limit its usefulness to the area of analogical classification. Yet even here the difficulties associated with relevant joins and fruitful analogies remain unresolved. We are reminded of Plato's insistence that no algorithmic technique for bipartite division could ever be devised (Plt 263a, 286d).

As we have seen by comparing Ross with Bochenski and in noting the crucial concession Hesse was forced to make to the internal demands of lattice theory, formal attempts to explain

11. Cf. N. R. Hanson, *Patterns of Discovery* (Cambridge, 1958), passim; J. J. C. Smart, "Theory Construction," in A. Flew (ed.), *Language and Logic*, 2nd ser. (Oxford, 1953), pp. 222–42; Mary Hesse, *Science and Human Imagination* (New York, 1955).

analogous usage seem self-defeating. They shunt from the formally correct but too narrowly stipulative to a more adequate but formally less acceptable scheme. The very recurrence of this pattern is revealing. Analogy, it seems, is closely linked to a purposive use of language. One of the serviceable features of analogous terms is their adaptability to diverse contexts. Yet the language we use to express our judgment about entire frameworks, and their adequacy to the more comprehensive purposes of inquiry, is also markedly analogical. Hence a formal characterization seems impossible in principle since formal logic constructs languages and tests their consistency but does not appraise them with respect to extralogical purposes.

This thesis is corroborated by Leo Apostel, in a careful discussion of the role of models in science.[12] Noting how scientific models are purpose-oriented so that their role may well modify the structure originally proposed, he does not fail to remark that isomorphy is inadequate to explain this role. Even scale models must be carefully weighed lest the change in scale alter relevant characteristics of the original (pp. 135–38). He proposes a modified "approximate isomorphism" relation, appropriately mathematicized in terms of neighborhoods (pp. 142–52). But *approximate* is a context-variable notion, depending on the purpose to be achieved. It is impervious to formal treatment except of the most schematic kind. So to speak of approximate isomorphism is to take what the substantive promises and cancel it with the qualifier. This would seem to be the destiny of any purely formal attempt to explain analogous usage.

12. "Towards the Formal Study of Model in Non-Formal Sciences," *Synthèse* 12 (1960) 125–61.

2. What Analogy Might Be

We have seen how the *a:b::c:d* scheme fails to supply or exhibit the proportional unity for which Cajetan's analysis of analogous usage called. If my subsequent reasoning was accurate, any attempt at formal analysis requires a kind of "common univocal core" which the best of traditional analysis has always denied to analogous expressions. Indeed Cajetan's very attempt to circumvent this by an interlocking use of proportions shows how well he appreciated the issues involved. His failure is a warning to philosophical analysis to sharpen its tools.

Yet if there is nothing in the *a:b::c:d* scheme that empowers it to justify these uses of language in an analytical fashion, it might be used as a criterion allowing us to distinguish expressions apt for use in metaphysical or theological assertions. If this is the case, however, there is a prior question: What characteristics do such expressions have that allow them to be used and properly used in these unusual contexts? Can we discover a set of terms whose ordinary usage suggests they might prove faithful in guiding us into less-charted territory? And if we succeed in identifying these terms, what can we learn of their status? Are they dispensable or integral to language as we know it? Even if it might prove difficult to answer this question directly, can we find indications to incline us strongly one way or another?

Should a certain class of terms prove indispensable to language, the characteristics they exhibit would be considered indigenous to the linguistic enterprise. Metaphysical or theological discourse would then show itself to be a quite natural development of ordinary usage. Whatever pecularities might be exhibited in these remote areas would already have been adumbrated in the "ordinary" behavior of the terms employed there. We would then be asked not so much to justify the move to a metaphysical order as to show, by a collation of ordinary uses embodying the same expressions, that there is hardly a "move" at all. If much of our ordinary usage is already quite "extended," it becomes superfluous to seek a justification of extended usage generally. But how can we characterize these key expressions? And why is a division between extended and normal usage inadequate?

The philosophic spokesmen of the Greek and medieval traditions explicitly recognized analogous usage as distinctive and attempted to explain why we are forced to have recourse to it. Their capacity for recognition, we shall see, outstripped their ability to account, leaving us with a set of problems sensitively delineated but still quite unresolved. Their linguistic sophistication encourages us to adopt their list of recognizably analogous terms, the so-called transcendentals: 'one', 'same', 'good', 'true', as a paradigm class. Many other expressions may qualify as analogous, but these will always form the most perspicuous subset. They mean different things in different contexts, yet this cannot be the whole story. The various meanings of terms like one and good are not unrelated, not *simply* different, as with the many senses of 'pen'. In the case of analogous expressions, then, the use of the same term is not merely arbitrary, so that another might do the job as well.

I am veering close to the overall question of calling different sorts of things by the same name. This is the thorny issue of general terms, usually misleadingly dubbed the "problem of universals." Of necessity, then, my first tactic must be to distinguish analogous expressions from generic ones. But we shall soon see that the attitude taken toward the meaning of general terms will normally strongly influence one's conception of analogous usage. If the formation of general terms is regarded as unproblematic and normal, then analogous usage appears as an extension requiring explicit justification. Aristotle's division of terms into univocal or equivocal tends to support this view. John Austin complains, "All that is to be found in traditional Logics is the mention that there are, besides univocal and equivocal words, 'also analogous words': which, without further explanation, is used to lump together all cases where a word has not always absolutely the same meaning, nor several absolutely different meanings." [1]

1. J. L. Austin, *Philosophical Papers* (Oxford, 1961), p. 42.

If on the other hand one is sensitized to the latent metaphor so prevalent in generic expressions and to the difficulty of finding a determinate set of criteria even for univocal usage, analogous expressions appear more acceptable and less in need of supplying their credentials. Austin introduces one discussion of analogous terms precisely to impress upon nominalists how vacuous a criterion of generic usage similarity turns out to be (p. 39). And when we add to these observations the fact that ordinary usage freely employs terms generally recognized to be analogous, the distinction between ordinary and extended usage blurs considerably. And when that distinction blurs, one falters in confidently legislating the limits of significant speech.

A preliminary distinction. Nonetheless we must distinguish, at least preliminarily, analogous from generic usage. Taking the transcendentals as prime examples, we may say that analogous expressions exhibit: (1) a resistance to definition and to an account that will not vary from one context to another; yet (2) a propensity to employment in diverse contexts in spite of the acknowledged differences in meaning. Both features are necessary, but the second will turn out to be the more important. The remarks just made suggest that even generic expressions may not always be amenable to definition. But for all their vagueness and "open texture," the characteristic role and utility of general terms demand that they function within a congenial context unless forcibly and appositely removed, as in metaphor.

In fact, the recognition of vagueness in generic usage, threatening as it appears to this initial distinction, cannot but contribute to my general aim. For by undermining the mystique of definition as a search for an underlying common element, it helps reduce the demand for locating a core of meaning common to the varied uses of an analogous term. What *is* common to these diverse yet not unrelated uses seems to lie more on the side of intent. And this is related to the essential difference between generic and analogous usage: the *need* to use certain expressions in widely diverse contexts, coupled with the fact that we do so use them and use them freely. As may be suspected, the need will turn out to be more significant than the fact, though the facts confirm that the need is not esoteric but indigenous.

LINGUISTIC: THE ROLE OF PARADOX

Because analogous usage is queer usage, we might expect philosophers taken up with language to be fascinated by it, much as the strange and bizarre makes news. The following brief samples suggest an early attitude toward it. The tone of their treatment differs as they are struck by the oddity of such discourse or by its expediency. Margaret MacDonald, for example, inveighed against an uncontrolled extrapolation; she focuses on the danger of analogies that can lead to a philosophical jargon thoroughly removed from ordinary empirical usage, as in "prime matter." [2] And the danger is twofold. The subject/predicate paradigm is systematically extended from 'that man is gentle' to 'that is a man' to yield an "ultimate subject of predication." Then reference is made to that ultimate subject as though its claims upon us were parallel to that of any empirical individual, quite forgetting the subject's origin in an (analogical) extrapolation of a form of ordinary discourse. This second danger is confirmed only when a philosopher, being advised of it, insists that there is not an ordinary subject in this case but an ultimate one. The expressions used to refer to it become part of a metaphysical language, and failure to recognize the "existence" of such a subject amounts to refusing to admit a "metaphysical order." (Not every philosopher, of course, will retort in this way; but we shall see that Scotus did and doubtless we know others who would. Their presence gives bite to this negative function of language analysis.)

Another tack is available, however. It is illustrated in John Wisdom's *Philosophy and Psychoanalysis,*[3] roughly contempo-

2. "Philosopher's Use of Analogy," in A. Flew (ed.), *Language and Logic,* 1st ser. (Oxford, 1951), pp. 80–100. For a detailed if not exhaustive treatment of the "prime matter" issue, cf. Milton Fisk, "Prime Matter and Unqualified Change," in E. McMullin (ed.), *Concept of Matter* (Notre Dame, 1963).

3. New York, 1953.

rary with MacDonald's writings. Wisdom firmly grasps the cutting edge of the critique from oddity. He feels its force yet deflects its intent, for he finds this doubly dangerous employment of language useful. At least he is anxious to show how it can be useful, without questioning for a moment that it may also be objectionable and even yield falsehood.

A falsehood can often succeed in drawing our attention to a likeness or to an unlikeliness concealed by ordinary parlance and can show up continuity and difference in a novel way (Wisdom, pp. 48–50). The example Wisdom chooses is the bald contention: "The laws of mathematics and logic are really rules of grammar." This, he concedes, is obviously not true. Yet the statement is more illuminating than the tailor-made "mathematical propositions are necessary but synthetic." For though this latter may be true, it stands isolated, incapable of exercising the properly philosophical role of calling attention to the relations between different styles of inquiry (pp. 37, 39, 42). The original example, on the other hand, intimates an "unlikeness to the laws of hydraulics," and a "likeness but not an exact likeness to the functioning of rules." And this is necessary to offset the continuity and difference suggested by speaking of *"laws* of mathematics and logic" in the first place—a usage urged by the omnipresent demand of simplicity for common grouping.

It is telling to notice the different conceptions of language operating in MacDonald's and Wisdom's accounts. MacDonald's model, though ever so accommodating to common usage, is nonetheless quasi-scientific: ordinary language offers a kind of normal form. Wisdom's, on the contrary, is dramatic. The control is not usage so much as usefulness—"not the merely unusual but the pointless" becomes suspect (p. 43). And for those untruths which make a point, "the curious thing is that their philosophical usefulness depends upon their paradoxicalness and thus upon their falsehood" (p. 50). So not just any falsehood will do; it must have a point, and the most pointed form we know is paradox. Enter Wisdom's flair for drama: "thus the metaphysical paradoxes appear no longer as crude falsehoods about how language is actually used, but as penetrating suggestions as to how it might be used so as to reveal what, by the actual use of language, is hidden." (p. 100). This is more poignantly felt in psychological paradoxes, of the love/hate variety, which "force us to recognize things familiar but unrecognized" (p. 263).

So "psychoanalysts in order to reveal to us things about ourselves modify and sophisticate our conceptions of love, hate, jealousy, envy, sympathy, sense of responsibility. They use familiar words not with a disregard of established usage but not in bondage to it" (p. 271). Ironically enough, it is not always useful to call attention to such employment of paradox, for the force of any one of them lies in taking it at face value: "Only in the shock of taking a paradox literally will people give that attention to concrete detail which will enable them to break old habits of grouping and recognize not merely *that* an old classification blinds and distorts but *how* it does" (p. 273).

Thus the torque Wisdom elicits from the considerations of Wittgenstein: if "a philosophical answer is really a verbal recommendation," nonetheless "a philosopher's statements have not a merely verbal point." Their point is rather "the illumination of the ultimate structure of facts, i.e. the relations between different categories of being or . . . the relations between different sub-languages within a language" (pp. 36–37). Hence a "philosopher draws attention to what is already known with a view of giving insight; . . . he intimates his point," saying surprising things "in trying to lead someone else to the unusual associations he has come upon" (pp. 38–39, 264).

This tactic is motivated by the psychological observation that "to gain a new apprehension of any part of reality we have to shake off old habits of apprehension crystallized probably in a well-known mode of presentation" (263). Applied to metaphysics and metaphysicians, this means that "we have to do little more than remove the spectacles through which they look at their own work. Then they see how those hidden identities and diversities which lead to the insoluble reduction questions about forms, categories and predicates, have already been revealed, though in a hidden way" (p. 101). Directed to the

verificationist dilemma regarding ethical and metaphysical statements, Wisdom's recognition of the utility of paradoxes allows
him to conclude that they "are not merely expressions of mud-
dle, but also expressions of a new grasp of the peculiarities of the
justification procedure proper to statements about right and
wrong, the minds of others, etc." (p. 269).

Viewed from within my inquiry, Wisdom harnesses the full
force of Plato's insistence that dialectic is dialogue, and thereby
releases the cramping pressure on "analogy" by spreading it to
analogies. As the history of philosophy illustrates abundantly,
paradoxes "are dangerous and need to be balanced by the re-
assertion of the old truths in their opposites." Whether they are
metaphysical, ethical, or psychological, all such paradoxes "call
for a dialectical process in which they are balanced" (p. 263).
Otherwise their usefulness will be seriously compromised. Coun-
terpoint of this sort results from discussion open and discerning
enough to allow the inadequacies of one formulation to show
themselves and suggest corrective measures. Indeed there is no
other way of adjudicating analogies, for no single one can claim
to be adequate to the task of sorting the relevant similarities and
dissimilarities from common speech.

Talk of analogy, then, turns to analogies and their respective
utility relative to the needs of a particular stage and style of inquiry. Whether some analogies prove more permanently useful
than others because they better express the drama inherent in
paradoxical usage, I shall discuss when appraising metaphor.
For an objection to Wisdom's procedure is that it inevitably
conflates what have traditionally been distinguished—analogy
proper and metaphor—by subsuming both under the dramatic
rubric of paradox. It may also be that Wisdom has succeeded
in betraying some artificiality in the distinction between analogy
and metaphor; but in so doing he could well have overlooked a
facet needed to redress the balance.

Dorothy Emmet, writing just after Wisdom's earlier papers,
makes a direct and imaginative application to metaphysics.[4]

4. "Use of Analogy in Metaphysics," *Proc. Aris. Soc.* 41 (1940) 27–
46.

After criticizing any attempt to give a comprehensive theory of analogy, she focuses on the role *analogies* can play: they afford a creative influence on the intellectual imagination by offering different models appropriate to different times (p. 41). One's choice of analogies then would not be governed by consistency but guided by a sense for the appropriate, and hence be subject to discernment through accumulating and discriminating insights (p. 42). Her explicit reference to the Platonic myths reinforces the tie with Wisdom and suggests a new note of her own. Such a use of analogies, in myth and paradox, helps to make their function manifest and shows that "metaphysical analogies point beyond themselves." This statement alone is not very helpful, of course, because its own highly metaphorical pitch conceals many latent ambiguities: Does not every statement "point beyond itself"?

A further remark gives Emmet's comment more body and suggests a definite direction: "We express in the analogy the way in which we find ourselves impelled to respond to the impact of the transcendent term upon us." This attitude, while radical enough to resemble a compulsion, need not be blind or native. Quite the contrary, "it must be disciplined by respect for the empirical sciences, and . . . sensible to such more concrete responses as are witnessed to in poetry, moral experience, and the historic religions" (p. 45). Finally then, the choice of analogy expresses the manner in which we *must* respond. As Wittgenstein quipped in commenting on the selection of an appropriate metaphor: "Often I might only say: 'It simply isn't right yet.' I am dissatisfied, I go on looking. At last a word comes: 'That's it.' *Sometimes* I can say why. This is simply what searching, this is what finding, is like here." [5]

MacDonald, Wisdom, and Emmet were writing at a time when the prevailing opinion seemed assured of a normal form for language and its proper expressions. Hence they were concerned to bring to light other linguistic uses. If we wonder why they did not explicate these uses more clearly, we have only to

5. L. Wittgenstein, *Philosophical Investigations* (Oxford, 1953), p. 218.

recall how much effort it must have taken simply to bring them to light. The cumulative pressure of Wittgenstein's *Investigations* has produced a different contour map of language itself. In the present climate I can move beyond the tentative suggestions of these earlier authors to offer (in Part Four) a more clearly delineated linguistic account of various types of analogous expressions.

The writers reviewed here serve this stage of the inquiry, however, by reminding us of those uses of language with a propensity to escape from any procrustean attempt to limit their boundaries. They also offer testimony in favor of my approach to historical figures: that closer attention to the ways in which language is used and has been used frees us to consider more closely the writings of the ancients and to recognize in them concerns similar to our own. For by approaching their writings with a feeling for what they were getting at, we might be sufficiently liberated to consider these issues ourselves. Whether that be the result or not, we can at least come to appreciate that philosophy is an ongoing affair, with a set of issues which continue to arise in quite diverse idioms. The ubiquity of analogous expressions offers to philosophy an effective antidote to its own pretensions to doctrine.

A WAY TO UNDERSTANDING THE TRADITION

We may conclude then that the distinctive dimensions of analogous usage are indeed significant. Not that any technique may be distilled from them which will justify metaphysical or theological discourse. But the peculiar and pervasive qualities of this usage should nonetheless cause us to reflect upon ourselves as language users and the discrimination and judgment we exhibit in speaking the way we do. Analogous usage may not prove so privileged a feature of language as some have thought, but it remains a provoking one, especially in the way it intimates the capacity of men to judge and discriminate.

The various attempts to account for analogous usage, for all their sophisticated and subtle approaches, seem determined to turn something up. Each is probing for something common, for, despite a variety of contexts, the same expression is employed. The presumption is, of course, that something is recognized to be the same; there must be some "ground" for the predication. Historically, accounts of analogous usage represent a set of increasingly refined proposals to satisfy this presumption. Indeed, refinement was demanded from the outset since the terms first labeled analogous were those without a home in the categories. If we presume that categorical predication rests on certain features or clusters of features, then transcendentals were already bereft of this basis.

Aristotle suggested some ways out, turning for guidance to established forms of expression like metaphor, which did not respect settled categorical habits. Such a tack inevitably leads us to wonder how settled the categories themselves might be. And then it is but a short step to question the presumption: same term, same referent or ground.

Yet the presumption is not Aristotle's; we feel it in our very bones. If this mooring goes, it seems, language is cut loose to mean whatever we want it to mean. The boundless rushes in to induce intellectual vertigo. No one thinks to ask innocently: Moorings are necessary, but why put in here? Same term, same referent or ground? This presumption may not be Aristotle's, but his careful attention to langauge, coupled with his tendency to be guided by it in crucial decisions, certainly leaves the impression of someone tying up to the sameness of words. But we shall have the opportunity to see just how superficial this impression is. Aristotle's distinction between sheer ambiguity and a reasoned (or analogous) kind should put a critic on his guard. The "ground" for deliberate and opposite ambiguous usage is neither a common referent nor a common formula (or meaning) but rather, I shall suggest, the demands germane to reason itself.

What are these demands? They are not clear in Aristotle, though clues abound, particularly in those threads linking philosophical inquiry with poetry. I shall argue that the demands are precisely those of appraising, of passing judgment. The transcendentals—'one', 'true', and 'being' (or 'object')—seem to label different dimensions of the intellectual activity of judgment where it is to be distinguished from consideration, classifying, and sorting. For it is not a foregone conclusion that the object we are considering is indeed one; the decision to consider it so manifests a position taken. Nor can anyone inquire how many objects there are on my desk. That a proposal is good and an assertion true are obviously appraisals, but so is the decision to consider something as the object of our inquiry and hence as possessing that kind of unity.

Judgment is called upon at the beginning of any inquiry to establish the appropriate context and idiom, and is later required to bring that inquiry to a satisfactory term. We shall see how Plato's preoccupation with Socrates, the examined life, and the peculiar logic of ethical appraisal laid the groundwork for Aristotle's treatment of transcategorical terms. Plato's studied manner of exhibiting the logic peculiar to appraisal language will provide a richer context for appreciating Aristotle's linguistic considerations. With this much of a hypothesis in mind, it is time to turn to the tradition. While the hypothesis is vague at present, vague it must remain. For more precise meanings of 'judgment' and the 'intellectual demand' it represents will be forthcoming as the documents of philosophical history are read from this standpoint. The more precise the interpretative standpoint, the more one risks prejudging the documents; initial vagueness gives greater liberty for the tradition to speak and promises greater fruitfulness and accuracy in the end.

THE WORKING HYPOTHESIS

With the vagueness appropriate to a working hypothesis, I wish to argue that the tendency of the philosophic traditions stemming from Aristotle to distinguish a set of expressions as analogous has proven to be a useful strategy. These terms are distinguished not merely by their resistance to definition but even more significantly by our propensity to employ them in quite diverse contexts. That propensity seems linked with the human demand that we make assessments, and the ambiguous character of the terms we use to make them indicates something of the shape of this activity.

The generic strategy is the normally unspoken one of any philosophic inquiry which orients itself by language usage: grammar reveals the essential contours of the subject. The subject in this case turns out to be the very activity of doing philosophy, and especially that role of assessing, which has been the heart of philosophizing from Socrates to the contemporary penchant for "philosophy of . . ." Grammar, as it is used here, refers to something like a set of rules outlining the appropriate ways of employing an expression. These are not immediately evident nor are they always formulable into rules, but it is possible with some artistry to assemble enough reminders that a person learns how to codify his capacity to discriminate among suggested ways of using certain expressions. In fact, the generic strategy contends that this is precisely what much of philosophy has always been up to: delineating the "depth" grammar of certain key expressions by distinguishing it from the "surface" grammar. The purpose of my sustained reflections upon Plato, Aristotle, Aquinas, and Duns Scotus will be precisely to test that contention.

I have selected analogous expressions as a proximate subject for "grammatical" analysis because of the avowedly central role they play in this philosophic tradition. A special subset of these terms—the transcendentals: 'one', 'good', and 'true'—have been given pride of place and accorded particular scrutiny. Yet other less spectacular but more discriminating terms of assessment share much of their grammar: 'fits', 'controls', 'organizes', or 'fruitful', 'elegant', and 'simple'. Analyses designed to meet the peculiarities of paradigms of analogous usage like the transcendentals turn out to shed much light on the wider set of expressions as well. And grammatical similarities suggest similarities in the activities involved in using these terms. I have chosen the vague expression "assessment" to group the activities for purposes of this inquiry.

Examining the four philosophers will afford a greater feeling for the diverse activities covered by that single term and also illustrate how a study intent upon language uses can reveal the contours of the activity, which is doing philosophy. The final systematic section will offer a linguistic account congruent with the actual usage of these philosophers and propose it as a more general elucidation of the roles played by expressions of this sort in the ongoing activity we call philosophy.

Part Two

Origins of the Question in Classical Philosophy

3. Plato: Inquiry as Dialectic

GOOD AS GOAL AND THE ROLE OF METHOD

What impressed Plato above all was the ideal. This betrays itself most clearly in his search for *what things are,* the quest for complete clarity in our use of language. The ideal is always to know what one is talking about, even though this may only be recognizing that we do not realize what we are saying. The dialogues attempt to translate this ideal into a form of speech that exhibits its own lacunae and acts out its own failures in an effort to overcome them.

Plato would have had the dramatists of his own day banished from his *Republic* for failing at their proper task to create a linguistic form that could exhibit its own limitations. Philosopher and poet alike were drawn to speak of the divine. In their attempt to help man search for himself, they had to make some sense of man's tendency to outreach himself in searching for himself. To move beyond the human ken, however, required as much humility as intelligence, for no man could dare presume to speak of the divine and presume his speech adequate. Hence if an individual finds himself engaged in this sort of discourse, he had better find a way of speaking which exhibits due reverence by constantly reminding listener and speaker alike that they know little of which they speak. Since the dramatists of Plato's time were not up to this task, they settled for straightforward stories about the gods. The result was a body of vulgarities about divinity. By failing to shape a linguistic form sensitively to the subject in question, the poets failed to do what poets are supposed to do, hence failed to be poets. Perhaps Plato's disappointment, coupled with some pique at having to do the job himself, galvanized his resolve to banish poets from his state. However that may be, inquiry is intimately connected with turning up the proper linguistic form or method. And this method, for Plato, is inseparable from the person of Socrates.

Socrates liked to show that everyone has already some idea

of what he is talking about—enough anyway to be led on to a clearer grasp of it. And this not merely passively, but in a journey plotted by both "teacher" and "student," by appropriate agreement and disagreement. Such discussion, it is true, rarely if ever comes to a conclusive end, but progress can be made. Socrates had shown this. But what singles out the method was not a series of handy formulae so much as the person of Socrates and the attitude he inspired. For Socrates' challenge bears fruit even if he never ceases to inquire, while contentious argument (= *eristic*) is both endless and fruitless (R 454ab; Sph 216*b*, 259c; Tht 167e sq; Grg 515b).[1] What is the difference? Socrates? In part, yes, but not alone, for Socrates communicates something to his companions as well. It seems that under the influence of "Socrates' art" one is drawn to bend personally, as it were, in the direction of the object sought after, and (at least temporarily) to order one's own life according to the order inquired into (Sph; Phdr 276–77; Grg 495e).[2] Socrates both inspires and impels, but always toward a goal. He seems a man devoured, become the slave, the single-minded instrument—of what? Plato will call it "the good."

But the very appellation is misleading, and Plato was quick to discover this. As he examined more carefully the indispensable role of language in inquiring into "what is," he could not fail to turn up the peculiar pitfalls of "the good." As a noun, it appears to name something, and Plato will always struggle with this difficulty (Sph 244).[3] For us, the term is readily restricted to the goal of human development. (Settled usage here reflects Aristotle's penchant for division. "Good" is not treated in his metaphysical lexicon, *Metaphysics* V, but reserved for the

1. Dialogue references will be according to the Stephanus pagination and the accepted abbreviations: *Charmides* (Chrm), *Euthydemus* (Euthd), *Gorgias* (Grg), *Laches* (La), *Seventh Letter* (7Ep), *Meno* (Men), *Phaedo* (Phd), *Phaedrus* (Phdr), *Philebus* (Phlb), *Republic* (R), *Symposium* (Smp), *Sophist* (Sph), *Statesman* (Plt). *Theatetus* (Tht).

2. R. S. Brumbaugh and N. Lawrence, *Philosophers on Education* (Boston, 1963), pp. 30–34.

3. I. M. Crombie, *Examination of Plato's Doctrines*, vol. 2 (New York, 1963), pp. 350–52.

Ethics. Its appearance in Book XII of the *Metaphysics* is almost
adventitious.) A better translation of *ton agathon* for us might
well be 'order' or 'principle of order'. For vague though it is and
must be, this term pervades intellectual as well as moral concerns. And for Plato, the fact that communication—disagreement, agreement, and palpable progress in inquiry—is possible,
testified to the presence of order (Grg 487; Phdr 277–79; Phlb
64e-e). Order alone could ensure the worth of a just life without advantage, for such a life would then represent an endeavor
to embody something of this good or order. The order, of course,
must correspond to what man most truly is (*ta ontōs onta*), but
since man is but the universe conscious, a privileged microcosm,
order cannot but be found everywhere.

Order—man's demand for it, and the devious ways Socrates
employs to uncover it wherever we turn—is the burden of all
the dialogues, illustrated in the "likely story" of the *Timaeus*
and variously articulated in others as well (Ti, esp. 90d; Smp
205–23; Plt 311e; Grg 507e–8d). What is manifested, however,
is not the nature of this order, which Plato dubs "the good," so
much as our inability to bring it out into the light of day. The
very reason (*logos*) which testifies to its presence fails in every
attempt to come to grips with this order as good, to yield a
reasonable account (*logos*) of it. So we can only believe in
order. Yet belief does not crowd out every attempt to articulate
what it is we find it necessary to believe in. Belief, Plato insists,
simply cannot mean trading in one's intelligence for a promise
of mystical identification of the object of one's faith. The order
that Plato identifies with the good, then, has little affinity with
Dionysus. The most transparent traces of order are to be found
in reason, especially in reason's most lucid exercise, mathematics. So it would be illogical to break faith with reason in
order to proclaim one's faith in what reason had revealed. And
consistency is one of the most obvious manifestations of order.
One frees oneself from its rigorous demands only to find oneself
swallowed up by the boundless and formless (Ti 52e sq, 69b-e;
Phlb 23c, 31a; Plt 273d-c; Grg 465d).

But on the other hand, how is reason to speak of the very

order which it exemplifies? In spite of the apparently straight-forward account of gazing on the sun in the *Republic,* the fact remains that whenever we are directed to look at a source of light, the result is not vision but blindness. Taking knowledge on the analogy of vision, then, as Plato tended to do, can only make us wary of assimilating talk about "the good" to the form used in giving an account of good things—as though we could see light in the same way we see lighted objects. It will be my contention that Plato realized this quite clearly, that he wished to communicate it in a manner that would not shake our faith in "good [order] itself," and that his addiction to the literary form of the dialogue was an attempt to find a way to do just that.

To reconstruct Plato in somewhat more modern terms, I wish to show how his Socratic concern that we understand the ex-pressions we do use forced him to an acute awareness of method and gradually led him to recognize that certain expressions enjoy a unique status and demand a peculiar method to articulate their many uses. This development was accentuated by Plato's keen eye for presuppositions and received a particular direction from Socrates' predilection for moral subjects.

The moral context, it seems, suggested that we call the object of this unique mode of inquiry, "the cause of knowledge and of truth in so far as known . . . , the *idea of the good*" (R 508e). We have seen that 'order' would qualify as a candidate, perhaps even a better one. The expression Plato used to demonstrate the need for a peculiar method is "the One," or "unity," as Ryle has suggested we translate it.[4] Given the fact, however, that 'good' carried the connotations of 'order' even more strongly in Greek than it does in English, the heavily moral associations of good did not confine so much as amplify its applicability. 'Unity' is clearly more adapted to show the logic at play, but good has the advantage of suggesting that more than logic is presupposed to rational inquiry. All three expressions share a certain self-reflexiveness: to inquire into their meaning is to probe into inquiry itself.

4. Gilbert Ryle, "Plato's *Parmenides,*" *Mind* 48 (1939) 142.

Plato insisted often on the affinity of inquirer and object, but nowhere more pointedly than in the *Seventh Letter* (cf. also R 486d, 487a, 494b, 501d; Sph 265a; Phdr 257b, 278a; Grg 495e). Here the process of "pupil and teacher asking and answering questions" which testifies so eloquently to the presence of order is mentioned to recall that all must be carried out "in good will and without envy. Only then, when reason and knowledge are at the very extremity of human effort, can they illuminate the nature of any object." And even then, "it is barely possible for knowledge to be engendered . . . ; and if the qualities he has have been corrupted, then not even Lynceus could make such a man see. In short, neither quickness of learning nor a good memory can make a man see when his nature is not akin to the object." [5] It is this kinship between inquirer and object which discussion with one already "in love with the good," like Socrates, is meant to engender. Those of us who had not the opportunity to know this education firsthand are invited, via the literary form of the dialogue, to compose ourselves in the manner of the dramatis personae and personally participate. The introductions are designed to provide a setting sufficiently individualized to make ourselves at home. The myths evoke a response archetypal enough to be universally shared, yet vague enough to encourage varying interpretations—just at that point where recourse to technical usage might have severely restricted the inquiry by offering what appeared to be an "account."

A Peculiar Method Required

But all this is to anticipate the argument, though in a useful way. For we may say now that if inquiry into the "true meaning" of any term requires such genuine give-and-take and a readiness to shape oneself in accordance with the conclusions reached, how much more is demanded of the inquirer into the "good itself" as the presupposition of inquiry itself? The personal pliancy required of any inquirer implies a willingness to reconsider his hypothesis in the light of relevant counterevidence, but the

5. Seventh *Letter*, 344a–b (Morrow trans.); on Lynceus, cf. Robert Graves, *Greek Myths* (Harmondsworth, 1955), nn. 60, 74.

dialectician inquiring into the good must be ready to examine every assumption, insofar as this is humanly possible (R 511b, 533).[6] Clearly more than mere mental agility is called for here; something rather more akin to "stoutness of mind and heart."

At least the mind (and presumably the temperament) of the mathematician will not suffice. This is what Plato states in explaining the divided line, and what he shows, I wish to argue, in the *Parmenides* (R 510–11, Ryle; and Crombie, p. 532). Nor does such a statement, coming from Plato, degrade mathematics. It rather seems to exalt the fourth member, dialectic, quite beyond the human ken; for Plato's respect for mathematics, as the science most transparently manifesting the order of reason, is notorious (Ti 31e; Phlb 18ab; R 522 sq). The difference between the third and fourth divisions of the line most germane to my thesis is a methodological one. Consider the diverse logical requirements for two accounts: one of the possible ordering relations among sets of elements, and another of order itself. In more sophisticated parlance, the first would be mathematics, the second metaphysics. But no one handed Plato these distinctions, and the point of the second half of the *Parmenides* was to show that one does not give an account of order in the same style that one analyzes ordered sets, even should such an analysis lead quite naturally to the more fundamental question. The expression chosen in the dialogue is not 'order', of course, but Parmenides' 'unity'. Plato shows that the kind of logic which works so successfully in developing a well-defined domain like geometry simply fails when confronted with a notion such as *one*. And it fails not by some extrinsic criterion—as though we were possessed of a more privileged statement—but by leading us to say contradictory things about the *one*. Since the very least we can demand of any account is that it not be contradictory, it seems that no account at all is possible of *unity*.

Such at least is the interpretation of Ryle and of Brumbaugh.[7]

6. Crombie, p. 566; Richard Robinson, *Plato's Early Dialectic,* 2nd ed. (Ithaca, 1953), pp. 77–83.

7. Ryle ("Plato's *Parmenides*") and Brumbaugh (*Plato on the One,* New Haven, 1961), are supported by F. M. Cornford (*Plato and*

Besides illuminating the dialogue itself, this interpretation allows us to glimpse the extensive trial and error underlying Aristotle's awareness of the unique logical status of terms like one and being. His insistence that we not attempt to assimilate them to his standard categorical form reflects a hard-won sophistication of logic.

To say that Plato was showing the kind of type distinctions necessary to deal consistently with notions "richer than" mathematical, and establishing these distinctions in the only way possible to logic—by generating antinomies—satisfies the reader of the *Parmenides* on at least two counts. First, such an explanation accounts for the presence of "obvious" logical fallacies (such as predicating an attribute of itself), and second, it reminds us that someone had to show that moves like these were fallacious before anyone could so label them. These fallacies arise in the *Parmenides* because the style of inquiry which is taken as the model—mathematics—is not subject to the ambiguities from which a more comprehensive account of *unity* suffers. For one

---

Parmenides, London, 1939): "The key to the understanding of the second part must be sought in the unmistakable ambiguity of the hypothesis, 'if there is a One' [p. 109]. A main purpose of the whole exercise must be to point out that even the apparently simplest terms, such as 'one' and 'being', which will appear at the threshold of any metaphysical discussion, are dangerously ambiguous [p. 110]. The appearance of fallacy is chiefly due to Plato's deliberate reproduction of the deductive form of reasoning characteristic of the Eleatics, and exemplified in Parmenides' *Way of Truth*" [p. 114]. A. E. Taylor firmly adheres to the 'exercise' thesis: the latter part of the dialogue exemplifies the degree of logical sophistication required to meet the kind of objection raised in the first part (*Plato: The Man and His Work,* London, 1926). Harold Cherniss also considers the dialogue to be primarily a demonstration of method ("Parmenides and the *Parmenides* of Plato," *Amer. J. Philol.* 53, 1932, 129). The antinomies rest on an abuse of 'to be', and 'one' is chosen only in deference to Parmenides [p. 135]. In Gallican manner, Jean Wahl sees no reason for opposing an exercise in dialectic to a search for understanding, and considers it the achievement if not the aim of Part Two to have shown that unity and diversity are unthinkable without each other (*Etude sur le Parménide de Platon,* Paris, 1926, pp. 81, 101).

thing, no triangle is more a triangle than the next, but any single item can be more or less *one* than the next, depending on the set of criteria proposed. Again, a fallacy common to the *Parmenides,* the confusion of quality with relation ("they differ from one another in virtue of being *different* or *other*"; 143b) simply does not arise in mathematics, where quality is irrelevant.

Plato takes us through the tedious exercise of the *Parmenides* to convince us that fruitful as the geometric method may be, certain notions are not amenable to such an account. And since geometry tends to be the paradigm for an explanatory system, we may say that notions like unity are not susceptible of any systematic account. But cannot a purist insist that this is the case with every general term? How many people can settle on a definition for "swan"? There remains a crucial difference, however, between swan and unity. Few definitions can claim to be irreformable, but it would be abnormal for a proposed definition of a general term to generate antinomies. Vagueness *may* conceal contradictions, but need not. Closer attention to the difficulties of concept formation, however, generally does seem to sensitize one for more semantically unusual notions like unity and good.

How are we to come to an understanding of these notions (or realities) which correspond to the fourth division of the line? What is *episteme,* in this restricted and exalted sense (R 533d, Crombie, pp. 70–102)? The *Parmenides* shows that a logic tailored to mathematics and abstract relations will not provide a method appropriate to it. For *episteme* is not merely a "higher-level" science, as though its objects—unity, good, order, and the rest—were overarching generalities. The dialogue illustrates this by submitting the expression unity to a logical analysis designed to determine the range and significance of general terms. The method illustrated in the *Parmenides* manifested its own inadequacy by generating antinomies. But whatever one's interpretation of this dialogue, there are numerous other indications in Plato that *episteme,* with its method of dialectic, is quite another thing from *dianoia,* which relies on hypothesis (Phd 99–102; Men 86–89; R 532–34). Since the method of hypothesis is forced from time to time to take a critical look at its own hypotheses, and to decide for nonformal but relevant reasons to alter them, the two methods are not altogether separate. But what counts as a good reason for inferring the consequences of a hypothesis would not be decisive in criticizing that same hypothesis. Criticism calls for a different style of reasoning, and that is enough to count the two methods of hypothesis and dialectic distinct.[8]

Method or Intuition? How can we indicate more positively the kind of knowing appropriate to "objects" like unity and good? Plato sometimes spoke in a way that assimilates *episteme* to a vision of its object, an intuition of "the good" (Smp 210e–11a; R 516b). This is disconcerting, of course, because intuition is never an answer. For an answer must culminate an inquiry by apexing previous avenues of thought and illuminating still others. Intuition bypasses all that and in doing so fails to abide by the rules of inquiry. But there are other reasons more proper to Plato for mistrusting intuition as *his* answer. The first is the emphasis Plato lays on method: the Socratic method of dialogue and the rigorous formation in different methods proposed for philosophers in the *Republic*. The method found appropriate for an inquiry provides some insight into the reality being considered, since success reveals a certain affinity with the object. Intuition, as immediate vision, leaves no traces of method and hence no clues to the structure of its object. Even worse, by adopting so closely the model of vision, intuition opens Plato to Aristotle's objection that the forms are merely superentities, for our knowledge of them is but a refined version of the knowledge by "direct acquaintance" familiar to us in perception (Meta VII, 16. 1040b35).[9]

But beyond what Plato might say about the importance of method is the method he employs. His recourse to literary form and careful composition of place and person, his addiction to

8. For support of this unobtrusive principle, see Aristotle, *Metaphysics*, 995a1–10; R. Carnap, *Meaning and Necessity* (Chicago, 1956), pp. 214, 221; S. Toulmin, *Uses of Argument* (Cambridge, 1958), pp. 141–45.

9. Crombie, pp. 125–27.

dialogue and its demand that any proposed answer be submitted to a further and often devastating set of questions—in fine, Plato's sensitivity to the inadequacy of any discourse—all this bespeaks a method and has little to do with immediate intuition as the epistemological deus ex machina it normally represents. In fact, one of the signal facets of Plato's method is the dramatic: the dialogue would show what it can only unsuccessfully say. Hence each level of discourse in the *Republic* will be introduced by a different interlocutor. Socrates in *Hippias Minor* defends the position that it is more virtuous to prevaricate deliberately than to unconsciously do so, thereby weaving the liar paradox into the very form of the dialogue. This device is often coupled with irony, as in the *Euthyphro,* where Socrates, accused of impiety (toward the gods), manifests by his earnest desire to uncover its "true reality": the very piety in whose name Euthyphro is compelled to prosecute his own father.[10]

The role of such a method is to show at once the inadequacy of a straightforward account and to supply a more complete one. In other words, the purpose of this method is to break through to a new kind of account (*logos*), one no longer beholden to geometric method but nevertheless giving that method and its logic their full due. Rather than simply remark that 'account' may be used properly for different styles of reasoning in diverse contexts—that it is (in Aristotle's terminology) an *analogous* expression—Plato proceeds to construct a mode of discourse which will account for those notions not amenable to geometric treatment.

Engaging the subject. In Plato's dramatic style of discourse, the inquirer must become involved from the outset in a pursuit. Hence the careful composition of persons in a setting, and the engaging play of question and answer.[11] The participant is forced to commit himself one way or the other, is urged to say what he

10. I owe the suggestion of these dialogues to Professor Robert Brumbaugh, whose predilection for this style of interpreting Plato lent valuable support.

11. Paul Desjardins, "The Form of Platonic Inquiry," unpub. Ph. D. dissertation, Yale, 1960; R. Robinson (n. 6 above), pp. 75–78.

thinks, and while properly attentive to consistency, must strain toward the mutual grasp of rational agreement (Grg 447c, 459a–e, 474ab, 487a–e, 495b, 497b, 500b–d). The new mode of discourse required for a thoroughgoing search after wisdom announces the fact that philosophy cannot be content, as mathematics is, with an account in words alone. Authentic philosophy entails a pursuit in deed as well. And since this fact must be reflected in the very style of the account offered, one does not speak of *the* answer but of the *best* answer; never the only or inevitable consequence, but the one meeting the fewest objections, the answer showing awareness of its inherent inadequacies.[12]

Plato has recourse to the dramatic and literary form of the dialogues to construct this special style of account which exhibits its own inadequacy. It is particularly in evidence when he deals with analogous expressions like order, good, and unity. For among other logical idiosyncrasies, these notions behave in so obviously self-reflexive and "recursive" a manner that we can expect to find them operative everywhere. One may always ask whether it is *good* to be in a well-ordered state. With *order*, we can either insist that it is impossible to speak of absolute disorder (since the very notion presumes some order) or assert with Peirce that utter randomness would be the most perfect order since the distribution would presumably be completely homogeneous.[13] But as these examples show, statements containing these terms easily tend to paradox. Hence Plato had to control the context of the statement, so as to show what could be said only clumsily if at all. The tendency to reversal and paradox is translated into the dramatic setting. The characters themselves embody, often ironically, the very characteristics whose "true reality" the dialogue would uncover. (The ironic twist, of course, heightens our sense of a statement's inadequacy. Think, for example, of the presence of Anytus in the *Meno,* the

12. E. V. Kohak, "Road to Wisdom: Lessons on Education from Plato's *Laches," Class. J.* 56 (1960) 123–32.

13. C. S. Peirce, *Collected Papers,* ed. C. Hartshorne and Paul Weiss (Cambridge, Mass., 1931–35), 6.401–6.405.

very man who would engineer Socrates' execution. His refusal
to engage in Socrates' *paideia,* his obstinate clinging to the
shadow of conformity, his petulant and untimely exit, all starkly
contrasted with the docility of Meno, certainly show what virtue is and what one must overcome in order to acquire it.)

When forced to speak about a pervasive or originative fact,
like our ability to recognize the adequacy of an account or
man's affinity for the harmonious and beautiful, Plato tends to
a mythical form or acknowledges an inspired source. In either
case, the implication is that we are dealing here with something
archetypal, something that could properly speaking be revealed
only from a perspective outside our own. For any account we
might give would invariably presuppose what we were seeking
to account for (Grg 523–27; Smp 201–12; Phdr 246; R 506e
sq; Phlb 65a).

The literary form, then, contributes to establishing this new
mode of discourse by pointing up the limits of an ordinary, geometric account. And the need to have recourse to this new style
of account suggests something of the nature of the object. By
eliciting a fuller participation of the inquirer, the very genre of
discourse suggests that the more fully one is engaged in pursuing
an object, the more adequately can one come to know it. In
this way, the literary style helps point statement beyond what
it can properly say, helps give it a bearing on an object to which
it is inadequate, and does so by showing this very fact. For the
crucial maneuver in analogous discourse is to be able to show
the dissimilarities without canceling the suggestions of the intial
similarity. This requirement (which will become clearer when
we consider Aquinas) demands an ingenuity sufficient to incorporate a negative judgment into the account so that the actual
accounting it gives manifests its inadequacy to the task. The dis-
trust Plato expresses for the doctrinal statement, the care he
takes to re-create a dialogic situation inviting the reader to grow
up into the question, and his recourse to dramatic irony and
to myth show how deeply aware he was of the limits of language
as well as the need to exploit those very limits. We have seen
at least some of the techniques Plato found useful in tackling

the logic of linguistic usage at the limit of discourse, which he dubbed dialectic. Other facets remain, but let us first marshall what has been said to confront the texts supporting intuition.

Intuition reconsidered. My argument will amount to little more than calling attention to Plato's preoccupation with method and asking whether this can be squared with a doctrine of immediate intuition. If one responds that all the talk is a preparation for an act of direct vision, altogether discontinuous with all that led up to it, then we must ask how necessary a propaedeutic dialectic is? If it is said to be absolutely necessary, then it matters little whether one asserts that it is merely extrinsic to the real knowing act conceived by analogy with vision and quite innocent of method. We may well believe that this is but a method of purification removing all obstacles from the way of the soul's direct contact with reality itself, but such a doctrine (which does seem to be Plato's) would be at variance with his working epistemology (R 475e, 500c, 532c, 507c–09b).[14] A doctrine of intuition could plausibly be dismissed as a mythical account embodying in ambiguous and popular language what defies rational explanation: the sui generis relation of known and knower. And it should be thus interpreted because Plato's practice belies his words here; by his own reckoning, we are to pay more attention to what one does than what one says at times like these (Euthd 289b, 290c; Grg 482b; 7Ep 340c; La 188de).

There are other pressures, though, favoring the intuition formulation as a handy one. There is the prima facie analogy of knowing with seeing which pervades ordinary language, ours as well as Plato's. We have seen how Plato used this quite uncritically in the cave analogy, and know also that his usual strategy included espousing the popular idiom as a plausible starting point, trusting that subsequent discussion would bring any latent ambiguities to the surface. Even if the conflict between method and intuition managed to escape his own notice, it would certainly have made itself felt in time. But what if Plato's very attention to method in the dialogues were his re-

14. E. A. Havelock, *Preface to Plato* (Cambridge, Mass., 1963), p. 275, n. 41.

sponse? And perhaps we failed to recognize it because we insisted upon an explicit account where Plato would more wisely prefer to leave a "likely story." The fact that his words were canonized as a doctrine of direct acquaintance, as they also became the doctrine of reminiscence in the *Meno,* would mark another act in the tragic denouement of the Socrates story.

There is of course the further pressure of the forms, which Plato introduced to preserve objectivity and to give a certain body to discourse by providing a stable referent for general terms. That very objectivity lends the impression that one has but to look with the properly prepared power to find the referent there.[15] The thrust of the middle dialogues, however, is certainly to trim the possible implications resulting from too literal a conception of the forms and to deter one from speaking of them in a straightforward and objective fashion.

We acknowledge all these pressures yet recognize the fact that Plato's own description of dialectic in the *Republic* (as well as the *Seventh Letter*) quite "avoids the metaphor [of vision], stressing instead the search, the question-answer. . . . and the effort of ratiocination." Noting that his attention to method belies immediacy, and that the middle dialogues were designed to expose the most immediate source of pressure, we can hardly accept Plato's doctrine of direct acquaintance at face value. We may safely regard his remarks in this direction as a case of being misled by a pervasive metaphor, with the proviso that he may well have allowed himself to be misled (as in *Hippias Minor*), prudently settling for the likely story.[16]

But there is a kernel of truth in the intuition position, which very much concerns Plato, and which we ought not let pass. Seeing the point of an argument or presentation does show a certain logical discontinuity with the discourse leading up to it. The teacher can at best offer an avenue of approach; teachers might well be graded by their sensitivity to this fact. The better the teacher, the less confident he will be that his mode of exposition inescapably leads to illumination, the more willing he will

15. Havelock, pp. 263–64.
16. Havelock, esp, pp. 268–71; 275, nn. 41, 42.

be to entertain questions, to supply yet other arguments, and to welcome variations in approach.

This innate dimension of knowledge has many facets. Plato was overwhelmingly impressed with the fact that we all "know" what it is we are seeking, that we can come to an agreement or know enough to disagree, that we are able through discussion to spot the inadequacies in a preferred account. The ability to communicate is so closely linked with the pursuit of knowledge, then, that it not only marks out a dimension proper to man but also links him in a unique manner to the entire cosmos.[17] It is tempting to hypostatize this mysterious power as soul. And in the face of other more pedestrian facts about man (his body), the ensuing dualism would also reinforce the tendency to regard knowing as seeing: knowledge at its best (*episteme*) becomes the soul's vision unalloyed (Phd 836; R 516b, 518c; Phdr 249e).

We cannot allow our dissatisfaction with a simplistic account, however, to blind us to the facts. Coming to know certainly involves something we might call discernment or discrimination.[18] It is akin to judgment and leads us into a closer look at the method Plato usually employed when engaged in a dialectic. This method involves a careful process of collating instances, and deciding whether they embody the notion in question by trying to discern how they do it. Such a process is intended to bring us to a certain understanding, regulated by a style of inquiry which upon reflection will itself reveal still more about the object sought.[19]

Dialectic: From "What Is X" to "The Good"

As Plato uses it, dialectic seems to denote a crowd of procedures rather than a family, and sketches more of an ideal

17. Cf. the "likely account" in the *Timaeus* 90d; and A. E. Taylor, *Philosophical Studies* (London, 1934), pp. 216–21.

18. Crombie, pp. 129, 564.

19. Crombie, pp. 559–60. The power and reach of this method will be examined more closely in Chap. 10, with the assistance of contemporary linguistic tools.

than delineates an actual inquiry.[20] Dialectic is inescapably dialogic in form and demands of the participants utter fidelity to pursuit of their object (Sph 263e; Phdr 231–34; Grg 495b, 497b).[21] This faithfulness to the quest, as we shall see, turns out to be a crucial requirement. For when dialectic moves out beyond any account, there is no pattern, no other control than the mutual sincerity of the inquirers. But what is it that forces one to investigate beyond any hope of finding out what x is? What explains the double focus Plato assigns to dialectic: (1) the search for what x is, for the "true nature of x," and (2) the mode of inquiry carrying us to "the good" (Phd 58; R 503–07, 532 sq; Plt 309; Phdr 265; Sph 253, 259; Grg 500)? [22]

Of the many possible answers to this question—as various as metaphysical systems—I shall propose two, and opt for the second as more faithful to Plato and more illustrative of the intellectual activity involved. The first answer is already familiar: where x ranges indiscriminately, the yearning to clarify what x is (for every x) will inevitably find us asking what we mean when we use expressions like existence, unity, same as, or different from. We wonder what these "things" might be. A thorough discussion will show that such terms resist an ordinary account which relies on a logic useful for more straightforward clarifications. Yet we cannot dispense with terms like these, and a discussion of their logical peculiarities usually leads us to yet other notions, apparently just as pervasive: measure, harmony, proportion ($=$ *analogia*), and the like.

One might suggest that Plato employs 'good' as an honorific term for the family of such expressions and the inexplicable yet

20. So R. L. Nettleship: dialectic seems to denote the ideal of human discourse, the end toward which science works as well as what impels it to this end (*Lectures on the* Republic *of Plato,* London, 1910, pp. 278–80). This section owes more than can be estimated to the perceptive accounts of Nettleship and of H. W. B. Joseph, especially in *Knowledge and the Good in Plato's* Republic (Oxford, 1948).

21. Robinson, pp. 79–89.

22. Nettleship, pp. 278–86; Robinson, p. 74.

indispensable role they play in discourse. Their role, Plato suggests, is akin to the organization that forms words into statements (Sph 261d–63d; Phlb 64c–65a). Since this organization alone allows for words being counted true or false and gives them a "bearing on reality," expressions functioning similarly in discourse enjoy a privileged status (Sph 263–64; Tht 189).[23]

Such a response is illuminating; it cannot be brushed off as merely linguistic. It suggests the line of development taken by Aristotle—where we shall rejoin it. But in treating language as an object, as logic must, this response cuts off another line of inquiry. That line recognizes language to be a "way of life" as well, and leads to a response at once more probing and more able to elucidate Plato's various concerns as they converge on "the good." [24]

This second response to our question of what moves one to inquire beyond the hope of discovering what x is, may be sketched as follows. The search for the true nature of x is invariably a search for some unifying characteristic or principle (Grg 448e, 465a; Plt 309bc; Phlb 61, 64; Euthph 6de). So if one were to know the whole truth about x, one would also know why the quest to understand it proceeds in this fashion. Giving an account is necessary but not yet sufficient, for we would also like to be able to say why we insist on so accounting for things. It is this latter question, this demand for full intelligibility, that moves us toward "the good."

In more objective terms, the question can be put by wondering how the various forms are united among themselves. Then it merely transposes to a higher level the same style of inquiry that led Plato to postulate the forms: What accounts for the multiple facets an object displays? What gives them intelligibility by ordering the forms, and so would better be dubbed 'order'? [25] But this term and the highly objective treatment it reflects would associate the demand too closely with that satisfied by

23. Cf. Aristotle, *Categories* 3, 2a5; *De Interp.* 1, 16a12.
24. Robinson, pp. 75–78.
25. Joseph, p. 73; Nettleship, pp. 252–57.

a straightforward account. For Plato insists that "the good itself is not essence but transcends essence," quite beyond the reach of an ordinary account (R 509b).[26]

If he feels competent to show that good must comprise beauty, proportion, and truth, Plato is quite at a loss to know how they are to be combined. The most he can propose is that we "regard these three as one"; no account of their conjunction will be forthcoming (Phlb 65a). To entertain any hope of articulating a principle of order promising full intelligibility would mean squandering the gains made in the *Parmenides*. As much as 'order', then, would help to offset any narrowly moral connotations, 'good' remains the better term. For it succeeds in signaling the turn dialectic can take at this level to satisfy the demand for a complete account. For good alludes to the manner in which order (measure, harmony, and proportion) elicits a response and finds an affinity in every inquirer.

Good becomes an illuminating term, then, as it connotes attraction and affinity: "what every soul pursues and for whose sake does all it does" (R 505e). The more radical and pervasive the affinity, the more central the role good plays in inquiry, but the less it is apt to show on the surface. (This is not a necessary truth but an ascertainable fact about men; one that Plato pictures by his tripartite soul.) The *good* must be cultivated, and to live according to it requires a degree of honesty tantamount to a conversion (R 499–501, 517–20; Sph 265; Euthph 15; Phdr 257b; 7Ep 340c, 344b). Finally, when the style of questioning designed to issue in an account is pursued beyond that limit to inquire into rationality itself, one can no longer count on the guidance of axioms, postulates, and definitions. One is inquiring into their grounds, and the only control left is the willingness to give oneself over fully to this radical affinity for

26. It cannot be denied that most of Plato's treatment is of the more objective sort (cf. Phlb 64–65, Sph 253, 259). But Havelock suggests that the need to establish a rational and united front against the poets pressured this strategy. My view would be similar to that of Crombie (pp. 550–67) and to that suggested by A. E. Taylor in his "Analysis of *episteme* in Plato's Seventh Epistle" (*Mind* 21, 1912, reprinted in his *Philosophical Studies,* London, 1934, pp. 216–21).

order. Plato calls it "love of the truth" and considers the touch-stone of its presence to be the mutual sincerity manifested in dialogue.[27]

How dialectic reaches its terms. But how does dialectic ex-hibit something like a radical affinity of inquirer and inquiry with a unity which is ordered, a proportionate unity, unity *kat'analogian?* And what sort of a fact is this affinity? The an-swer to the second turns on the first: How de we come upon this affinity? Plato would insist from many directions and with dif-ferent styles of reflective analysis. (Consider the number of "fresh starts" he undertakes: Plt 268d; Phlb 34e; etc.) Plato would not claim to be able to give an exhaustive list of ap-proaches, nor a foolproof method for following any one of them; for there is no method for discriminating relevant features from incidental ones even though we do it every time we propose a definition (Sph 227d, 235d, 237b; Plt 283d). Some reflections about knowing are germane, however, in the absence of a strict method.

1. We might reflect on the fact that we know, in a measure, what we are looking for when we agree to begin an inquiry. This is the express subject of the *Meno* but is a live awareness in other dialogues as well (190c sq; Grg 495e; Phdr 242c; Phlb 58d). One of the indications that we anticipate our conclusion each time we initiate an inquiry might be expressed as knowing what form an account will take in explicating a specific subject matter, and hence knowing (within limits) where and how to look.[28] Roughly speaking, the problem of any inquiry is to find the appropriate ordering principle (Phlb 22, 61; Ti 31; Plt 277d–78e, 284b–85b). Mathematics is the most perspicuous, and hence proves eminently successful where its kind of order is appropriate. To judge any one set of ordering relations in-adequate to a task is never to renounce the search for an order-

27. Robinson, p. 226; Plt 262–63; Grg 500; reflected in Aristotle's "formal object" (*Posterior Analytics* I 7–10).

28. An apt contemporary example is the proposal to extend a relative frequency theory of probability from events to hypotheses; criticized in P. F. Strawson, *Introduction to Logical Theory* (London, 1952).

ing principle but simply to recognize that the one proffered provides a pseudoorganization, an arbitrary arrangement (Phlb 45, 53b; Plt 262).[29]

2. We can also notice that certain accounts are more satisfying than others, and that we are able (again, within limits) to recognize one style of inquiry as more adequate than another. This recognition is not immediate; initially it requires a working familiarity with the subject and then an honest effort to engage in a critical, often mutual search (Phd 276–77; St 263; La 187e–88e, 194). And the reasons given for selecting one mode of discourse (or "conceptual framework") over another are usually couched in terms like expedient, fruitful, simpler; terms whose semantic structure is quite similar if not identical with those Plato considered: existence, sameness, unity, and the like. The former are quite as pervasive as these latter terms, and every bit as resistant to definition, at least to one that claims to be context-invariant. Here again we are not granted a privileged language by which to adjudicate the fit of any other. This judgment of appropriateness cannot be guided by a set of axioms precisely because it varies from one context to another. So some might be tempted to call it a mere (and presumably blind) option; yet the terms describing the judgment are unmistakably epistemic. Perhaps the capacity these terms announce is akin to that of learning a language; but whatever it is, such a capacity remains a fact of inquiry.

3. Finally, we might recognize that there is no other norm for inquiry outside this undefinable affinity of the intellect for order. There is simply no sure method outside of giving oneself over to inquiring by a willing engagement in critical questioning that is as searching as it is honest (R 494e; Grg 487; Phdr 257b).[30] The rules of logic are merely formulations of the inner exigencies of inquiry, an assurance of order of a minimal sort. And when one moves beyond the axiomatic account—in physical science or more ordinary investigations—to inquire into the relevance

29. Cf. the remarks of C. S. Peirce on affinity of mind with its object as a norm in *Collected Papers*, 6.477, 5.589.

30. Robinson, pp. 224–27; E. V. Kohak, "Road to Wisdom," p. 131.

of the account itself, one can uncover only different facets of the object sought. One can bring forth examples—show the object operating, that is, in diverse contexts or examine the characteristic ways of referring to it—and try to judge their relevance, in dialogue with oneself or others (R 580).[31] (This picture is necessarily sketchy. It will be filled out, particularly as we examine more closely the role of examples in the section below on the program and its realization.)

All this points to a disjunction: either there is a radical affinity for order in man as inquirer or there is no sense to inquiring. But if inquiry is senseless, then many if not all human aspirations are void or absurd, for each presupposes the power of discrimination native to inquiry (R 611e; Phdr 242e; Phlb 58d; Sph 253, 259; Grg 487e, 495e). It is clear that these aspirations exist, that we admire, let us say, the conscientious head of state and despise his assassin; consider his spending himself for the country *comme il faut,* and find his murder baffling. But beyond this Plato insists that our only salvation is to believe in these aspirations and take them seriously, for they ground man's image of himself and guarantee our humanity (R 621c; Phdr 255 ff; Phlb 64c–e; Grg 523–27; Plt 311c).

Dialectic and the limits of discourse. What sort of facts are these we have been attending to? They are obviously of some special sort, ingredient as they are in every situation, yet constituent of the inquirer himself as well as the object sought after. The normal thrust of inquiry carries it directly to the object— What is x?—and Plato's inquiry was no exception. But we are pointing to a similarity of structure between the knower and the object of knowing. Both must be shaped, a superficial reading of Plato might suggest. Then one would simply have to sketch the features of several candidates, and within a reasonable

31. For the work preliminary to defining, cf. Phdr 273; Men 71 ff.; Plt 277–78, 297–99, Grg 493–94. See also Aristotle, *Posterior Analytics* II 13; "Perspicuity is essential in definitions, . . . and we shall attain it if we can collect separately the definition of each species through the group of singulars we have established, . . . and so proceed to the common universal" (97b33).

amount of time we would have been able to piece together a
composite of the dialectician and to that extent, at least, know
what it means to be committed to truth. There is something of
this in the program of the *Republic:* write the just man large in
the harmonious state, and the picture itself will be an eloquent
response to Thrasymachus. But I have suggested this is a one-
sided and misleading formulation for knowing. Another side requires us to go along with the inquiry. Unless we are willing to
respond candidly, and take up the search with some hope of
illumination, the most we can hope to show is that ordinary
ways of speaking fall short of their target. If one is to move
beyond this skeptical sophistication, one must be faithful to the
spirit of inquiry, as were Glaucon and Meno. Justice will show
itself for what it is only to the person given over to inquiry, to
the one sensitized to recognize his own deepest aspirations in
the "objects" answering to them.

It is not intuition, then, but inquiry that authenticates itself
for Plato. This has less to do with "self-evidence" than with a
pervading spirit, an orientation, an engagement of the entire
person (Smp 210; Grg 487e; R VI–VII; 7Ep 340–44; Phdr
255–57). By pursuing the question arising most naturally to all
men upon encountering any object: "What is it?", Socrates can
guide us on skillfully to the very presuppositions of questioning
itself. By laying bare the structure of this connatural query,
Plato succeeds in laying out guidelines for metaphysical discourse which incorporate and explicate Socrates' lifelong ad-
monition: "Know thyself" (Phdr 230).

THE PROGRAM AND ITS REALIZATION

My aim is to discover the élan of inquiry itself by faithfully
following its spirit as far as it will lead (Chrm 169, 175;
R 532–34). The method is to begin with the common conceptions of ordinary usage, subjecting them to critical examination
of various sorts. Candidates are sifted out by testing their consistency with notions more firmly held as well as by weighing
their power to illuminate experience, until one reaches a more
or less adequate account. Then, if one's stamina holds, one will

question the very process of "giving account" and pursue it to rock bottom, that is, to notions that force themselves upon us because inquiry itself is at stake. One may try to give examples of these; or if this is impossible, supply a likely story or a myth. All this is designed to test our grasp of these ultimate conditions, to find out whether we really know what we mean when we use expressions like harmony, proportion, and the like.

This procedure, we shall see, is the strategy of the *Republic*. And it is worth noting that, by offering examples in such a way, Plato is telling us he is doing the very best he can, calling upon the power of discernment native to inquiry to function on its own, at it were, where an account of the usual variety is no longer feasible. We are not so much asked to see as to judge the relevance of the examples offered and, by reflecting on the relative weight we are willing to give them, arrive at some notion of the object sought.

Plato has found a way to offer an account of that "sort of object" which defies imagination and even definition. His method consists in renouncing hope of any direct knowledge and having recourse instead to an indirect technique: offer a number of examples, come to a certain appraisal of their relevance to the topic, and then, by reflecting on the relative importance of one over another, gain a certain "proportional" grasp of the object. This explains why Plato says that dialectic dispenses with images and moves in the realm of "pure thought"—yet in a region beyond that of axiomatic accounts. He is not referring to a yet more abstract mode of consideration but to a use of the powers of discernment or reflective judgment that defies a systematic form (R 511, 532–34). The method—appraising examples—is similar to that of concept formation, the stage preliminary to definition, except that the issues at stake here will not admit of an account as objective as definition, for they lie at the point where subject and object meet in the very ground structure of inquiry.

Metaphor and myth play an auxiliary role in this method by announcing that any straightforward account would be inadequate to the realities involved. Plato's very recourse to them suggests something of the nature of the object by inviting and invoking a fuller personal participation in the inquiry. I have called this role auxiliary because, while it does not directly contribute anything to the account, it is nonetheless cognitive in the sense that it helps attune or "proportion" the inquirer to the object. By providing and suggesting a particular style of inquiry, these figures of speech presage something of the structure of the object sought. (This would class poetic usage generally somewhere between music—note the use of 'attune'—and science, which is no startling advance; but the clear recognition that poetry can play a cognitive role, especially in those areas where any scientific account is inadequate, will prove helpful.) That careful attention to similarity and difference, which made up for want of a method in sifting formulae proposed for definitions, again proves reliable for ascertaining the relative roles played by metaphor and myth, by model and "likely story." For where a systematic account is no longer appropriate, everything depends upon the use made of these literary devices.[32]

Dialectic in the Republic

Before illustrating the movement of dialectic in a large-scale analysis of the *Republic,* let us recall how intimately reflexive a movement it is. The move to "the good," we have seen, takes the demand that *many,* whenever we find them, be *one;* it raises the question of how the ensuing unities themselves might be one. We cannot question *whether* explanatory unities are interrelated, only *how* they are, for the original thrust of the inquiry demands that they be ordered. This primordial fact about human inquiry leads us to call the principle of such order (whatever it may be) the good, as if to point to the roots of this order in man's aspiration to be human.[33] The root metaphor operating throughout

32. H. W. B. Joseph (n. 20 above), p. 73.

33. Identifying the first division of the line (*eikasia*) as the level of uncritical acceptance, of slogans willingly adopted and easily passed on, allows us to capture Plato's concern for knowledge as a social reality, and to catch the main thrust of Socrates' prodding the community to critical awareness. I am conscious of disagreeing with D. W. Hamelyn's carefully constructed interpretation: *eikasia* is the state of mind of one

the transformation is that of harmony or concord. It signals the kind of unity one might hope to find by remarking the peculiar affinity mind has for a unity of order.

The *Republic* illustrates the harmonious unity which is the true state, thus displaying "the good" through a picture or model so that we may recognize it, *Meno*-fashion. It is necessary, of course, that the good be displayed under some aspect—here as the harmonious interchange within the body politic, or as justice—but equally necessary that this aspect manifest enough of the same logical peculiarities to be said to reveal something of the good.

Justice proves an admirable choice. The model account is established via discussion, according to the pattern sketched in Book VI as a divided line. Beginning with the common associations of the word 'justice' and cognate expressions ($=$ the level of *eikasia*), the inconsistencies manifested in our use of them force us to appeal to actual experience to clarify the confusions of proverbial usage.[34] The result is a kind of "right opinion." The next step is to show why the resulting opinion might be said to be right, by giving an account of the central expressions. Then if one should demand the credentials of our account, we can show the inadequacy of alternatives, call attention to the pervasive character of our assumption, and finally note the limits of knowledge by recalling that an *ultimate reason* cannot itself be accounted for. If we have come this far by fidelity to the demands of order and harmony as ingredient in every account, then it would be eminently reasonable to believe in an

---

who holds that sense-data appearances are all there is, and is unaware or does not acknowledge the existence of material objects such that interpersonal standards of description and identification apply to them (*"Eikasia* in Plato's *Republic," Phil. Quar.* 8, 1953, 23). Not that such a reading could not serve to interpret the line; but the terms of the problematic outlined strike one as just too foreign to Plato. Mine is more in line with pages 41–44 in H. W. B. Joseph.

34. This explains in large part Plato's polemic against the poets. They were the only or at least the accepted source of theology, and the gods that resulted held no ontological status. They could not function as God just for a philosopher (cf. *Euthydemus*).

ultimate harmony. Plato would show that we must be content to believe so—there is no reason why the universe is reasonable —and would argue that we can settle for nothing less.

Knowing Plato's fascination with self-reference, we should expect to find this very same scheme operating in the *Republic* as a whole. The first clue would be transitions roughly corresponding to the divisions in the line. And these are forthcoming. At the end of Chapters 1, 4, and 7 we have three possible terminations of the dialogue, each challenged by one of the interlocuters or by Socrates himself as leaving something up in the air, containing grounds for objection, inconsistency, unsupported premises, and the like.

That the first possible termination of discussion appears in Chapter 1 of the *Republic* shows how contradictory common conceptions of justice are. It also indicates how hopeless it is to try to resolve anything on this plane. Thrasymachus, who typifies the initial stage, is so blind to true inquiry as to accuse Socrates of contentiousness. Nor has he any intention of keeping within the spirit of inquiry. Thrasymachus begins to treat it as a game, professing to be doing so out of respect for Socrates, yet really of course fearing to be dragged out of his complacent opinion by the sheer logic of ongoing inquiry. The outcome of a discussion like this for the honest inquirer, on the other hand, can only be to recognize his own ignorance of the true nature of this object which everyone talks about in a different way (354b). Though quite a negative result, it does represent a gain, say, over Thrasymachus, and Socrates is willing to stop. The implication is that he must stop, unless a kindred spirit more resolute than Thrasymachus stir him on. This will be Glaucon, "an intrepid, enterprising spirit in everything," who will not be persuaded that the flaccid pseudoinquiry with Thrasymachus could really convince anyone. And since Socrates would really convince, the dialogue takes up again, on a new level.

Glaucon proves his seriousness of purpose by proposing a thought-experiment, a symmetrical model of a completely unjust man thought to be the paragon of justice, and his dual, the perfectly just man considered by all to be unjust. Socrates takes up the challenge, but to do so offers a model of his own, a republic. By this model he proposes to lead us to what justice really is, and so respond to Glaucon's puzzle. The next three chapters develop the analogy of a republic and then project it onto man himself, until, toward the end of Book IV, Socrates can say: "Well, if we should affirm that we had found the just man and state and what justice really is in them. I think we should not be much mistaken. . . . Let us so affirm" (444a). A handy place to stop, after tying up a loose end or two.

But if we have found what justice is in the just man and state, we have not yet given an account of it. By blowing man up large into the state, we have been able to clarify the relationships we know ought to be present and have succeeded in unraveling many a confusion. But we have gone no further than common opinion. The very appeal to an image, outsized though it be, signals this. So even if we know it to be right, what has been discovered about justice remains opinion.

Now when faced with a set of propositions proposed as right opinion, we may accept all, some, or none. And presumably we may ask for an account of any one, since at this level it is not clear how they might cohere one with another. It is Adeimantus this time who objects, taking exception—as one might expect— to the radical and doubtless offensive stipulation that wives and children be held in common. Socrates' reaction shows that his objection is highly relevant. Meeting it will carry us from what we have found justice is to the reason why what we have found is justice. In short, it leads to an account. For after Plato defends the coherence of his unpopular proposal—as an organism the state cannot tolerate (the exclusive) 'my' and 'mine'—and when he reaffirms the necessity of having a class whose happiness lies solely in serving the needs of others, Glaucon wonders whether this is not all a dream. Will it ever be possible to find any men willing to renounce all claim to personal happiness to find it in their role-well-executed? Glaucon's question leads to an explicit identification of the guardians as philosophers, for these alone will be able to function as true guardians must. Understanding that unity is organic, they will be influenced to expand their appetite so as to take in the whole of the state. This would forbid them from seeking any exclusively individual happiness, for they would *know* that well-being is organic.

The philosopher *is* the account we sought. He is the part which accounts for the whole and must govern the whole, because the philosopher alone can be at once part and whole. This is what Aristotle was later to call the "formal element."

The next two chapters of the *Republic* present the philosopher's "true nature" by considering what contributes to his generation and his corruption, the odds against his developing, and the painstaking formation he requires. Because the distinguishing —or formal—aspect of the philosopher is his knowledge of the good, the treatment of dialectic as the method of pursuing the good comes in these chapters. And here again we are offered analogies; one cannot give an account of the good. We are "unable to apprehend its nature adequately," but Socrates is "willing to speak . . . of what seems to be the offspring of the good and most nearly made in its likeness" (505e, 506d). There follow the three likely stories of the sun, the line, and the cave; the best one can do in an objective account of the pervasive affinity for order Plato calls the good.

And who would dare question whether knowledge of the good were a suitable underpinning for the just state? Not Glaucon, who is satisfied: "I think we have finished." Only Socrates dares move further, beyond the account given, to display why it can serve as an account. The tactics, as I have already outlined them, consist in contrasting the perfect state with its corruptions, and finally with an utter tyranny, the complete inverse of the state "harmoniously ordered according to reason." But this defense is in its turn once more on the level of opinion: we are asked to judge degrees of happiness as displayed in states and souls (580). We must now offer an account why the just state *must* be so ordered, and we are given yet another analogy for the soul: it is tripartite and composed of reason, spirit, and desire (588c). Yet the fact that this triune model must be ordered by reason, and not one of the other two parts, can be established only by recalling how pervasive are order, harmony, and concord, and that we invariably associate them with reason. What we cannot know, then, but must believe, is that the soul, and specifically its rational element, is "itself akin to the divine and the immortal and to eternal being" (611e, 591c), not however, the gods of the poets, but to whatever it is that accounts for order itself.[35]

SUMMARY

This brings us to Plato's central contribution: showing that a search for the ultimate goal of all inquiry is in reality a laying bare of the rational principles we find pervading inquiry itself. In relentlessly pursuing our recognition of the fact that we seek for a kind of unity in every object we would understand, Plato is able to map the move from "What is *x?*" to "What is the good?" through "What does it mean to explain (or account for) *x?*" By paying close attention to laws of language—some of which Aristotle will formulate as logic—Plato can show that these are questions of different sorts, calling for different styles of response. But by keeping his eye as well on the élan common to them all, Plato is not overwhelmed by the logical diversities. This, we shall see, is the central issue for analogous discourse: how to show the uniqueness of any final or ultimate account. Or put more exactly, how do we incorporate the inadequacy within the account itself to show that one recognizes its pretensions, yet without losing the initial thrust, and hopefully directing and transforming it?

Plato succeeds in highlighting the uniqueness of dialectic by refusing it the status of a "super-account." Dialectic is not a direct knowing of a higher sort (hence it can only be misleadingly referred to as intuition) but rather a critical reflection on the accounts we do give. Such a reflection remarks the inadequacies of each account, yet recognizes that the deficiencies of one

---

35. Compare Phdr 270d with 271d–272a, and R 525d–526b with Phlb 62a. This approach is examined in detail by Paul Desjardins, "The Form of Plantonic Inquiry," pp. 297–308.

may well be complemented by another.[36] And this generous pluralism is preserved from an indecisive academicism by the further realization that an ultimate account must be rendered not in word only but also in deed (La 188de, 7Ep 340c).

Nor is this demand esoteric. It simply acknowledges the exigencies of man's heart and spirit as well as his intellect. This comprehensive conception of inquiry—as a style of living, as a way of being personally engaged in pursuit of the truth—explains and is explained by Plato's insistent recourse to the dialogue form, to figurative speech and artistic imagination. Each of these devices helps engage the inquirer and reminds him that neither the pursuit nor the goal can be rendered intelligible independent of engaging upon it. The sign that we are faced with something different comes with expressions like good, order, unity, harmony, and their like. Since these terms resist a formulation modeled on that of mathematics, they can be understood only in our pursuit of them. Since they name the standards governing any inquiry, there is no particular inquiry capable of tying them down. Finally, their presence as a demand in every inquiry—that it be conducted in an orderly fashion to a single end—suggests that a form which solicits the inquirer to engage himself in the pursuit is the form proper to philosophy.

Aristotle will be more impressed by the linguistic issues raised, and so will direct his energies to clarifying those moves central to language itself, which collectively come to be known as logic. And in the interests of a similar clarity, Aristotle will carefully distinguish good from true, and inquiring from doing; intellectual from moral, intellect from will. He will show that all these moral qualities may predispose us to understand, but they are not understanding. But a gain in clarity is not always an unequivocal gain. We shall see how Aristotle's bifurcation diverted his own attention and that of his followers away from the regions where language embodies life to the structures of language (and thought) as something laid out before us. To say that 'good' is

36. Notably L. B. Geiger, *La Participation dans la philosophie de S. Thomas* (Paris, 1953), and C. Fabro, *Participation et causalité selon S. Thomas d'Aquin* (Louvain-Paris, 1961).

analogous includes but does not employ the fact that good specifies the subject as well as the object in an inquiry. The logical
device of analogy merely acknowledges that good has many yet
related uses. Our attention is diverted from the unique role it
plays in linking the inquiring subject with the object sought after.
Aristotle is thus permitted the pose of a linguistic pluralist quite
neutral to the nagging questions surrounding language-users.
Yet as we survey his manner of employing this acquisition, we
shall see Aristotle presuming a privileged role for the inquirer,
not unlike Plato's "affinity for the true." Unless this be the
case, the logical pluralism suggested by "analogy" would prove
so radical that we could never successfully engage in inquiry as
Aristotle wishes it.

4. Aristotle: Inquiry and Its Method

Plato could not help being fascinated by the peculiar logical behavior of certain expressions. Yet in elucidating some of the notions expressed, he found that he was required to speak of the knowing subject as well as the "things" referred to. When Aristotle confronts the same type of notion, he tends to focus on the logical peculiarity of the expression itself. After proposing three ways of accommodating these notions he will reject one, apparently opt for the second, but actually use the third. This discrepancy between the solution proposed and the one actually used arises more readily when the account proposes clear-cut and decisive criteria. Plato's dialogic style attempted to overcome the limitations of what can and cannot be said, but when Aristotle confronts the same type of notion, he tends to focus on the expression. He prefers a more straightforward formulation —a solution. His solution of the logical puzzles surrounding expressions like good, being, and true has been summarily called a doctrine of analogy. The resolution is, however, more apparent than real. In fact, the discrepancies between the solution Aristotle proposes and his actual practice will reappear in a thinker of the status of Aquinas, and stand accentuated when we contrast Aquinas' usage with that of Scotus.

We have noticed the dual focus of dialectic for Plato: the clarification of general terms (What is x?) and the elucidation of the more elusive, all-pervasive notions that outstrip even generality. I remarked how the latter arose out of the inquiry about general terms by Plato's substituting expressions like good and one in the general schema: What is x? Then these pervasive expressions went on to usurp more and more of dialectic's attention. Yet this very shift forced Plato's dialectical inquiry to mine the dramatic, ironic, and self-reflexive resources of language. Aristotle also focuses on the clarification of general terms and uses his results to break up the business of coming-to-know into manageable departments.

Aristotle's aim is to establish conditions for knowledge (*episteme*) in a manner appropriate to different areas of inquiry. Yet his *episteme* does not correspond to Plato's *dianoia* (where one gives an account of one's object); Plato's paradigm of such accounts was too mathematical, too little adapted to the specific subject for Aristotle's taste. In fact, Aristotle departs from the divisions of the divided line to arrive at an entirely new style of account. This is the burden of *Physics* I and *Metaphysics* I, where the four causes are isolated; and of the *Posterior Analytics,* which sets out the logical conditions for seeking after the causes. Yet Plato's insistence that common notions be "tied down" via the forms had secured an indispensable logical point: if one were to use the causes to explain, one could use them only within the boundaries of a generic type. It was not necessary that the types be given; the very pressure of inquiry would reveal the divisions more clearly. But one could recognize their outlines from the outset by structural and functional samenesses which varied only in more or less (HA 486b19; PA 644a18–b11, 645b6–27).[1]

To look at our discourse with these logical demands in mind, and with an eye to common nouns or names, preliminary division suggests itself: those terms used to refer to any object exhibiting a common set of general characteristics (*sunōnuma*), and those making reference without regard for such general types (*homōnuma*) (C 1a1–11). The background is the "doctrine of forms"; the foreground, a concern for a linguistic clarity conducive to a formal account (or definition). The polemic en-

1. Reference to Aristotle will ordinarily be incorporated into the text, with Bekker pagination preceded by an abbreviated reference to the work according to the following scheme: *Analytica Posteriora* (AP), *Categoriae* (C), *De Anima* (deAn), *De Interpretatione* (deInt), *Ethica Eudomenia* (EE), *Ethica Nicomachea* (EN), *De Generatione Animalium* (GA), *De Generatione et Corruptione* (GC), *Historia Animalium* (HA), *Metaphysica* (M), *Meteorologia* (Meteor), *De Poetica* (P), *De Partibus Animalium* (PA), *Physica* (Phy), *Rhetorica* (R), *Topica* (T).

visages anyone who purports to give an account outside the proper limits of scientific discourse—to construct a superscience of those things exhibiting no set of characteristics in common. Aristotle's concern for common nouns betrays the background of the forms; his discussion of scientific demonstration and its propadeutic in the *Posterior Analytics* and the *Topics* shows the requirements for scientific discourse. The very examples used in the *Categories,* together with Aristotle's sustained attack on an overarching science in the *Metaphysics,* underscores the polemic. The only kind of terms that will carry the weight of demonstration are the univocal (*sunōnuma*)—or to speak more precisely, only expressions employed univocally can assure the validity of a demonstration.

But this division of Aristotle groups together under equivocal uses such odd company as 'pen' used of a writing instrument and an enclosure for pigs, 'man' referring to type and to token, as well as the Platonic favorites of 'one' and 'good'. From the point of view of language as an instrument of scientific discourse, then, the only response to one's desire for a unified view is to deny there can be one. For Aristotle, scientific knowledge (*episteme*) is irreducibly pluralistic: there are many sciences but no way of unifying them, no hope of grasping (scientifically) what it is they are all about.

But such a complete pluralism is obviously unsatisfactory. Why should we cut off the very animus impelling us to science when it comes to reflection upon the sciences themselves? The pervasive desire to unify multiplicity is at the heart of science as an enterprise. And besides this, we do ask further questions. It is not enough to warn a person that terms like being and one are used differently in different contexts. If he is a genuine inquirer, he cannot help but wonder why it is the same term that is so used. As Plato recognized, the demand for unity is imperious. And as if to manifest this need, poets show a blithe disregard for the legislation of philosophers and usually find a receptive public. The fact that this response comes from the instructed as well as the multitude forces a consideration of the poet's tools of discourse, and especially of metaphor.

First Proposal: Metaphor

Aristotle undoubtedly singles out metaphor because its structure is most akin to logic; it is a device the poet shares with prose writers. Metaphor arises quite naturally as a way for Aristotle to mediate the neat but inhospitable division of univocal/equivocal. (Metaphor is defined in P 1457b5; used in prose, R 1405a5; and offered as a mediating category, T 140a6, 158b10.) Indeed, in the *Topics,* metaphor provides the only hope that some equivocal terms might be less so than others, and that some of them might even be cognitively expedient. (G. E. L. Owen used this point about metaphor as evidence for inverting Jaeger's thesis. Owen shows how Aristotle swung from an initial anti-Platonic polemic against "metaphysics"—strengthened by an exhaustive univocal/equivocal division—to a metaphysics of his own when he could find a satisfactory semantic device to engineer it. Owen argues persuasively, but there is at least one counterindication to his interpretation. Nonetheless, whatever be the facts about the development of Aristotle's metaphysics, Owen's structuring and analysis of the three modifications of the univocal/equivocal dichotomy rings very near to Aristotle and has shaped my entire discussion.[2])

But what of metaphor itself? Can it sufficiently redress equivocity to provide us with some hope of using transcategorical words responsibly? Aristotle's views on metaphor are distinctly ambivalent. On the one hand it is a "sign of genius"; on the other, the very mark of obscurity (P 1459a6; T 139b34). And while such views can be explained by Aristotle's diverse con-

2. The counterindication to Owen's thesis on development—that the only alternative to equivocity recognized in the *Topics* was metaphor—is found at 110b16: "consider those expressions whose meanings are many, but differ not by way of ambiguity of a term (*kath homōnumian*), but in some other way," for example, as "end and means to that end." Cf. H. A. Wolfson, "Amphibolous Terms in Aristotle, Arabic Philosophy and Maimonides" (*Harvard Theol. Rev.* 31, 1938, 151–73), for a tripartite division of Aristotle current among Arabian commentators and bearing upon the medieval interpretation, even if Aquinas' disregarding it would suggest he found it inadequate.

cerns, there are other oppositions still more revealing. His concerns are poetry, on the one hand, and disputation preliminary to scientific definition on the other, Speaking of the poet, Aristotle insists that "the greatest thing by far is to be a master of metaphor . . . ; it is a sign of genius since a good metaphor implies an intuitive perception of the similarity in dissimilars" (P 1459a5). But there is no place at all for metaphor in dialectical disputation, and if not here, then "clearly metaphors and metaphorical expressions are precluded in scientific definition" (AP 97b37). Yet "perspicuity is essential in definition," and this is the precise quality Aristotle lauds in those who know how to use metaphor properly (AP 97b30; R 1458b13–17, 1410b32, 1412a10).

Would Aristotle have in mind a different kind of perspicuity for scientific definition, one that notices similarities only and not "similarity in dissimilarity"? But this would be preposterous if not impossible, for to be quick to recognize sameness *is* to grasp difference, and the road to definition leads through careful distinguishing (*Topics* I, 15–18). Perhaps, however, a radical similarity in requisites does not exclude diversity of focus. Aristotle recognizes the common qualification—"metaphors must be drawn . . . from things that are related to the original thing, and yet not obviously so related"—but speaks of perspicuity in defining in quite different terms from a perspicuous use of metaphor (R 1412a10). What is required for defining is akin to facility with inference. He suggests that "we shall attain perspicuity if we can collect separately the definition of each species through the group of singulars which we have established . . . and so proceed to the common universal with a careful avoidance of equivocation" (AP 97b33). In the context of this final requirement, Aristotle precludes metaphor from definition. Science requires a certain degree of clarity about its basic types (T 123a33).

A perspicuous use of metaphor, on the other hand, must satisfy criteria of liveliness more than exactitude. The division is, however, misleading. While metaphor is said to be the best way to "get hold of something fresh," and is best because it presents something in a fresh manner, metaphor "must be drawn from kindred and similar things—so that the kinship is clearly perceived as soon as the words are spoken" (R 1410b12, 1405a34). Nonetheless, metaphor should not be drawn from things too obviously related lest it want in surprise, which is a distinct advantage in "seizing a new idea promptly." Surprise is the cardinal distinction of metaphor from simile for Aristotle, and this suggests an opening for the contemporary reflection I shall sketch out in chapter 9. But my concern here is rather with the demand that the kinship and resulting transfer of characteristics be appropriate.[3] A metaphor, Aristotle insists, "must be fitting, . . . i.e. fairly correspond to the thing signified" (R 1405a10). It cannot be too farfetched and demands a feel for the proper context: "the heroic, for example, as the gravest of metres, is more tolerant than the rest of strange words and metaphors" (P 1459b34; cf. R 1410b32, R III, 7, for the fittingness of language to subject). A sense for appropriate fit is particularly necessary with metaphor, since the harmony or "want of harmony between two things is emphasized by their being placed side by side" (R 1405a11). Such verbal proximity requires attention to sounds as well; in fact "the materials of metaphor must be beautiful to the ear, to the understanding, to the eye or some other physical sense" (R 1405b17, 1405a30–35). It is no wonder, then, that facility with metaphor cannot be taught and is a mark of genius, demanding as it does a sensitivity to similarity in dissimilarity ranging over language as well as subject matter and the elusive relation between them (R 1405a7; P 1458b13–17, 1459a5).

Yet for all this, Aristotle does not want to say that metaphor lacks any structure at all. If it proves misleading when we are expecting univocity, the similarities metaphor evokes are not completely spurious; it will not do to class metaphorical usage with the merely equivocal, The solution Aristotle invokes is

3. Aristotle compares and contrasts metaphor with simile, R 1406b20, 1410b12, 20. Consult IX. 1 *infra* for more contemporary treatment.

proportion, or "analogy." [4] By insisting on proportion, he can give oblique recognition to the formal demands of definition (P 1457b5, where Aristotle lists analogy as one of the grounds for transferring predicates in a responsible use of metaphor). Yet in another context altogether he calls proportional metaphor the "most taking" and attributes liveliness in speech and reasoning to the graphic use of proportional metaphor (R 1411a1–b30). The reasoning here seems to be that the fairest manner of "corresponding to" (*ek tou analogou*) the thing signified is *proportionally* (R 1405a10). Simile displays the proportion most transparently, but its 'as . . . so . . .' form makes the comparison all too obvious, sacrificing the immediacy, the verve of metaphor (R 1410b18). So, for example, "successful similes . . . are in a sense metaphors, since they always involve two relations like the proportional metaphor" (R 1412b33).

But since liveliness, attractiveness, and verve—however desirable they may be—are not logical characteristics, metaphorical usage is set apart from equivocal usage by what it holds in common with simile: a proportional structure. This does not entail, however, that every metaphor be compressed into an *a:b::c:d* mold. All that is required is an appropriate similarity. Yet Aristotle will insist that the "most taking" metaphors will display a proportional structure, at least upon analysis.

We can now locate the three ways Aristotle proposes to mitigate the univocal/equivocal division, as well as the tensions apparent in reconciling them. (1) Metaphor stands out from merely equivocal usage as an initial candidate. An analysis of its successful usage uncovers quite stringent conditions of fittingness, yet these are manifestly elusive and hard to formulate. The closest paradigm (2) is the mathematical schema of proportion. There is much to recommend this formula—it can boast of a rich history already—but the philosopher hesitates to apply it in procrustean fashion. So he will not demand that every meta-

4. That metaphor can be misleading where no relevant similarity is present, is the burden of T 140a6–17; that it proves useful in scientific inquiry is manifested in PA 645b5–27, 652b24–53b35, 681b16–29.

phorical likeness be proportional but will insist (3) that a privileged subset, the "most taking of them," is.

It is commonplace to refer to the mathematical origins of the proportionality schema (*a:b::c:d*) and fashionable to speak of other uses of 'proportion' as extended. While the mathematical model is certainly operative, Aristotle's usage cannot support so convenient a reconstruction. Aquinas noted that proportion knows several senses, and his interpretation seems to be more faithful to Aristotle.[5] Mathematical proportions are equalities; ordinary and poetic usage employ proportions to signal similarities. Nowhere does Aristotle betray a penchant for analyzing 'similar to' as a weak or extended form of 'equal to'. He would rather inveigh against analysis of that sort for demanding in one area of discourse the exactitude appropriate to another. Our sense for relevant similarity so readily exercised in ordinary speech and so carefully refined in poetry needs no mathematical justification.

If it is out of place to harp upon the mathematical form of proportion, though, one might ask how a "sense for relevant similarity" differs from the "fitting poetic (or rhetorical) use" of metaphor I set out to elucidate? Aristotle apparently thought the schema could shed some independent light on the question. And the tradition that has groped for a formal criterion of properly analogous usage certainly thought so too. We shall see that Aristotle's employment of the schema actually presupposes that ability to grasp relevant similarities which is at the heart of his final justification of a responsible equivocal usage: the principle of focal meaning. The formal affinity with mathematics will prove more misleading than helpful. But first we must see why he tended to place so much faith in proportion.

Second Proposal: Analogy

Platonic background. Something of Aristotle's predilection for *analogia* can doubtless be explained by its role in Plato. According to the "likely account" given in the *Timaeus,* analogy or

5. Aquinas' remarks may be found in *Sum. Theol* I 12 1 ad 4, 64 1 ad 2, *de Ver* 12 3 ad 13, 14.

proportion makes for the "fairest of bonds," is "best adapted
to effect a union" (31a). As the principle harmonizing the elements of the world, proportion imports to it the "spirit of friend-
ship" (32c). Plato settles on proportion as the most adequate
image for the relation of many to one and one to many; what
is totally unrelated (or only irrelevantly so, like politician, philosopher, and statesman) is said to "defy all . . . mathematical
expressions of proportion" (*Statesman* 257b). 'Proportion' and
its cognates, 'measure' and 'harmony', tend to image intelligibility itself and so end up every bit as pervasive as 'one' or 'being'. Thus creation is pictured as the act whereby "God [estab-
lishes order by] creating in each thing in relation to itself, and
in all things in relation to each other, all the measures and har-
monies which they could possibly receive" (69b). "As far as
necessity allowed or gave consent . . . God has exactly per-
fected and harmonized in due proportion the ratios . . . , mo-
tions, and other properties" of the elements (56c). While the
Timaeus immediately refers to the world, the language over-
reaches the cosmos. To speak of proportion, harmony, or
measure is to touch a sympathetic chord in reason itself. It signals a basic affinity imaged by the stipulation that the circles of
the same and the other "are divided and united in due proportion" so that "when touching anything which has being, the soul
is stirred through all her powers to declare the sameness or difference of that thing and some other" (37a). So knowledge, in
the *Republic,* is imaged by a line proportionately divided, in an
effort to grasp its nature (509e). And on the true earth—the one
fulfilling our aspirations for complete intelligibility—"the trees
and flowers and fruits . . . are proportionately beautiful"
(*Phaedo* 110d).

Mathematical connotations. In more structural or systematic
terms, Plato's use of proportion reflects the intermediate role
reserved to mathematics, linking instance with type, limitless
with a bound (Phlb 23c; Ti 56c). Now if Aristotle felt compelled to temper Plato's excessive reliance on mathematics, he
also inherited his mentor's great respect for it. This comes to
the fore in two apparently quite unrelated cases: in the proposal

at hand for regularizing a subset of equivocal expressions, and in his discussion of virtue. Ironically enough, both treatments place a reliance on notions mathematical in origin which far surpasses any claims made by Plato. For Plato carefully distinguished dialectic and its method from that of mathematics by manifesting the logical peculiarities of objects like unity, and refused to speak mathematically of the unity-of-opposites which virtue represents. Instead he speaks of virtue (in the final pages of the *Statesman*) in terms calculated to display its precarious nature: the dominant image is that of a unity-in-tension, or a weaving together of mutually opposed characters (Plt 306–11). By translating what appears to be the very same insight into terms of a mean, Aristotle tends to betray the psychological force of Plato's observations by casting them into a more static, arithmetic context.[6]

Perhaps the reason for this choice lies with Aristotle's excessively objective cast of mind. But whatever it may be, the tenacity of the mathematical context can be gauged by the measure in which it has infected the tradition in spite of Aristotle's express qualification regarding the mean of virtue: "the intermediate not in the object but relatively to us—and this is not one nor the same for all" (EN 1106b8, a33). *Virtus stat in medio* has come to be synonymous with middle of the road. And if the eminent role of prudence for Aristotle was to discover the mean, prudent has become an easy cloak for an indecisive and overly cautious temperament. This is quite the opposite of Aristotle's meaning, to be sure, but no amount of expository prose can fully undo the connotations of a mathematical notion so misused. Indeed, in speaking about virtue, Aristotle uses it in a sense so extended that it might well come under his own strictures in the *Topics* against cutting too many threads of common usage (139b32–40a17).

It is instructive that a contemporary illustration of Aristotle's

6. Aristotle's treatment may be found in EN II 6, and EE II 3. This critique is shared by H. W. B. Joseph in "Aristotle's Definition of Moral Virtue and Plato's Account of Justice in the Soul" (*Philosophy* 9, 1934, 168–81).

doctrine of the mean speaks of a conciliation of opposites more akin to Kierkegaard's dialectic than the notion of mean would appear to warrant.[7] And there is a venerable precedent for such an exposition in Aquinas' careful but resolute identification of the rational mean with the virtuous man himself.[8] It is quite clear that interpretations such as these are more faithful to Aristotle's use of the notion. We may also observe how Aristotle's elaboration of the role of the middle term in a syllogism offers a precedent for an extended use of 'mean'. Yet the very need to supply so elaborate a defense for this usage ought to make us question whether the notion itself is appropriate to describe moral decision. For the present, however, we may be content to have traced Aristotle's predilection for mathematics as an ordering principle to his background in the Academy, and look more closely at some typical uses of *analogia* or proportion.

Uses of analogia. A careful study of the use and meaning of the term *analogia* in Aristotle divides the usages into three: (1) mathematical, (2) applied (or extended) beyond the limits of mathematical proportion and usually functioning without reference to ratio as such, and (3) acting as a principle of unifi-

7. H. B. Veatch, *Rational Man* (Bloomington, 1962), pp. 91–101.

8. "Every man of moral virtue is a rational mean," he insists, "since moral virtue is said to observe the mean, through conformity with right reason. But it happens sometimes that the rational mean is also the real mean, for instance, in justice. On the other hand, sometimes the rational mean is not the real mean, but is considered in relation to us: and such is the mean in all the other moral virtues" (*Sum. Theol.* I–II 64 2). "These virtues are chiefly concerned with the passions, the regulation of which is gauged entirely by relation with the very man who is the subject of those passions in so far as his anger and desire are vested with their various due circumstances. Hence the mean in such virtues is measured not by the proportion of one thing to another, but merely *by comparison with the virtuous man himself,* so that with them the mean is only that which is fixed by reason with regard to ourselves" (II–II 58 10, emphasis added). In a passage cited by Pieper and reminiscent of *Summa Theologiae* (II–II 64 1 ad 2), D. Feuling invites us to "adhere to the great and fundamental moral truth that virtue lies in the mean, but not in an abstract, levelling mean, rather in the mean according to the circumstances, conditions, spiritual states, principles, and above all according to the person acting" (*Prudence,* New York, 1960, p. 77).

cation or identity.[9] We may dispense with the strictly mathematical use, for its function is well defined and its meaning clear. This very clarity accounts for the primacy many have assigned it in calling uses of *analogia* (proportion, correspondence, analogy) other than mathematical ratio, extended. I have questioned whether such an ordering does not reflect a prejudice in favor of a certain kind of clarity. It is certainly the case that we make ordinary classifications and judgments on "correspondences" hardly reducible to mathematical terms. Yet "analogy" is proferred as an explanation of the validity of at least some of these judgments. Its apparent power to explain, however, seems to derive from a promise of clarity associated with the mathematical uses of 'ratio'. In this sense, then, in which the nonmathematical use of analogy is distinctly promissory *because* of its mathematical connotations, one may speak of its mathematical origins.

Considering the second and third classifications of Muskens together—extended (or applied) uses and unifying uses—we may distinguish five styles here. These divisions are of course heuristic and hardly meant to be adequately distinct. Arranged in order of relevance for our concerns, 'analogy' is used: (1) to extend a theory so as to suggest a still more unified understanding; (2) to call attention to certain similarities, to include a limiting case under a common term; (3) to provide an image for the order required of a social unit; (4) as a handmaid to insight for introducing new notions and establishing first principles; (5) to express the manner in which the first principles of the physical world can be the same (i.e., spoken of as one).

The first two are more useful in natural science or in practical reasoning; the third is indispensable for thinking in politics; the last two are more directly related to metaphysical or dialectical notions. The first points out that a theory is more than classification and aims at a yet more unified understanding (e.g. as used to extend the theory of sensing in the critique of *Timaeus, De Caelo* 300a2). Its use in Aristotle—to call attention to pos-

9. G. L. Muskens, *De Vocis Analogias Significatione ac Usu apud Aristotelem* (Louvain, 1943).

sible unities beyond the categorical—is more suggestive than scientific. In this first style of usage there is the echo of Plato's warning that such unities may not be real ones. But there is little hint in Aristotle of a procedure that could minimize the dangers involved: to recognize these classes as hypotheses and devise methods to verify them.[10] The second division collects those uses of 'analogy' coordinate with 'similarity', 'resemblance', and 'metaphorically speaking' (GA 715b20, 779a3; PA 662b25; EN 1138b5, 1148b10; EE 1240a13; R 1387a28). It reflects the scientific bias against metaphor. Or better, the second style of usage acknowledges that "metaphor" covers a spectrum from a "certain correspondence" to a "proportional likeness," and opts of course for the latter as paradigmatic (R 1387a26, 1411a1–b22). Although this treatment of limiting cases and of introducing common names via mataphor is pregnant with metaphysical issues, Aristotle does not bring them into the light of day. He shelves them too easily by the arbitrary stipulation that even here the only respectable uses will be expressible in a proportion. The same may be said for the third set of uses which insist that political equality be expressed in proportional terms. Although these three ways of using analogy will affect our judgment of Aristotle, more would be served by focusing on the ways he employed analogies in regions more clearly metaphysical, domains reserved by Plato to dialectic. The last two usages of the fivefold division pertain to these.

In fact, the fourth division is quite akin to Plato's dialectic: it collects the use of comparisons to illustrate a common use (or introduce an unfamiliar usage into an alien context). The

10. Cf. I. M. Crombie, *Examination of Plato's Doctrine* (vol. 2, New York, 1963, pp. 380–83); *Statesman* 262–3; PA 644a18; M 1093b6. Frederick Crowe, in contrasting Aristotle with Aquinas, notes that he "did not advert to the necessity of verifying his concepts on the explanatory level," whereas "St. Thomas was not unaware that science on the level of understanding is hypothetical (cf. *Sum. Theol.* I 32 1 ad 2, where he expressly characterizes his trinitarian theory as an hypothesis similar to a scientific hypothesis that gives understanding but does not settle the question of truth)" ("St. Thomas and Isomorphism of Knowing and its Object," *Sciences ecclésiastiques,* Montreal 13, 1961, 184).

technique of adducing examples to offer some insight into first principles is also employed. I am reminded of Plato's gathering instances from apparently unrelated domains to isolate and explicate a general term, like virtue (*arete*), as well as his predilection for pervasive expressions like unity. There is a crucial difference, however, between using comparisons or examples to introduce new terms and using them to illustrate first principles. Common terms will eventually be incorporated into their own account so that examples here are merely heuristic or propadeutic. But first principles, if they be truly first, must be present in every category, and so cannot be explicated by any account whose very power depends on respecting the limits of a subject genus.[11]

The meaning, then, of notions as pervasive as *first principles* must be formulated so that analogy is not merely propadeutic but *constitutive*. Witness Aristotle's insistence that "the causes and the principles of different things are in a sense *different,* but in a sense, if one speaks universally and analogically, they are the *same* for all" (M 1070a31). They are not the same in the sense that we speak of common elements, since "specifically different things have specifically different elements." Yet "one might say that there are three principles—the form, the privation, and the matter. . . . But each of these is different for each class," so if we say they are the same for all it is "only analogically" (M 1070b17). He says only analogically to emphasize that when "analogically identical things (like actuality and potency) are principles, . . . they are not only different for different things but also apply in different ways to them" (M 1071a5).

By remarking this penchant of certain terms to appear everywhere yet function in a fashion that varies with the context, Aristotle not only describes a certain set of notions most felici-

11. The first characteristic of such terms is their presence in every genus; see the discussion of possible scientific treatment in M III, and the statement about axioms of demonstration in AP I 10–11; the role of the "subject genus" in Aristotle's treatment of science (AP I 7–9, 28, 32).

tously but also shows why their meaning must be established via examples. It might even be taken as a definition of analogous or analogously identical terms. But there is another explicit definition in *Metaphysics* V of things that are "one by analogy": whatever cannot be comprised in a genus and is "related as a third thing is to a fourth" (M 1016b32–17a3). Here we have an obvious reference to the schema of proportion, even to the fact that we usually place the *explicandum* (or *illuminandum*) first: "actuality is to potentiality *as* the waking is to the sleeping"; or, "the relation of master and servant is [as] that of an art and its tools" (M 1048a37; EE 124a30). (The order is of course irrelevant to the mathematical schema, hence: "as the bronze is to the statue or the wood to the bed, . . . so is the underlying nature (*hupokeimenon*) to the substance"; Phy 191a10).

But the proportional schema cannot explain what I mean by analogously identical; it serves at best in an ancilliary capacity, as an image would for Plato. When speaking of the difficulties attendant upon elucidating actuality, Aristotle recalls that "we must not seek a definition of everything," but rather "be content to grasp the analogy, that it is as that which is building is to that which is capable of building, etc." (M 1048a37). We would never speak thus of *ratios,* but rather simply of "recognizing the equality" of the ordered couples (1, 2) and (3, 6). Similarly, the proportional schema fails to give any clues whatsoever to the fact that the analogously identical terms are applied in different ways to different things. Finally, this quasi-mathematical way of speaking is never employed with reference to the completely pervasive terms of 'one', 'being', and the like; but only with reference to the principles of physical nature.[12]

Aristotle asks in the *Nicomachean Ethics* whether *good* must be explicated proportionally, or whether there is another way of elucidating it: "by being derived from . . . or by all contributing to one good?" (1096b23). He prefers explaining our use of good by reference to a paradigm instance: "actions are called 'just' and 'temperate' when they are such as the just or

12. Muskens, p. 91.

temperate man would do," and, "the man who has received an all-round education is a good judge in general" (1105b5, 1095a1). Circular as this looks, the subsequent history of ethics has hit upon no better answer. The apparent circularity vanishes when we see that Aristotle is employing yet another method of elucidating the use of a term which is neither common nor equivocal but may be said *with reference to a single instance.*[13] This device is recognized by Joseph Owens as a peculiar subdivision of equivocals (*pros en* equivocals) and dubbed "focal meaning" by G. E. L. Owen. It offers the final and most successful of Aristotle's proposals to mitigate his original division of terms into univocal/equivocal: "there are many senses in which a thing may be said to 'be', but all that 'is' is related to one central point, one definite kind of thing, and is not said to 'be' by a mere ambiguity" (M 1003a33).[14]

Third Proposal: Focal Meaning

Joseph Owens' monograph, *The Doctrine of Being in the Aristotelian Metaphysics,* details Aristotle's way of assuring that metaphysics enjoys a single subject matter. *Being,* as he summarizes it, is a "group of *pros en* equivocals of which the primary instance is form in the sense of act" (p. 470). Everything, that is, all beings, are derived from the primary instance in the sense that they imitate its duration in a manner proper to their nature: sensible things by propagating the species or any other contribution to the good of the whole, man by contemplating it (pp. 462–66; M 1003b17). Owens accentuates the fact that this primary instance of being—highest act, form par ex-

13. Contrast R. M. Hare's *Language of Morals* (Oxford, 1952) and P. H. Nowell-Smith's *Ethics* (Harmondsworth, 1954) with H. A. Prichards "Meaning of *agathon* in the *Ethics* of Aristotle," *Philosophy* 10 (1953) 29–39. The last is rightfully singled out in J. L. Austin's *Philosophical Papers* (Oxford, 1961) as a paradigm of textual misreading and ethical misunderstanding (p. 39).

14. Joseph Owens, *The Doctrine of Being in the Aristotelian Metaphysics* (Toronto, 1963), pp. 118–23; G. E. L. Owen, "Logic and Metaphysics in Some Earlier Works of Aristotle," in During and Owen (eds.), *Aristotle and Plato in Mid-Fourth Century* (Göteborg, 1960), p. 189.

cellence—is the knowing of knowing (pp. 458, 466, 471; M 1074b34). These identifications allow Aristotle to give his primary instance of Entity a peculiar and fitting nature: intelligence. Does this mean then that Entity in its primary instance is a self? Aristotle's answer is not completely clear, and even were it clear, it would not be enough just to say so. One would have to show how its being *self* makes Entity the paradigm of being and how as paradigm its selfhood is made manifest. This want of articulation is betrayed by Owens' proposed solution of "imitation." It is not Aristotle's, for Owens readily admits that Aristotle nowhere succeeds in characterizing this relation (*methexis*) of secondary instances to primary. But it is offered *ad mentem Aristotelis* (pp. 462–66).

Yet would not Aristotle retort that to talk about other things imitating the primary instance of being is but "to use empty words and poetical metaphors" (M 991a20)? "Imitation" does not look different from "participation," and cannot logically differ from it. Each is an attempt to characterize the kind of unity attendant first upon instances of a common type and then upon that kind of usage neither common nor merely equivocal. Would it not be more accurate to say that Aristotle eschewed any such characterization, and that this was his contribution? True, any solution attempted will have to be of the same order as Plato's "participation"—it is Owens' merit to have shown this, albeit unwittingly. But perhaps in trying to do what Aristotle eschewed, Owens has missed the decisive point: that Aristotle saw that this relationship must never be said but can only be shown—"our meaning can be seen in the particular cases . . . and we must . . . be content to grasp the analogy" (M 1048a35).

If this be the case, then Aristotle may be said to have operated on a level of awareness consonant with Plato's use of dialectic, but found himself impelled to criticize the doctrines of the forms, participation, and the rest. Shaped by his own semantic bent of mind, Aristotle's critique was undoubtedly fanned by developments in the Academy after the death of Plato, developments normally in the direction of codifying. But what singles out a philosopher as great is not his peculiar approach so much as his sensitivity to ground-level issues. In hitting upon "the concept of a word as having many senses pointing in many ways to a central sense," Aristotle achieved a genuine logical breakthrough. And if he realized as well that "its scope and power are to be understood by *use* and not by definition," then we may agree with G. E. L. Owen that this represents "a major philosophical achievement." [15]

Guided by G. E. L. Owen's short but incisive study of "focal meaning," we can try to determine the scope and power of this device by tracing Aristotle's use of it. Owen catalogues the places where Aristotle sheds light on a particular expression by displaying some of its senses as extensions of a primary usage. In the physical works, 'new' is defined most properly as a potential division of the time-continuum, other uses being approximations of this one; " 'contact' *in the proper sense*" is said to apply "only to things which have position," though there may be "various meanings *either* owing to a mere coincidence of language, *or* owing to a real order of derivation in the different things to which it is applied" (GC 322b30–36).

The clearest examples, however, are to be found in *Metaphysics* V. In the analysis of 'one', Aristotle insists that the "things . . . primarily called 'one' are those whose substance is one—and one either in continuity or in form or in definition." Other "things are called 'one' because they either do or have or suffer or are related to something else that is one," and so finally, to substance (1016b6–10). The treatment is manifestly schematic and preliminary, for one would have to decide which of the three senses in which substance may be said to be one is itself primary. Similarly, for 'contrary', Aristotle must give five distinct proper meanings, adding that "other things that are called contrary are so called, some because they possess contraries of the above kind, some because they are receptive of such, or are producing or suffering them or are losses or acquisitions, or possessions or privations of such." But the style of solution is the same, for "since 'one' and 'being' have many senses,

15. G. E. L. Owen, ibid.

terms which are derived from these, like 'same', 'other', and 'contrary' must correspond, so that they must be different for each category" (M 1018a31–37). A like treatment can be found for 'capable' or 'possible', where "the senses which involve a reference to potency all refer to the primary kind"; for 'quanta', where "some things are called *quanta* in virtue of their own nature, others incidentally"; for 'complete', where "the others presuppose the first two kinds, and are called *complete* because they either make or have something of the sort or are adapted to it or in some way or other involve a reference to the things that are called complete in the primary sense" (M 1022a1–3).

An argument for development in Aristotle's position might be gleaned by comparing his warning in the *Topics* that there is no general definition of 'life' with the same statement in the *De Anima*. The latter is modified by the demand that we nonetheless explain why the diverse senses of life display an *order* of "potential containment" (T 148a23–36; deAn 414b25–15al). While the difference in focus of the two treatises would allow for an explanation other than that of development, a temporal shift of position would certainly be advantageous for Owen's argument.

ANALYSIS AND SUMMARY

Now to focus on a privileged meaning so as to derive others from it is a Platonic tactic. Form functions as the paradigm for Plato, answering to a need to tie down the meaning of a term used of an indefinite number of individuals. But the motivations of the two philosophers are different, and this suggests why Aristotle had to rediscover the tactic after his original polemic against the doctrine of the forms had made its mark. For the Academy looked for a focal meaning for every general term, coupling it with "participation" to link type with instance, original with copy.[16] Aristotle's concern to establish general terms without the metaphorical note of participation turned him away from this style of analysis. (Indeed the very terms of his polemic

16. G. E. L. Owen, "A Proof in the *peri ideon,*" *J. Hellenic Stud.* 77 (1957) 103–11.

employ a favorite Platonic example, the relationship of a picture to its original, as an instance of mere homonymy or equivocation (PA 640b29; de An 412b20; Meteor 390a10; C 1a1).) Some such shift was necessary, for a direct translation of Plato's employment of "focal meaning" into Aristotle's more semantic framework would have led to the demand that every general term be explicated by reference to a primary use. This requirement proves too strict, as discussions of dead metaphor indicate. We are quite capable of using 'comprehend', for example, without reference—explicit or implicit—to the physical imagery latent in its etymology and similarly for the "collar" of a machine and hosts of other extended terms in common usage, whose reference is quite clear (cf. p. 254).

Aristotle's related polemic against dialectic as a superscience led him in turn, as we have seen, to set up too strict a requirement for responsible discourse, for certain notions inevitably arose which defied a division into either common or ambiguous, univocal or equivocal. By hitting upon focal meaning as a tool for handling this peculiar class of terms, Aristotle was able not only to account for them but could also construct a "first science" which escaped his own objections. Not claiming to function deductively, this science would eschew any form of general proof, contenting itself with a general analysis of those terms which defied a categorical one—terms like one and being, and "others derived from these." [17]

Yet peculiar as notions like one or being may be, when Aristotle speaks of grasping the analogy which constitutes them, he makes reference to the same power that operates in the formation of general concepts: induction (M 1048a35; AP 99b30–1000b5). But to remark this is to recall the force of Aristotle's use of 'induction'. Where we would be tempted to think of Mill, the connotation is rather the *Meno* and the insoluble problem of coming to know what we know not. Plato's recourse to myth indicates that he recognizes this to be insoluble as a problem. Aristotle stipulates after the manner of a transcendental deduction that it simply must be the case that "the soul is so consti-

17. G. E. L. Owen, "Logic and Metaphysics," pp. 178–79.

tuted as to be capable of this process" (AP 99b32, 100a13). The process refers immediately to concept formation but also to "recognizing the analogy" in terms like one and being. Furthermore, by expanding the reference to the constitution of the knowing subject we may distinguish between just any common term and these peculiar ones, as well as solve an obvious ambiguity in focal meaning, namely: what is to count as a primary sense.

What sets terms like one and being apart from common terms is their peculiar quality of appearing in various contexts and functioning variously in each. What distinguishes them from mere homonyms is that a primary sense addresses itself to us in their regard and does so in such a way as to allow us to grasp the analogy by relating other uses to it. At least Aristotle presupposes this to be the case, and it is necessary that it be so in order to find a unifying principle for his conceptual pluralism. For if the most one can say is that " 'being' has many senses . . . different for each category," then nothing distinguishes its use from any other homonym. And if one proposes to give such terms a privileged status by noting that at least a subset of their uses is related to a single use which is primary, then the primary use must be perspicuous—lest the number of primary uses be as numerous as the uses themselves.

The issue comes more sharply into focus once we reflect that "the primary use" is a notion quite uncongenial to us. 'Primary', we would tend to say, makes sense relative to the concerns of a particular inquiry, but to speak of *the* primary sense of a term is gratuitous. Like 'simplicity', no definition is forthcoming that will work for every context; its meaning is relative to the inquiry at hand, plain only to the expert in the field. Primary, in short, is itself one of these peculiar notions, as Aristotle had already remarked in the *Physics* (260b16). So to say that one can grant these notions semantic status short of equivocity, by the fact that their many senses point to a primary sense, presupposes that one be able to identify which sense is primary. Only if these notions were to possess an affinity with the knowing subject as such could we be assured that this were possible. This, as we have seen, is Plato's solution.

What could possibly give these terms the capacity to sustain the use to which we put them? Could it be that in use they manage to reflect in some fashion the very structure of thought, and in this way bespeak something connatural to the subject? Such a proposal amounts, of course, to a variant on the myth of reminiscence, especially by retaining Plato's basic insight that the issue will remain insoluble so long as it is posed exclusively as a problem of plotting objective shifts in meaning. One feels that Aristotle would have liked to be able to lay it out so, but by his recourse to induction—the mind's innate capacity to be led on to understanding—he showed that he realized it could not be done.[18] Nowhere in the *Ethics,* for example, does Aristotle define the good man; it is rather presumed that he will be recognized as one cajoling, mocking, or threatening *me.* We are in quite a different atmosphere now from the quasi-mathematical solution of *analogy,* and it is worth remarking that Aristotle himself does not relate the two proposals. *Metaphysics* IV uses focal meaning; *Metaphysics* XII, analogy; each is proposed in the *Nicomachean Ethics* as a separate alternative (M 1003b8–11, 1070b19–21; NE 1096b23).

The relation of derived uses to primary use need not be pressed into the proportional form, nor is there any suggestion

18. James Ross so characterizes *induction* in *Aristotle* (London, 1937), p. 40, n. 1. It seems a generous interpretation of Aristotle and nicely avoids the anchronistic label of "intuitionist." Aristotle remains ambiguous, of course, about the character of this *recognition,* as he does about "grasping the analogy" or the unity of a general term. In contrasting him with Aquinas, I shall trace this obscurity to his failure to distinguish judgment from consideration generally. Just as the *Posterior Analytics* omits all reference to verification, so is the question "whether x?" inevitably subsumed under the more formal "What is x?" Existence seems merely to be instancing form, and so pertains to the material aspect of a thing. Since this defies knowledge, the more subtle cognitive modalities of discernment, discrimination, and judgment simply do not come up for a distinct analysis.

that such an arrangement would necessarily elucidate the relationship more effectively (M 1016b6–17a3, but see 1093b18–
23). This is yet another indication that the proposal of focal
meaning took precedence over that of analogy for Aristotle.
And it can be interpreted as a further recognition that the proportional schema does not offer so secure a control as it appears
to. In fact, as we have suggested, the schema can be positively
misleading and so "worse than metaphor" since it looks like a
formal criterion and plainly is not (cf. T 140a6–17). Once this
fact is exposed, the search for a formal criterion for a responsible use of focal meaning may prudently be called off. For as
G. E. L. Owen concludes, "the concept of a word as having
many senses pointing in many ways to a central sense is a major
philosophical achievement, but its scope and power are to be
understood by use and not by definition." [19] And the most significant fact we can uncover about the distinctive usage of these
peculiar terms is that it must respond and correspond in some
way to the very reach and rhythms of the mind itself.

This conclusion is not expressly Aristotle's. But it is the contention of a number of contemporary studies that some reformu-
lation of this sort would be required to make a firm case for his
privileged instance of *substance*.[20] These studies are reconstruc-
tions via Aquinas, it is true, but certainly not unfaithful to Aristotle. I shall examine his reworking of Aristotle in due time.
More immediately, however, there is another medieval who felt
compelled to reject analogy as an account of metaphysical and
theological discourse. And what made him reject it was a presentation much closer to the received account of Aristotle than
to ours. The philosopher is Duns Scotus. His reasons for re-

    19. "Logic and Metaphysics, p. 189.
    20. More recently, Michael Novak's "A Key to Aristotle's 'Sub-
stance'," (*Philos. Phenomenol. Res.* 24, 1963, 1–19), which depends explicitly on B. J. F. Lonergan's systematic *Insight* (London, 1957) as well
as his historical analysis: *Verbum: Word and Idea in Aquinas* (Notre
Dame, 1967). Cf Yves Simon, "Order in Analogical Sets" (*New Scholasticism* 34 1960, 1–42) and my accompanying note (ibid. 36, 1962,
225–32) for the role of the privileged instance in analogical usage.

jecting analogy, and his own alternative proposals, will help us see more clearly the virtuosity of Aquinas' proposals as well as the instrument of their realization: the central role of critical judgment.

Part Three

Contrasting Medieval Positions

5. John Duns Scotus: The Univocity Of Analogous Terms

Plato and Aristotle had firmly established the fact that certain expressions in our language, notions we cannot help but use, manifest a peculiar logical behavior. Neo-Platonism (and gnosticism generally) was to fasten on these terms as carriers of theosophic insight. For the medievals, however, the problem shifts. The transcategorical or "transcendental" character of these terms secured, they seemed to offer the most promising way for saying something of Him of whom man can properly speaking say nothing, the transcendent God of Moses, the Hebrew prophets, and Jesus Christ.

The terms involved—'one', 'good', 'being', and expressions akin to these—are transcendental in the sense of pervading every category and hence defying definition; but the Judeo-Christian God is utterly *transcendent* in the sense that he can never be fully or properly known and indeed could hardly be reached at all had he not revealed himself. So the proposal to speak of God in these terms was not a simple case of transferral or "application" for a medieval. In using them so, in stretching them to cover God and creature, one was consciously exploiting their range, even proposing something prima facie ridiculous, as Aquinas noted: "wishing to speak of the names of something which cannot be named." [1]

At least one notable medieval, however, modified the suggestion that transcendental equals transcendent by insisting that 'being' and related terms which we would want to use of both God and creatures did not in fact possess the analogous structure hitherto identified with transcendentals. Indeed, Duns Scotus felt that they could not be so explicated if one expected to use them with such maximal range. The argument then was not

1. In I Div. Nom. 3, 77 (= Aquinas' Commentary on *De Divinis Nominibus* of Pseudo-Dionysius, Turin, 1950).

whether we could use such terms of God, but rather what structure they must possess to be able to be so employed. For we do use them of God, yet we always count on a significance derived from their use among creatures. Scotus was dissatisfied, presumably, with Aquinas' treatment of the issue, doubtless wondering whether one would be able to say anything at all about God on a theory like that. And he saw through the theory of analogy current in his own time, realizing it could not accomplish the task set for it.

So Scotus proposed a new interpretation of the transcendentals which explains their presence in every category. This ability to function with any category cannot be accounted for by a set of related uses, for the very unity of the set would raise the same questions all over again. For Scotus, therefore, it must be that such terms refer to something ingredient in every other notion. This conviction becomes his famous doctrine of the univocity of being. We shall see how Scotus is pushed to a position so notorious by certain models of concept formation and inquiry. The sheer force of the contrast with Aquinas will help show how much a viable philosophical treatment must depend on the light Plato can throw on the proposals of Aristotle.

The teaching of the "most subtle Doctor" actually presents fewer difficulties of exposition than that of Aquinas. Hence I have chosen to invert the historical order in the interests of clarity. The fact that their method and concerns were quite dissimilar minimizes the danger of distortion. The cardinal point—that Aquinas deftly avoided many logical (or semantic) howlers of which Scotus seemed quite oblivious—is actually accentuated by inverting the chronology. What especially impresses us in contrasting the two, however, is not a relation of before/after, but sheer divergence on basic issues. Scotus may have been motivated, for example, to develop a univocal account of 'being' by what he felt was Aquinas' excessive "agnosticism." At least, I suspect that if he had understood Aquinas, Scotus would have reacted so. But actually the conception of analogy he labors against is not that of Aquinas but of Henry of Ghent; and in elaborating his own position, Scotus will hearken back to Avicenna.[2]

From "Analogy" to Univocity

Before arraying his arguments against analogy—arguments attesting to the widespread acceptance of the Aristotelian problematic and general style of solution—Scotus identifies his opponent quite precisely. The "doctrine of analogy" he feels it necessary to refute is extraordinarily simplistic. It speaks of "an analogous concept" that is really two concepts, but two which "we may consider as one because of their proximity."[3] Of course this means that using an analogous concept involves two distinct acts of concept formation, plus the recognition of some similarity or proximity between the two. This was apparently the teaching of Henry of Ghent, as it would be that of John of Saint Thomas, at least by implication, some three centuries later.[4] When employed to explain the transcendent use of terms like

2. Cf. Ovon 1, d 8, q 3, n 23; IX, 616; E. Gilson, "Avicenne et le point de départ de Scot," *Archives hist. doct. litt. de M-A,* 2 (1927) 89–149; J. Owens, "Common Nature: A Point of Comparison," *Med. Stud.* 19 (1957) 1–14. For reference to Scotus: the *Opus Oxoniense,* containing the Commentary of John Duns Scotus on the Sentences of Peter Lombard done at Oxford, has been reissued in a critical edition under the editorship of Carl Balic, as the *Ordinatio* (Vatican City, 1954). Since most readers, however, will have at their disposal the *Commentaria Oxoniense* (Quarrachi, 1912) or the Vives *Opera Omnia* (Paris, 1893), the references to the *Ordinatio* will be given in full, with Vives volume and page citation following, as: Oxon 1, d 3, q 3, nn 18–19; IX, 587b–98a, for *Opus Oxoniense (Ordinatio),* book 1; distinction 3, question 3, marginal numbers 18–19, vol. IX of Vives edition, pp. 597 (right column) to 598 (left column) of Vives edition. Since the Balic edition retains the marginal numbers of the *Opus Oxoniense,* this apparatus will readily locate a text therein.

3. Oxon 1, d 3, q 2; IX, 13–14; d 8, q 3, n 6: IX, 583b. For the background, cf. M. Schmaus, "Zur Diskussion über das Problem der Univozität im Umkreis der Joh. Duns Scotus" (*Sitzungsberichte Bayerischen Akad.,* Phil-Hist Klasse, 4, 1957, 1–32).

4. For the teaching of Henry, cf. E. Gilson, "L'Objet de la métaphysique selon Duns Scot" (*Med. Stud.* 10, 1948, 84); for John of St.

being, however, we can readily show how this doctrine demands an insight into the very nature of God, thus violating a finitistic theory of concept formation. Scotus recognizes this, of course, claiming in words reminiscent of Aristotle and Aquinas that the second concept is a mere velleity and could never successfully be formed.[5]

But why should Scotus trouble himself with an account so self-refuting as Henry of Ghent's—one which if true would obviate any need for a special logical feature like "analogy"? We are tempted to see the influence of the formal $a:b::c:d$ paradigm at work here. That scheme suggests Henry's theory and if someone were to apply it literally, the difficulties Scotus notes certainly would arise. Wise:man::wise:God, for example, will readily be explicated as $wise_1$:man::$wise_2$:God. A mathematical mind would also note that we must know how 'wise' is used on both sides if the ratio is to work, since (1) God can never be known, and (2) the mere proportion wise:man cannot give clues of itself unless we know which of the relations is relevant. Normally, an analogy or model proposed to illuminate another relationship initiates an inquiry into the second, so that the relevant features of the analogy are gradually delineated. In the case of divine predication, however, no such inquiry is possible, for many diverse conceptions of God's wisdom are compatible with the same set of terrestrial events.

But why does Scotus insist on "applying" the paradigm so literally, or why bother with such a simplistic account as Henry of Ghent's? What kept him from considering Aquinas' other proposal of "focal meaning"? The answers to these questions will make the shape of Scotus' reasoning stand out and will show us a philosophical temper that can only be called Aristotelian yet is as far removed from Aristotle as Aristotle is from Plato. If we think of Aristotle translating as much of Plato as he could into common-sense parlance, Scotus is performing the same service for Aristotle. And if we can wonder whether Plato

Thomas, cf. *Material Logic* (trans. Y. Simon et al., Chicago, 1955, pp. 179–83.

5. Oxon 1, d 3, q 2, nn 8–9; IX, 19–20a.

always fits into the mold of philosophical common sense, we can say the same for Aristotle at the hands of Scotus.

Yet the fact remains that the Aristotle familiar to us through the British empiricists had been quite thoroughly refracted through Scotus. The same may be said of Scotus' relation to Aquinas, and the role that he has played in transmitting Aquinas to us. Gilson's remark, for example, that a real point of conflict is lacking because analogy for Aquinas denotes an act of judgment while for Scotus it refers to concepts, is not very illuminating to those who view Aquinas as proposing an "abstractive" theory of concept formation more akin to Scotus.[6] My analysis of the manner in which Aquinas employs analogy will explicitly bring out the feature of judgment or use which allows him to espouse both proposals of "focal meaning" and "proportionality" quite indiscriminately.

We are fortunate in having Scotus' commentary on Book IV of the *Metaphysics* where Aristotle proposes focal meaning as the way of unifying the consideration of being.[7] Scotus' transformations are at once far-reaching and telling. The text of Aristotle as reproduced by Scotus reads: " 'being' is said in many ways, but with reference to one, indeed to one certain nature, hence not equivocally" (M 1003a33). Scotus acknowledges: of course not equivocally, else how could we have a science of metaphysics; one *science,* one univocal subject genus?[8] The requirements of the *Posterior Analytics* are invoked with little sensitivity to the problems involved in transferring them from a particular science to the "science of all." Nor does

6. E. Gilson, "L'Objet," p. 84; for a discussion of Aquinas and "abstractive theory," cf. Wilfred Sellars, *Science, Perception and Reality* (London, 1963), pp. 41–59; and P. Geach, *Mental Acts* (London, 1957), pp. 130–31.

7. On focal meaning, cf. G. E. L. Owen, "Logic and Metaphysics in Some Early Works of Aristotle," in During and Owen (eds), *Aristotle and Plato in Mid-Fourth Century* (Göteborg, 1960), pp. 163–90; and J. Owens, *The Doctrine of Being in Aristotelian Metaphysics* (Toronto, 1963), pp. 118–23, 470–71; Aristotle, *Metaphysics* IV 1.

8. In Meta 4 q 1, n 2; VII 146a (= *Quaes. Super Libros Metaphysicorum Aristotelis,* Paris: Vives, 1893, vol. VII).

Scotus find anything problematic in metaphysics as the first science from which all others are deduced. In fact, the requirement of univocity seems designed to assure deducibility.

This suspicion is corroborated when Scotus lays down the first principle of metaphysics and of all science as "it is impossible that the same thing be and not be at the same time," and then insists that if *esse* were equivocal, all principles would be placed in doubt. This could be the case for two reasons: either because these principles would be deduced from a first principle whose predicate is ambiguous, or because each principle would contain some form of *esse* and hence share its ambiguity. In either case, the one word, one meaning adage rules the discussion, and the privileged position of the key word (*esse*) in the first principle of all science demands that its meaning be unambiguous.

Scotus opts for Avicenna's description of the role of *esse* as the most likely one: " 'being' is said of everything under one formality" (*per unam rationem*).[9] This means that being is a concept present in our conception of anything. It would give a determinate meaning to the scholastic adage that the "first things we understand are the most common principles of all." [10] Being then becomes what is "unqualifiedly most common" (*communissima simpliciter*), and presupposed to building all other concepts.

On such an account, we dare not vacillate about our ability to be clear about being, for everything else hangs on it. And there is the requirement of epistemology that each faculty have its proper object: the intellect's is *being*.[11] If anyone feels suddenly out of his depth, Scotus simply bids him consult his own experience: "We are certainly aware ourselves that we can conceive *being* without conceiving *this being* in itself or in another;

9. Ibid., VII 146a, and n 5; VII 147–48.

10. Aristotle, *Post. An.* I 11; Aquinas, *In I Post. Anal.,* I 20.

11. *In Libros de Anima Aristotelis,* q 21; III 612–27; A. Wolter, *Transcendentals and Their Function in the Metaphysics of Duns Scotus* (St. Bonaventure, N.Y., 1946), pp. 74–77; C. Shircel, *Univocity of the Concept of Being* (Washington, 1942), pp. 69–86; B. Heiser, "The *Primum Cognitum* According to Duns Scotus," *Franciscan Stud.* 23 (1942) 210–13.

in fact doubt does not arise until we try to conceive whether being is in itself or in another." [12]

Such a style of thinking leads to a notion of *being* indistinguishable from "the most common genus." But this identification proves unwelcome for theological reasons: creator cannot share a genus with creature and still remain God; nonetheless we want to be able to say of God that he *is*. Philosophically as well, we can see that being cannot designate a genus since the *differentiae* which modify the genus from outside it, as it were, could not *be* differences. Scotus' response is characteristic: what differentiae do for genera, *intrinsic modes* do for being. Intrinsic modes turn out to function like specific differences but lack the problematic characteristics we have noted.[13] On Scotus' view we say of God that he *is,* prescinding from the modalities intrinsic to him, and this explains why our knowledge of him will never be perfect. Being remains, then, the "most common element" underlying all, but is no longer a genus. And for Scotus it must of course be so, since otherwise there could be no "absolutely certain principle." Apprehending being, however, "under one distinctive formality [viz., *communissima simpliciter*], we may then combine it with other [concepts] to form indubitable principles." [14]

AN EXEGETICAL HYPOTHESIS: ALL
SIGNIFICANT TERMS NAME

A sympathetic way of responding to any position which sounds utterly incredible is to try to reconstruct a theory that would make the position plausible. The approach is, of course, hypothetical, but successful to the extent that the complex of statements which have been given would follow from it as a matter of course. The hypothesis claims that one axiom and two

12. In Meta 4, q 1, n 6; VII 148b: "experimus in nobis ipsis quod possumus concipere ens, non concipiendo hoc ens in se vel in alio."

13. Oxon 1, q 8, n 16; IX, 595; Gilson, "L'Objet, p. 86; Wolter, pp. 24–27, 37–39; A. Marc, "L'Idée de l'être chez St. Thomas et dans la scholastique postérieure," *Arch de phil.* 10 (1933) 43–47.

14. In Meta 4, q 1, n 13; VII 154a.

models would suffice to give scholastic logic and epistemology a distortion peculiarly Scotistic. The axiom is one word, one meaning. It claims that the unit of meaning is the word. This principle has really been presupposed by Scotus in much of the teaching already examined here, and most explicitly in his remarks about the first principle. It is laid down expressly in his definition of a "most certain principle" as one composed of terms "known for certain," and amply corroborated in the commentary on *De Interpretatione*.[15]

Some form of 'is' would doubtless be the most ubiquitous word in a language lacking articles. Even were this not strictly the case, certainly the set of paronyms of 'is' would be the most significant of all terms enjoying such ubiquity. Taken together with the axiom—one word, one meaning—this fact about is gives a peculiar twist to Aquinas' assertion that "being is known in knowing any particular thing."[16] For the *being* which is known thereby for Scotus would tend to be what was named by is (or one of its forms) since words signify by naming. Being, then, would be something like "the common determinable element, the first and fundamental note of the essence of anything, . . . the ultimate *subject* capable of existence, the ultimate *quid*." And this is Wolter's description of Scotus' being.[17]

Strange though this notion of being might sound to ears medieval or modern, it becomes plausible given a certain analysis of our statements about things. If complex statements were regarded as built up out of elements, any statement about anything would presuppose that it is. The normal form of an assertion, for example, '*x* is *y*', might then be regarded as containing '*x* is', which is composed in turn of *x* and is. Such an analysis manifestly views concept formation as a process of building composites out of simples. And this is exactly the model Scotus employs, the first of the two models we find crucial to elucidating his train of thought. His assumption that there must be a con-

15. *In Opere 2i Perihermenias*, p 5; I, 591; Wolter, pp. 7, 17; cf. J. L. Austin, *Philosophical Papers* (Oxford, 1961), pp. 23–43.

16. Aquinas, *De Ver.* q 10, a 11 ad 10; cf. ibid. q 1, a 1.

17. Wolter, *Transcendentals*, p. 81.

cept of being common to all rests on a program demanding that all composite concepts be reduced to simples, from which they derive their meaning.[18] And Wolter defines the simple concept as "resulting from a simple act of apprehension," while the composite "results from the synthetic activity of the mind." [19] Now since the mind is said to be passive in the case of simples, and active only in producing composites, objective meaning may conveniently be anchored in the simples and revealed by analysis.[20] This would assure that simple concepts name objects, elements, or features of the world, and so yield *being,* the most common and certain of all our concepts, as the "ultimate determinable element in every essence." Or as Wolter (pp. 17, 71) conveniently puts it, "being thus becomes the core around which the mind is able to build up a proper notion of the whole object whose sensible qualities are immediately intelligible in the phantasm."

Lest this model appear too crude (and the sample analyses of sentences into their components too implausible), it is buttressed and supplemented by the more analytical model of a deductive system, after the fashion of Aristotle's *Posterior Analytics.* In fact, the two models seem to be used often enough in tandem and do enjoy certain affinities. But a latter-day Aristotelian would doubtless want to point out that the *Posterior Analytics,* however weak it may be on methods of hypothesis and verification, does not entail a building-block picture of concept formation and is quite compatible with a highly sophisticated semantics. True as that may be, Scotus employs the deductive model without regard for the special status of metaphysical statements. Hence the model's requirement that the conceptual beginnings of a science be the most certain of all lends support to his epistemological demand for an underlying concept of being.

So on both logical and epistemological counts, the study of

18. In Meta 4, q 1; VII 154a; cf. Marc, "L'Idée," pp. 35–36.

19. Wolter, *Transcendentals,* pp. 81–82.

20. Wolter, ibid., pp. 82, 51, 54; the latter two for use of "objects *causing* concepts."

being designates the protoscience grounding the special subject matters of every other science. Hence, being, while not susceptible of definition (as a first, indeed *the* first), must at least "possess sufficient unity in itself so that to affirm and deny it of one and the same thing would be a contradiction," for it must be stable enough "to serve as the middle term of a syllogism." [21] Scotus' stipulation of the univocity of 'being' reflects deductive demands. Another account hearkens back to the model of concept building: the univocal is that "whose *ratio* is one, i.e. which has no other formality (*ratio*) according to which it is said of this or that." [22] Thus one model reinforces the other, enabling Scotus to insist that "*x* is [a] being" is the most certain thing about *x*. For as the most simple and elemental bit of information about it—that it is a being—it is the most certain. And if *being* is not univocal, then no concept will be.[23]

Is Being the Primary Object of the Intellect?

The upshot of all this is the resounding assertion that the primary adequate object of human understanding is *being*.[24] I have tried to show how the axiom that words are the unit of meaning, taken together with the complementary models of building composites out of simples (epistemological) and deducing everything from an indubitable first premise (logical), might lend plausibility to such a counterintuitive statement. (The motive from philosophical theology is clearly secondary. Having rejected Henry of Ghent's self-defeating form of analogy, Scotus cannot see his way clear to any knowledge of God unless it be via some basal concept of being. But this very incapacity to discover another alternative betrays his epistemological blinders.[25]) But a claim like this one about *being* not only contrasts with the bulk of our experience, taken up as we are with sensible

---

21. Oxon 1, d 3, q 2, n 5; IX, 17a; Wolter, p. 20.

22. Oxon 1, d 8, q 3, n 14; IX, 593a.

23. Oxon 1, d 3, q 2, n 6; IX, 18a; q 3, n 9; IX, 109; n 12; IX, 111; q 2, n 7; IX, 18b; B. Heiser, "Metaphysics of Duns Scotus," *Franciscan Stud.* 23 (1942) 383–84.

24. Oxon 1, d 3, q 3, n 6; IX, 102; Shircel (n. 11 above), pp. 39–86.

25. Oxon 1, d 3, q 3, n 8; IX, 108b; n 12; IX, 111.

things—beings, not Being—but runs counter as well to certain deeply entrenched scholastic principles designed to do justice to that very experience. To cite but two: (1) Nothing is in the intellect that has not first come through the senses; (2) The primary object of human understanding is a sensible thing, or more properly: "a nature existing in corporeal matter." [26]

It could be philosophically significant if it were simply the case that Scotus rejected these theses and worked out a counter position. The fact is, however, that we find him explicitly espousing them while taking a stand against these very principles. A historian might appeal to a conciliating temperament and an early death which left positions underdeveloped; but a philosophical appraisal knows only two alternatives. The first is simply to indict Scotus for making contradictory assertions: for saying on the one hand that all knowledge, including that of being, *does* come through the senses—that we abstract the concept of being from accidents perceived—and yet insisting with Avicenna that "being is impressed in the mind in its first impressions." No question of abstraction would arise for Avicenna since being would be understood immediately as "naturally perfecting our intellect." [27] It is also possible to find him agreeing that the object most proportioned to human understanding is the quiddity of a sensible thing and yet insisting as well that the only object adequate to the cognitive power *as such* is the most common of all—being.[28]

Since contradictions are uncomplimentary and often easily amassed out of context, a more benevolent and usually more fruitful tack is to look for a context where their opposition contributes to a higher synthesis. A contemporary student of Scotus has attempted this by organizing into types the assertions I have recorded, to show that Scotus distinguished knowledge into two orders: distinct and indistinct.[29] (Indeed Scotus himself had distinguished the senses of 'proper object', as a glance at

26. Aquinas, *Sum. Theol.* I, q 84, a 7; q 85, a 1.
27. Oxon 1, d 3, q 3, n 24; IX, 148; *In de Anima* q 21; III, 614, 616.
28. Oxon 1, d 3, q 3, n 24; IX, 148; *In de Anima* q 21, nn. 3–5; III 613–15; cf. Shircel, pp. 45–53.
29. Heiser, "Primum Cognitum," pp. 197–200.

the documentation will indicate. However, this distinction into infra- and post-lapsarian objects, motivated by religious concerns, turns out to be philosophically inoperative and theologically unnecessary.) The scholastic theses can then be relegated to the order of indistinct knowledge; indeed they fairly define it. The fact of such an order, however, does not exclude another distinct order comprising logic and demonstrative science generally, where the demands are quite opposite from those of ordinary experience. In this order, as analysis shows, the basic building blocks are not sensations but indubitable pervasive concepts like *being, thing, one,* and the like. Hence the primary object will be radically different, depending on the indistinct or distinct order to which one is referring.

This approach is not only fairer to Scotus; it is also more representative of his own way of proceeding. But if such an account is more sophisticated than the terms of the first indictment, it will turn out in this case to be more sophistic as well. Indeed we have here an instance of the bad philosophy which turned 'scholastic' into a pejorative—bad, not in a narrowly technical sense of professional ineptitude, but ethically questionable, as indicated by the revolt of the untutored as well as academics against such procedures. In a treatment of Scotus, a brief aside on what one might call an ethics of the distinction does not seem out of order. Distinctions are offered to clarify the issue at hand by isolating the relevant concerns, pinpointing the sense of the question, with a view to meeting it better. Being at the service of inquiry, then, distinctions are not to be used as a pigeon-holing device; and as essentially subordinate to the issue at hand, they cannot resemble a formal mechanism of bifurcation.[30]

Here, as in many a move to different *orders,* Scotus invokes the distinction in such a way as to dissolve the problems rather than meet the issues. The crucial test asks whether the same problems do not arise upon comparing the two orders. And of

30. Cf. B. J. F. Lonergan on Aquinas' use of distinctions in *Verbum: Word and Idea in Aquinas* (Notre Dame, 1967), pp. 16–24; and Plato on the method of division in *Statesman,* 262b–63a.

course they do: how the two proper objects or the two manners of arriving at *being* might relate to each other simply becomes a question about the relations of distinct to indistinct knowledge. What makes such a misuse of distinctions ethically questionable is that the author fails to deliver what he promised. A clarification offers to meet the issues more squarely. Yet by neglecting to apply the crucial test to his own proposal, he leaves the unwary with the impression of having delivered without effecting any real advance.

The final judgment, then, must be that Scotus opts both for and against the theses noted, holding onto a dual primacy of the contents of perception and of the first principles of a deductive science without engaging in the rigorous job of reconciling one with the other. It is the systematic paradigm of scientific knowing which receives more prominence, though, encouraged by the model of concept building and the desire to assure to our knowledge a unified, deductive certitude. The psychological objections to a procedure that postulates a secure possession of concepts fundamental to a deductive schema are silenced by appealing to introspection, as we have seen. And a simple appeal to a process of abstraction conveniently inverse to that of concept building assures that the human mind will yield the simple and basal elements required for more complex judgments.[31]

Judgment as Composition

But what assures that these elements will be elements of the world? (The critical question was always lurking even before it became a central issue.) Scotus has silenced this threat by insisting that the concepts basic to the primary science of metaphysics be simple concepts. As simple concepts, they are the object of unerring simple apprehensions.[32] (Being, we recall, as the most fundamental of all concepts, is also the most simple and hence the most certain.[33]) Statements employing these simple concepts, then, cannot help but be true, so long as they are put

31. *In de Anima,* q 21, n 9, 616b; Marc, "L'Idée," pp. 35–36.
32. Wolter, p. 81.
33. Cf. n. 24 above; also Oxon 1, d 3, q 2, n 24; IX, 49–50.

together correctly. Judgment, often referred to by Aristotle and
the scholastic tradition as a process of composition and division,
is literally just that for Scotus.[34] To judge that a statement is
true is to decide that it is correctly composed. But on Scotus'
terms this is not much of a task, for one who knows the meaning
of the elements and puts them together with respect for the
logic of terms will presumably be doing so correctly. Experience,
of course, is not to be disdained, but this too is basically an
uncomplicated matter of looking to see how things stand and
then combining them rightly.

An initial decision that all the significant components of a
statement signify by naming leaves little for the judgment to do.
The ensuing lack of critical activity reinforces the demand that
each such component function as a name, for 'truth' has come
to mean an isomorphic sort of correspondence. It is simply presupposed that terms stand for aspects of the world to be represented adequately—as aspects—by their composition in a
statement. This assertion is borne out by Scotus' reading of the
De Interpretatione, where we find his discussion of the role of
'is.' Inquiring whether is functions as a copula, Scotus reviews
the opinions and answers no. The reason, however, is that the
is in '[some] man is' does not change its meaning when a predicate noun or adjective is appended: '[some] man is white'. The
res of the verb (presumably, what it signifies) is united with
the subject by the same manner of signifying in both cases.[35]
We can only conclude, then, that '[some] man is white' is to be
analyzed into '[some] man', 'is', and 'white'.

Analogy or Similarity?

Even should all the significant terms in a statement function
as names, however, this would not leave Scotus with a secure
"knowledge by acquaintance." For even the name signifies a

---

34. *De Interpretatione* 1; Aquinas, In VII Meta 17, nn. 1651, 1656–58;
also F. Crowe, "St. Thomas: The Isomorphism of Human knowing and
Its Proper Object," *Sciences ecclésiastiques* 13 (1961) 167–90, esp. nn.
32, 56, 79.
35. *In Peri Hermenias,* q 5; I 591; cf. Wolter, pp. 7, 17.

thing for the scholastics, and hence names through a concept (*nomen significat rem mediante conceptu*).[36] The concept was often described by scholastic as a similitude, and Scotus seems more disposed than most to taking this literally.[37] Adopting the scholastic account in this way allows him to frame the common retort to any proposal of analogy: if the same word names (or signifies) different things, then it must do so by a feature they hold in common. Analogical usage, then, must ultimately reduce to a solid univocal core of meaning as its justification.[38]

Note that this objection is fully compatible with admitting all the facts about analogical usage. Scotus need not and does not deny that 'being' et al. are used differently in different contexts, for of course they are. If we find Scotus' models unmistakably wooden, we cannot but marvel at his agility in employing them. Let this warn his critics to aim at the models themselves as the most viable and most fruitful tactic—fruitful especially in forcing one's own implicit models into the open. Many critics who know that 'being' must be univocal for Scotus have felt it necessary to edit the problem text where Scotus concedes that being is predicated neither univocally nor equivocally, but analogically.[39] But Scotus does not need that kind of defense. Nowhere does he try to explain facts away, even though on his explanation alone they might not be so effectively present.

His point is rather that there must be some explanation why 'being' is used in many ways, why one term is used; and that explanation must be something, viz., the common *ratio* of 'being'. I could have said: something must explain the fact that 'being'—i.e. one term—is used in many ways. This would have suggested why Scotus might move from 'there must be an explanation' to 'the explanation must be *something*'. Yet it would

36. Aquinas, *In Peri Hermenias,* lect, 2, n. 15.
37. Cf. Heiser, "Primum Cognitum," p. 195.
38. Oxon, d 8, q 3, n 27; IX, 626b; Wolter, p. 25.
39. The text can be found at In Meta 4, q 1, n 12; VII 153a; Wolter gives a detailed clarification at pp. 45–46, n. 35, although this is anticipated to a great extent in the commentary in the Vives edition, VII 619b–627b.

not suffice to explain this move as a simple confusion elicited by the scheme: 'something must explain . . .', for what we have here is rather an instance of a pervading type of confusion, as we shall see presently in greater detail.

Briefly, 'being' must stand for a common ground, an ultimate element in everything said to be, as well as the different manners of being: sick, man, red, related to, etc. This must be the case, since we cannot use a term unless there is a concept which it expresses, and a concept is a similitude permitting the term to denote a feature of the thing.[40] This explanation reflects the pressure of realism plus a model of composite concepts constructed from simple ones. Scotus locates the distinguishing feature of analogous names in the fact that they own both a common and a proper concept, for we can either prescind from or recognize the intrinsic modes associated with the notion. These modes function somewhat like layers, except that they are said to emanate from a common ground—the "common concept." In fact, the modes account for the existence of paronyms of 'being', one of the traditional ways of characterizing *pros en* equivocals, albeit the least satisfactory way.[41]

But without subjecting the technical solution of modes to the same criticism as distinct/indistinct orders, though it is every bit as vulnerable, let us rather isolate the need to have recourse to it. This seems to be the conviction that every analogy must, deep down, betray a core of univocity. Else why employ one term? In plainer language, there must be something common to a_1, a_2, a_3 . . . ; otherwise how can we call them all *beings*? Here we have the common-sense retort to analogy, and from what we have seen, there is much common sense in Scotus.

A Possible Resolution Rejected

Why could not Scotus have made the move that appears so readily to us—*what* the *a*'s share is a form, '*fx*', and the form

40. Oxon 1, d 3, q 6, n 13; IX, 253a; In Meta, 7, q 19, n 4; VII, 466a.
41. Cf. Wolter, pp. 24–27; Shircel, pp. 139–57; and on the identification of modes with paronyms, cf. Wolter, pp. 89, 96–98. For a discussion of paronyms, cf. index to Owens, *Doctrine of Being.*

is not a thing but states a fact about something, about x. The demand is not anachronistic, for this solution is in the style of Aristotle and was adopted by Aquinas as well: "the kinds of essential being are those that are indicated by the figures of predication, for the senses of 'being' are just as many as these figures." [42] For Aristotle, as for Plato before him, the study of being, metaphysics, begins in wondering about, asking questions about things. Logic, in the broad sense of the syntax of the language of inquiry, provides this study with its most salient clues by isolating the characteristic *manners* of responding to questions about x.

The basic style of the question, as Plato had noted, is "What is x?"; and this remains basic, even though (as Plato was quick to see) it resists a direct reply.[43] The informative answers are all facts about x, given in quantitative, qualitative, and relational terms. These are the "accidental figures of predication," each different but all related to one subject—the subject we sought to understand from the beginning, and had recourse to questions of this shape to try to grasp what it is. It is easy and tempting to slide from the "primary sense of 'being' as 'what x is' " to "something definite which underlies"—everything else we know about x. It is significant that Aquinas refuses to follow Aristotle (on at least one occasion) when he falls into this trap.[44] Aquinas seems to have realized Aristotle's signal achievement better than Aristotle himself, capitalizing on Socrates' question by focusing our attention on its form.[45] Rather than continuing to wonder about what x is (= its nature or essence) or asking about its *is-ness*, Aristotle notes that what is most common and pervasive is the manner of asking and answering questions about x. And these manners, by defining the shape of any inquiry, give us something common to all and so provide a basis for a "science of all," as well as suggesting a method appropriate to it.

42. Meta V 1017a23.

43. Cf. Phaedo, 101d–e, I. M. Crombie, *Examination of Plato's Doctrines*, vol. 2 (London, 1963), pp. 528–61.

44. Meta VII, 1028a9–b6; Aquinas, In Meta 1, nn.1247–51.

45. Cf. Lonergan, *Verbum*, pp. 11–16.

For Aristotle this will be one science, because every conceivable type of response is an attempt to meet (and avoid) the recurring question which will not be downed: "What is *x?*"[46] The shape of this question, then, supplies a focus for all the others, and so provides the primary subject of metaphysics: substance. (The Latin *quidditas* shows the derivation from *quid est x* most transparently.) As ammuntion against the Platonists, substance (= the what) is certainly "the existing thing," but more radically it is the answer to the question, what is *x?* The answer is discovered in the very shape of the question, as Aristotle's final argument for its primacy betrays. He maintains that "substance is primary in every sense: (1) in formula, (2) in order of knowledge, (3) in time." And arguing for the second, he notes that "we think we know each thing most fully, when we know what it is, e.g. what man is or what fire is, rather than when we knew its quality, its quantity, or its place; since we know each of these predicates also, only when we know *what* the quantity or the quality is."[47] And whatever the quantity or quality is, it is not *an existing thing.*[48] So if we are studious to follow Aristotle's insight and most careful usage, we need not come up with a "substratum" at all, and most certainly will not find one common to all, named *being.*[49]

For Scotus, however, being is not to be discovered from the shape of the question, *quid/quale est?* but from the answer to its primary form, *quid est x?* Now the only sure answer to this question is *aliquid* (something), and if one insists on starting in this way and believes also that concepts are formed by building

46. For the admission that the question "will not down," cf. W. Sellars, "Substance and Form in Aristotle," *J. Phil.* 54 (1957) 694, n. 11; also Lonergan, *Verbum,* pp. 15–16, 23–24, 35–36.

47. Meta VII 1028a37–39.

48. And such a view is compatible with Susan Stebbing's insistence that substance for Aristotle "is the individual thing" by the use of "focal meaning," (*Proc. Aris Soc.* 30, 1929-30, 285–308).

49. As a study to which I am indebted summarizes epigrammatically, "As soon as the metaphysician asks the question, he sees he already has the answer—or, if he be a pessimist, that there is no answer." James C. Doig, *Aquinas on Metaphysics* (The Hague, 1972), p. 260.

later ones out of earlier ones, then this something which comes at the very beginning will be an ingredient of all, and of course the only notion ingredient in every other.[50]

But we might object: there is nothing conceptual at all about 'something'. It is a mere index if it is that, or at best stands in for 'I know not what'.[51] And if this is the case, then 'something' is but a pronoun for the basic question/answer form. For the only invariant answer to "What is x?" would be "I do not know what x is," or "x is I know not what (x is)." 'Something', then, simply disguises the blank in x is . . . . All this linguistic detail is intended to provide some support for our feeling that there is no conceptual content to *something*—we can know nothing about "it." The only available option, then, is that it stands for the manner of talking about an object, any object.

CONFIRMING THE HYPOTHESIS

Yet this way of approaching the question seems never to have occurred to Scotus. How is it that an approach which appears to us and appeared to Aquinas as the classic Aristotelian manner could be so utterly foreign to Scotus? His reticence would readily be explained if, as we hypothesized, he considered every significant term as a name whose object was a component of the complex state of affairs named by a well-formed sentence. For then, each element of reality is more or less adequately represented by the names taken singly or concatenated, and nothing suggests that the concatenation itself might function in a representing sort of way—quite different from naming, doubtless, yet a role nonetheless integral to meaning.

For Aristotle, the difference is suggested by the dual yet complementary roles played by subject and predicate.[52] Aquinas

50. Cf. Wolter, p. 70.

51. C. S. Peirce lists 'something' as an indexical term at 2.289 (*Collected Papars*, ed. P. Weiss and C. Hartshorne, Cambridge, Mass, 1934), but it is clearly not a very satisfactory one, as it is indifferent to direction or other indicating criteria.

52. Meta VII 1043a5; Aquinas, In VII Meta 2, nn.1696–98; In Meta 11, n.1898.

ratifies this procedure by recalling the methodological affinities between logic and metaphysics.[53] Scotus accepts, of course, the general thesis about logic and metaphysics, and for this very reason must analyze the verb as another kind of name, for every significant term must function as a name.[54]

With this much said, I may consider my hypothesis to be corroborated, for it has shown admirably how a seeming anomaly might follow as a matter of course—the anomaly that everything said of a thing must name a part of it or, more neatly, that every *aspect* of a thing must be an *element* of it as well.[55] The semantic hypothesis that the unit of meaning is the term functioning as a name was supported by two models cognate to it, the first taking concept formation as a building-up process, the second assuming the geometric paradigm of science. Taking composite concepts as put together out of simples presents few complications and requires the least attention of all to synthesis, emphasizing as it does the materials employed. And the *Posterior Analytics'* ideal of science gives a surety to metaphysics as the first science by providing that its terms, univocal and most certain of all, be the foundation of those used by every other inquiry. It has often been assumed that metaphysicians coveted such a deductive primacy for their science, and it seems that Scotus did in fact satisfy this image.

An epistemological corollary follows which will prove illuminating in contrasting the approaches of Scotus and Aquinas. Knowledge, for Scotus, apparently reduces to two types: knowledge by acquaintance (or intuition), and knowledge by abstraction. Combined with Scotus' view of abstraction as a

53. Aquinas, In VII Meta 2, n.1287; 3, n.1308; In IV Meta 4, nn. 572–77.

54. But on this use of 'kind', Cf. L. Wittgenstein, *Blue and Brown Books* (Oxford, 1958, p. 64): "for those who say that a sense datum is a different kind of object from a physical object misunderstand the grammar of the word 'kind', just as those who say that a number is a different kind of object from a numeral."

55. On the corroboration of a hypothesis, cf. C. S. Peirce, *Collected Papers*, 5.189; for distinction of 'element' and 'aspect', see Aristotle, Meta III 6.

method of resolving complexes into their simple components, the result is a view of knowledge with little or no feel for diverse yet related uses of a term. For terms, Scotus insists, must have definite meanings, or science would not be possible. The meaning of a term may be known by acquaintance or by abstraction, but in either case, it is *the* meaning which is sought. Although preoccupations of this sort do not contradict the fact of multiple usage, they have to regard it as undesirable. Diverse yet related usage could be considered only as something for a reconstructive type of analysis to tidy up.

Summary and Application to "Divine Names"

This tendency manifests itself most clearly in Scotus' treatment of the problem of "naming God" in theological discourse. Glossing a typical passage from Augustine, where our understanding of "this good" and "that good" is said to lead ineluctably to that good *"cuius participatione illa sunt bona,"* Scotus takes this as claiming we "possess not only the concept of good-in-general" (*bonum in commune*) but also that of good-per-se" (*bonum per essentiam*).[56]

The interpretation squares with a textbook caricature of Augustine. It concentrates on the logical presuppositions (interpreted here in Scotus' own conceptualist terms), and fails to explain the "leading-up-to" aspect of the account, clearly the heart of Augustine's analysis.[57] This aspect will merit a special term for Aquinas, *manuductio,* and figure as the key to his treatment of naming God. Later we shall see how such a difference in style entails a quite diverse epistemology as well. Suffice it to mention here that Scotus, not Aquinas, qualifies as an "abstractive theorist" on the issue of concept formation.[58] This is corroborated by Scotus' need to invoke intuition (or knowledge

56. Oxon 1, d 8, q 3, n 3; IX, 591.

57. Cf. my "Reading the *Confessions* of Augustine: An Exercise in Theological Understanding," (*J. Religion* 50, 1970, 327–51).

58. For a critique of abstractive theory, cf. W. Sellars, *Science, Perception and Reality,* pp. 41–58; for an analysis corresponding to that criticized by Sellars, cf. Heiser, "The *Primum Cognitum"*, p. 208.

by acquaintance) as a separate and complementary way of knowing. The accusation of incompleteness by contemporary Scotists against Thomists who espouse an abstractive theory and reject intuition is certainly valid, but leaves Aquinas himself untouched.[59] He was not so much remiss, we shall see, as he was astute enough to avoid an abstractive theory. The accusation does support my contention, however, that much that passes for Thomist owes more to Scotus than to Thomas.

On an epistemology like that of Scotus, the move to naming God is quite straightforward. In fact, we detect that much of the preliminary work has been done to facilitate our using language in this exalted but indispensable fashion. All that we must do is to consider the formal *ratio* of a suggested predicate, e.g. wise.[60] If it is such that we may successfully remove all created imperfections from it, then the predicate is capable of being used of God, since in itself it is clearly indifferent to any particular mode of realization, and so transcendent.[61]

But when we do use the suggested predicate of God, we must add the proviso that it is perfectly realized in God. So God remains properly unknown to us. We can only attribute the formal *ratio,* perfectly realized, to God, without ever realizing ourselves what this might be like. Yet some knowledge of him remains possible. Scotus uses a distinction Aquinas will also employ but it is more at home with Scotus. When any predicate is ap-

59. Cf. Shircel, *Univocity,* pp. 39–44.

60. Oxon 1, d 3, q 2, n 10; IX, 21a.

61. Oxon 1 d 8, q 3, n 8, 19; IX, 598—in Wolter, *Duns Socotus: Philosophical Writings* (London, 1962): "kinds of predicates are those which are predicated formally of God, for instance, 'wise', 'good', and the like. I answer that before 'being' is divided into finite being and infinite being, it is common to the ten genera. Whatever pertains to 'being', then, in so far as it remains indifferent to finite and infinite, or as proper to the Infinite Being, does not belong to it as determined to a genus, but prior to any such determination, and therefore as transcendental and outside any genus. Whatever [predicates] are common to God and creatures are of such kind, pertaining as they do to being in its indifference to what is infinite and finite. For in so far as they belong to creatures they are finite. They belong to 'being', then, prior to the division into the ten genera. Anything of this kind, consequently, is trancendental" (p. 2).

plied to God, the *res significata* can be affirmed of God, for it is arrived at by prescinding from every indigenous this-worldly *modus significandi*. At the same time, the speaker explicitly attributes modes of signifying proper to God himself. The possibility of our arriving at any such formal *ratio* or *res significata* which we could employ in this way is challenged but avoided.[62] Presumably Scotus would resolve the problem with an appeal to experience like that invoked for the concept of being.[63] He concedes that such a concept is imperfect, since a perfect concept is always conceived together with its intrinsic modes, but in spite of this limitation the *res significata* is available and presumably quite distinct.[64]

Scotus' theory is designed to safeguard our knowledge of God from agnostic objections, while preserving the finitistic view of concept formation which forbids a proper concept of God. Hence Scotus must reject Henry of Ghent's theory of analogy as two concepts taken as one.[65] Of course the vocabulary and structure of Scotus' theory of naming God are very much indicative of his views on knowledge itself. Nothing brings this out more clearly than his remarks about negative theology. He cannot countenance anything like a *via negativa*. For a negation cannot be known as such, and in the absence of a "positive concept" we will have nothing positive to which we might "attribute the negation." Similarly, we *may* attribute perfections to God "by way of proportion," but they are said of him more perfectly when there is a similitude like the formal *ratio* of wise-as-such to provide the way. The reason for this is that attributing also requires a unity, since the privileged instance (God) is the measure of all the rest, and measuring requires a univocal domain. Even attributing, then, is a conceptual activity, involving a kind of comparison like that of measuring. Yet while God and creatures must be able to be compared con-

62. Oxon 1, d 8, q 3, n 8; IX, 598.
63. Cf. n. 12 above.
64. Oxon 1, d 8, q 3, n 27; IX, 626b; Wolter, *Duns Scotus*, p. 46, n. 35.
65. Oxon 1, d 8, q 3, nn 4, 6; IX, 582, 583b.

ceptually, as the only alternative Scotus sees to agnosticism, still they must remain totally diverse in reality.[66]

With this set of representative statements we may take leave of Scotus, confident that the very arena where his univocal concept of being with its related conceptual machinery was specifically designed to operate has succeeded best in displaying the inadequacies of both doctrine and method. If this is not yet the case, it will certainly appear so by contrast with the parallel treatment of Aquinas.

66. Oxon 1, d 8, q 3, n 9; IX, 585b; n 10, 586; n 12, 591a; n 11, 590.

6. Thomas Aquinas: Analogical Usage and Judgment

We have become so accustomed to Thomists' making extravagant claims for the "analogy of being" that the conclusions of recent research into Aquinas' own usage are somewhat disconcerting. Even though the prospect of calling a halt to the obscurities of *analogia entis* be a welcome one, it is dismaying that a major figure like Aquinas could have been misconstrued so thoroughly as contemporary critics claim. Perhaps, however, this is the most telling mark of greatness: Socrates experienced it in his lifetime; Plato anticipated it by resisting the pressure to compose a treatise. In fact, the clearest and most straightforward statement we possess of Plato's position is one explaining why he dare not express it so straightforwardly: the *Seventh Letter*. The same tragic tone accompanies many a reference to Aquinas in the voluminous corpus of "Thomist" commentary. Indeed the singular merit of recent studies has been their genuine attempt to reconstruct Aquinas' own teaching, without forsaking the systematic for a purely historical treatment.

RECENT RESEARCH: ITS CONTRIBUTION AND LIMITATIONS

Of recent critical studies, Lyttkens is certainly the most comprehensive, though repetitious and somewhat lacking on the systematic side. McInerny will prove the most illuminating once his carefully reasoned conclusions are worked into a more ample perspective. Klubertanz' collation of texts is of course useful, and the generalizations he feels they warrant afford a kind of control on the reading of any single text. But his own interpretative analysis inevitably suffers from an idiom so parochial that we often cannot help asking what it might mean. The most recent study, by Mondin, treats Aquinas only in part; however, it could be consulted profitably for a summary review of the current reappraisal, even if the crucial epistemological and semantic issues receive short shrift.[1]

The target of all these studies is Thomas de Vio Cardinal Cajetan, known simply as Cajetan, the sixteenth-century commentator whose divisions of analogy have furnished the very mold in which all subsequent Thomistic discussion was cast.[2] To realize Cajetan's role vis-à-vis Aquinas' teaching on analogy is to appreciate the scope of the present reappraisal. Cajetan is roundly and unanimously accused of having collated, classified, and clarified Aquinas' usage in classical procrustean fashion. Specifically, Cajetan is charged with having mischanneled centuries of speculative effort into defending what he called "analogy of proper proportionality" as the normal form of analogical discourse.[3] The magnitude of this misdirection can be indicated briefly as follows: ana-logical, according to Cajetan, suggests by its very form a procedure not to be contained by logic, yet sharing enough in it to escape contradiction and even to claim a certain legitimacy.

1. Hampus Lyttkens, *The Analogy between God and the World* (Uppsala, 1952); Ralph McInerny, *Logic of Analogy* (The Hague, 1961); George Klubertanz, *St. Thomas Aquinas on Analogy* (Chicago, 1960); Battista Mondin, *Principle of Analogy in Protestant and Catholic Theology* (The Hague, 1963). See also a summary article by M. S. O'Niell, "Some Remarks on the Analogy of God and Creatures in St. Thomas Aquinas," *Med. Stud.* 23 (1961) 206–15. My references to Aquinas will be to the *Summa Theologiae* unless otherwise noted. The other works will be cited by sigla: *Summa Contra Gentiles* (CG), *De Ente et Essentia* (De Ente), *Questiones Disputatae de Veritate* (deV), *Questiones Disputatae de Potentia* (dePot), *De Substantiis Separatis* (SS), *In Libro Boethii de Trinitatis Expositio* (deT), *In Libro Dionysii de Divinis Nominibus Expositio* (DN). The various commentaries on Aristotle will be cited by "In 8 M 3, 198," for example, to indicate that I am referring to Aquinas' commenatry on the eighth book of the *Metaphysics,* the third lesson, and paragraph 198 in the Marietti edition. The commentaries cited will be those on the *De Anima* (deA), *De Caelo et Mundo* (CM), *Nichomachean Ethics* (Eth), *Metaphysics* (M), the *Physics* (Phy), and the *Posterior Analytics* (PA).

2. Cajetan, *Scripta Philosophica: De Analogia Nominum,* ed. P. N. Zammit (Rome, 1952). Cf. Chap. 1.

3. Lyttkens, pp. 218–20; McInerny, pp. 1–2.

However Cajetan's proportional schema, $a:b::c:d$, together with his insistence that it is properly employed here, gives the impression that ana-logical means supra-logical. Thus *analogical* discourse, if not logical in the usual sense, owns a logic all its own—a "higher" logic for use in higher domains. The desire to be released from an accounting to ordinary semantics has ever plagued philosophy, and Cajetan's proposal was particularly welcome in that it appeared so systematic. (It is Kant's merit to have detected and exposed the temptation to engage in combinatorial play with highly abstract concepts. And the mere proviso that we are using them "analogously" cannot serve to mitigate his judgment. For we must show how different analogous use is.[4]) The proper proportionality doctrine suggests that one may simply switch to another level and be released from the demands of logic in the name of ana-logic.

But if this is the burden of their criticism of Cajetan, these authors (principally McInerny) would nonetheless concur with his focusing analogy on terms and their use. *De Analogia Nominum* is the title of Cajetan's commentary. His attention to language allows us to acknowledge affinities between Aquinas and contemporary Anglo-American philosophy which remained quite unsuspected so long as the Thomist idiom was one of "analogy of being." Aquinas' usual expression is "analogously speaking" (*analogice loquendo*), and we shall see how conscious he was of the semantic issues involved in speaking so.[5] In fact, the marked difference between Aquinas and Scotus appears here. However kindred their motivations may have been, the plain fact is that Aquinas betrays a logicosemantic

4. Cf. my "Kant and Philosophical Knowledge," *New Scholasticism* 38 (1964) 189–213.

5. That such a shift of focus from ontological to logical issues will bring clarity to the discussion can hardly be questioned, though I shall try to exhibit it as well. That some such shift means a betrayal of metaphysics could occur only to someone who had not reflected how much language is a "way of life." Cf. Joseph Owens, "St. Thomas and Elucidation," (*New Scholasticism* 35, 1961, 421–44), and the reply by Harry Nielsen, "Fr. Owens on Elucidation: A Comment" (ibid. 36, 1962, 233–36).

sophistication absent in Scotus. The divergencies come to light the more we recognize the role semantics enjoys in epistemology. The temptation to explain understanding on the model of seeing, and concept formation as intellectual process or construction, is all too enticing; its most effective antidote, it seems, is closer attention to language. Keeping Wittgenstein's admonitions in mind as we consider Aquinas' usage of analogous terms well prove incidentally helpful in clearing Aquinas of any remaining charges of "abstractionism" and highlighting his significant divergence from Scotus.[6]

The recent studies already noted differ from the bulk of Thomist commentary in their careful attention to Aquinas' actual usage. The case against Cajetan is documented from it. Difficulties encountered in making coherent sense of "proper proportionality" could have provided a strong case against Cajetan's insistence that it is the only permissible form analogy can take in metaphysics. But an even stronger case exists. The fact is that Aquinas' usage is frankly pluralistic while Cajetan's account is baldly procrustean. He accepts one or possibly two texts as normative for all the rest.[7]

Analogy, as Aquinas accepted the term from Aristotle through the Arab commentators, referred indifferently to Aristotle's proposals of "proportional similarity" or "reference to one" (= focal meaning).[8] Indeed, for Aquinas it seems to refer to any manner of establishing a notion too pervasive to be defined or too fundamental or exalted to be known through experience. More often than not, this is accomplished via examples designed to point up enough relevant aspects of these notions to use them responsibly. The word coined for this technique was *manuductio*.[9]

6. Ludwig Wittgenstein, *Philosophical Investigations* (Oxford, 1953), passim; Peter Geach, *Mental Acts* (London, 1957), pp. 130–31; B. J. F. Lonergan, *Verbum: Word and Idea in Aquinas* (Notre Dame, 1967), esp. Chap. 1 and 3. Contrast the last with Alan Wolter, *Transcendentals and their Function* (St. Bonaventure, N.Y., 1946), pp. 14–30.

7. Lyttkens, pp. 211–18; McInerny, pp. 3–23.

8. Lyttkens, p. 77.

9. Albertus Magnus, *Sum. Theol*, t 14, q 59, m 4 ad 3; *Mystica Theol.* 2 1 (Borgnet XXXI 597; XIV 840); Aquinas, deV 10 6 ad 2, 11 1; In

Now it is clear that this use of examples to "lead us on" to grasp a notion not susceptible of definition is also germane to the formation of universal general terms, and even to forming adequate definitions. (Indeed Wittgenstein would lead us to suspect that an account of analogous usage would not be so difficult as has been imagined if we were to recognize the play already present in ordinary generalization and definition.[10]) We have noticed how Aristotle recognized in metaphorical usage a power indispensable for defining as well as for moving beyond the arena of definition. Aquinas offers an explicit parallel: "as the mind is led on from what the senses apprehend to something further [i.e. *what* the thing is], so things understood lead it on to some knowledge of the divine (deV 10 6 ad 2). His insistence on the utility of examples to "take us by the hand and lead us on" reminds us of Wittgenstein's reflections on guiding.[11] The moment we ascertain that Aquinas' move to the *quiddity* does not depend on an intellectual intuition, and that his understanding of abstraction makes it more akin to an ongoing inquiry than a petroleum-cracking process, then dialectic discovery and recognition all become relevant to a discussion of concept formation.[12] The classical shortcuts have been illustrated in Scotus: understanding is a kind of seeing, and concept formation becomes an automatic process.

To the extent that Aquinas' positions have been shown for what they are, one may be content to refer to the studies and develop an interpretation consonant with them. Where the argument requires it, of course, I shall summarize as well as document the supporting studies. But the precise merit of the recent research into Aquinas' use of "analogy', as well as Lonergan's detailed examination of concept formation, is to release Aquinas from the systematic demands imposed by

---

1 Eth 4, 53; In 9 M 5, 1826–27; dePot 7 5 ad 3–4; *Sum Theol.* I 117 I 51 3 ad 1.

10. Wittgenstein, *Investigations,* ##59–67, 96–109; and from a more traditional point of view, A. Maurer, "St. Thomas and the Analogy of Genus" (*New Scholasticism* 29, 1955, 127–44).

11. Wittgenstein, *Investigations,* ##172–82.

12. Cf. Lonergan, Verbum, Chap. 4.

Thomism and allow him to speak more fully from his own usage. The result will prove most fruitful in preparing the general issues summarized in "analogical predication" for scrutiny by contemporary logic and semantics. Moreover, Aquinas will prove useful for bridging from old to new, combining as he does a deep respect for tradition and an active feeling for logical issues.

USE OF ANALOGIES AND SIMILARITIES
IN ORDINARY SPEECH

The twin testimonies of recent textual research and centuries of confusing commentary assure us that Aquinas had no clear-cut theory of analogical predication. The omission is all the more exasperating as he seemed to depend upon one, invoking it in the transcendent region of theological discourse. But as we study more carefully what Aquinas came to expect of analogical predicates and assess the semantic obstacles in the way, it appears that he was maneuvering better than he knew how to say in neglecting to put together a logic for analogy.

Aquinas' primary concern was theological: How to speak of both God and the world? He tended, as in most issues, merely to accept Aristotle's formulation of the terrestrial side of things. In this case he simply acknowledged that we can recognize proportional similarities among types of things. The acknowledgment is twofold: it envisages types of things and relations among them; it takes into account our ability to recognize and speak to them. The less we count on proper proportionality as paradigmatic for analogy, the less important loom questions about types (or genera) and how they might be said to be similar to one another.

It has been insisted that the existence of irreducible genera is a central and unwarranted assumption in Aquinas' theory of analogical discourse.[13] This might be true were it the case that Aquinas had a tightly woven theory, neatly meshed with an ontology of grades of being, or if one were anxious to construct

13. James Ross, "A Critical Analysis of the Theory of Analogy of St. Thomas Aquinas," unpub. Ph.D. dissertation, Brown University, 1958, p. 198.

such a comprehensive account on the foundations he may have laid. But barring such ambitions, it seems sufficient to admit the kaleidoscope of similarities-cum-differences which color our daily speech, and to acknowledge an entire spectrum of uses of 'similar to' from scientific classification to poetic metaphor.

In short, analogy as a logical or semantic account of our usage does not prejudice the issue of final explanation in favor of pluralism. The final account—whatever that is—may well be one of a unified science, but our ordinary talk trades on many kinds of similiarities. And what is significant here is the fact that we can recognize them where we have no notion of how to formulate them, and that we are continually discarding the less relevant of them in favor of others.[14]

It is this common fact of experience, rather than a metaphysical assumption about irreducible genera, that should provide the background for a discussion of analogical discourse. The more aware we become of the wealth of uses of similar or analogous to already in our possession, the better able we shall be to delineate their admittedly unusual employment in elucidating the ways we speak about God.

Peculiarities in "Naming God"

I have been speaking about recognizing types of things, and about speaking about them—speaking, in short, about predication. Talk about God raises special difficulties in this context because as principle of all he is beyond any genus, even that of substance.[15] Aquinas was extraordinarily aware of the host of semantic issues released by this assertion, as his commentary on the *Posterior Analytics* reveals. In more contemporary terms, such an assertion means that God is outside any of the universes of discourse that provide the contextual meanings for the terms we use.[16] It was a situation only adumbrated by Aris-

14. Wittgenstein, *Investigations*, ##182–83, ##602 ff., p. 218; also R. M. Hare, *Language of Morals* (Oxford, 1952).

15. DePot 7 3 ad 3–5; deT 1 2 ad 4.

16. This is of course the burden of much of the linguistic writing about theological statements. For an incisive reading of Aquinas in this regard, see Victor Preller, *Divine Science and the Science of God* (Princeton, 1967).

totle in his affirmation of an unmoved mover, though Aquinas will have recourse to some of the logical theorems employed there.[17] Aristotle's use of analogous to call attention to similarities among the biological genera themselves would suggest its use beyond any genus. But the situation is still more radical when we are speaking of the principle of all.

If God must remain outside of any genus, he is properly unknowable. Such an assertion would seem to end in pure agnosticism. Yet Aquinas refuses to settle for that and goes on to drive a wedge: then God must be improperly knowable, namely by analogy.[18] So far this says no more than the term *ana-logos* itself suggests: improperly knowledge yet still knowledge. The implication is, of course, that God is at all costs knowable; or rather, Aquinas implies that something must be able to be said about him. Why?

For a believer, or his theologian, the answer should be plain: there must be sufficient cognitive linkage so that he knows to what he is assenting. But if this much is plain, the assertion remains fraught with ambiguities, many of which have been exposed by Karl Barth's extreme stance on the subject. The upshot of the attendant discussion, however, has been rather to emphasize the complexities involved in trying to formulate the relations between faith and knowledge than to undermine the initial insistence that there must be some linkage.[19] That very insistence stands and must stand. Barth himself was led to see this when he realized that admitting "some knowledge" need not jeopardize the gratuity of faith, whereas

17. If we can say that the first mover is unmoved, then the mode of his causality can be described only metaphorically as being loved (or desired) (Meta 1072b3). Aristotle did not see this in the *Physics,* however, but only in the *Metaphysics.* Cf. *Preller,* pp. 117–22.

18. Aquinas will prefer the "focal meaning" (or *pros-en* equivocal) device to proportionality in seeking to explain our discoursing about the principle of all (Lyttkens, pp. 283, 355; Mondin, pp. 20, 24, 34).

19. See the way in which Hans Urs von Balthasar, in *Karl Barth: Darstellung und Deutung seiner Theologie* (Cologne, 1962; Eng. trans., *Karl Barth,* New York, 1971), and Henri Bouillard, in *Karl Barth* (Paris, 1957) expound natural theology and *analogia entis* in Barth.

rejecting all connection does threaten, if not destroy, the status of faith as an action of the believer.

But what if the presumption of belief is laid aside? Is simple (and hence complete) agnosticism still unworthy of consideration? Since Aquinas worked in the context of belief and breathed the very air of faith, it is difficult to answer this question directly. We must do our best to construct a reply faithful to his random observations. It will have two parts, the first epistemological; the second, broadly speaking, anthropological.

The first reply would deny that we can know simply *that* there is a God, yet know nothing about him. Positively, the assertion claims that if one can know that God exists, one must thereby know something about him. Thus if God is strictly unknowable, we cannot claim to know that he exists either. For Aquinas, however, such a definitive (as opposed to methodological or searching) agnosticism about the existence of God is intellectual suicide *tout court*. Or better, it is to cease (or refuse) to be a man. This startling statement will be examined in a moment. For now, we may be content to remark that analogy merely refers to a characteristic of our language which opens it to such an unusual use. Nor would it be very enlightening to insist that assertions like these belong to metaphysics, as though that were a domain reserved to a privileged few. In fact, it will turn out that Aquinas' metaphysics presupposes an epistemology. His epistemology in turn reflects a philosophical anthropology, a reflective understanding of man as the sort of being who makes claims open to a progressive sort of verification by men themselves.[20] But let us first examine the argument against a mere knowledge that God exists.

20. Lyttkens, pp. 201–14. Wittgenstein remarks that his study is "on the natural history of man: not curiosities, however, but rather observations . . . which have only gone unremarked because they are always before our eyes" (*Foundations of Mathematics,* Oxford, 1956, p. 141); and J. L. Austin consents to entitle his program one of "linguistic phenomenology" (*Philosophical Papers,* Oxford, 1961, p. 130). I would take these as intimations of what Continental philosophers dare to call a philosophical anthropology.

On Knowing That God Exists

It would be convenient if acknowledging that God exists were compatible with total ignorance about him. For this would square with the intial assertion that he is outside any genus, and would allow us to sidestep many apparently insurmountable semantic hurdles. Besides, it would seem to formulate Aquinas' own insistence that we cannot know of God what he is but only what He is not (I 3 1; deV 10 11 ad 4–5; 13 DN 3, 996). Doesn't he say as well that "of God we cannot know what He is but only that He is" (deT 1 2 ad 1–2)? This last statement— so similar to the proposition we would deny—has even been accepted as the best formulation of Aquinas' arcane position on the whole subject, a position dubbed agnosticism of definition.[21]

But the statement is unstable and incomplete as a description of Aquinas' intent, as a parallel assertion reveals: knowing that God *is* entails knowing "what necessarily befits Him as first cause of all and beyond all He causes" (I 12 12). Why must this be so? The argument proceeds as follows. Any knowledge that God exists must either be immediate or mediate, by a vision or revelation of some sort, or by a process of reasoning. If it is immediate, the revelation must be self-authenticating and hence reveal something of God. (We see that Smith is here, which involves seeing someone whom we can identify as Smith, or what are clearly traces of him.) If the knowledge is a conclusion, then the reasoning process must proceed conceptually (via predication) and hence betray some features of its terminus.

"Ground of Being"

To understand what Aquinas is up to, let us reconstruct what he seems to be doing. Let us look at a schematic proof that God is the *ground of being*. This appellation is quite similar to the name Aquinas considers most appropriate for God, *ipsum esse*. To speak of God as *being itself* succeeds in

21. Sertillanges as cited in Etienne Gilson, *Christian Philosophy of St. Thomas* (New York, 1956), pp. 107–08.

conveying his transcendence, since being, construed as existence, leaves no features to tempt us to univocity (I 13 11, 4 1
ad 3). Certainly obvious and explicit disparities separate Tillich
and Aquinas. But it would seem legitimate to call attention to
the similarities between them so that we might employ the contemporary phrase "ground of being" as more suggestive than
the venerable *causa in esse.*

The very expression ground of being, however, assumes that
x's existing needs an explanation. This amounts to treating
existence as a formal aspect, a "perfection" of *x*—a regularity
or specific kind of orderliness—for these are the kinds of things
we seek to explain. So while it may have been specifically
designed to be featureless and to conclude to the fact that God
exists and nothing more, the argument to God as ground of being can use the principle of sufficient reason only because it
presumes that existing is intelligible, and so demands that something account for it.

But what impresses us about existence, if we may put it so,
is its brute "thereness." Peirce tried to handle this by creating a
special category, *secondness;* but the inherent tendency to make
this lack of character a characteristic is revealed in the '-ness'
construction, and even more tellingly in an expression like
facticity.[22] Though Aquinas does not resort to a mystification
like facticity, he does recognize as nearly inevitable that "existence be considered as if it were a formal [aspect]," and that it
is hard to resist making a feature out of what is precisely no
feature at all (I 4 1 ad 3). But the fact remains that existence
is not just another feature of a thing; '. . . is' is not a predicate

22. For my use of existence as shorthand for 'that *x* exists' and the
context of my remarks about this stubborn fact, cf. C. S. Peirce (*Collected Papers,* ed. C. Hartshorne and P. Weiss, Cambridge, Mass., 1931–
35, 6.395–427, 1.322–37). For 'facticity', cf. Heidegger, *Being and
Time* (New York, 1962, p. 56): "Whenever Dasein is, it is as a Fact; and
the factuality of such a Fact is what we shall call Dasein's 'facticity'
[Faktizität]. The concept of *facticity* implies that an entity 'with-in-the-
world' has Being-in-the-world in such a way that it can understand itself
as bound up in its 'destiny' with the Being of those entities which it
encounters within its own world."

in the sense of a further descriptive note.[23] And if not, then existence does not ask to be explained. If we insist, however, that existence be intelligible, it must be that we are forcing the issue in this case. For we are demanding more than "matter-of-factness." We are asking why, even though we know the response must be of a completely different kind precisely because *that x exists* is not a further fact about it.

The distinction between regularities as the type of phenomena that ask for an explanation, and existence, where the demand must originate more from the side of the inquirer, is not of course a clear-cut one. Yet it helps reveal a difference in the mode of questioning, a difference which will be reflected in what shall count as an explanation. If this tack is inspired by Kant, it stops short of identifying the differences as "objective" or "subjective," simply because we need not be preoccupied with so dividing knowledge. We shall see, however, that there is a difference in the style of questioning when one inquires why something exists, and that we must call attention to this difference if we wish to grasp the role which transcendent intent plays in Aquinas' assessment of types of meaningful statements.

We must be extraordinarily careful in staking out the path here, however, as this generation's work in the logic of our language has taught us. The way of the ontologist, whoever he may be, is too easy. He speaks of 'Being,' and proceeds to argue schematically: if we seek to explain the regularities *of* being, order *in* being—if these form the object of inquiry and are therefore presumed to be intelligible—then why not ask the same of being? Is it not illogical, he would ask, to refuse to go the whole way? [24] We might retort that we have methods for inquiring into regularities and the like, but none yet for 'being.'

23. Both Aquinas and Kant make this point in refuting Anselm; more recently G. E. Moore, *Some Main Problems in Philosophy* (London, 1953), pp. 312–31; *Philosophical Papers* (London, 1959), pp. 114–25.

24. For a classic example see Robert Neville, *God the Creator* (Chicago, 1968), and my review in *Review of Metaphysics* (22, 1969, 690–95).

For being is simply not a feature at all, qualitative or quantitative; being *never appears*. And if this is so, as most all will admit, how can we inquire about it? What will ever count as an explanation of it? Until these questions can be answered, we have little choice but to treat it as a mere fact.

But however impassioned the retort, it has never succeeded in quenching our desire that existence too be intelligible. Antimetaphysical arguments trade on the inability of ontology to come forward with a method, and capitalize on the common realization that it must be a method utterly diverse from any we employ to explain regular recurrences. The question: "Why is there anything at all?" arises without apparent lineage and offers no directions for responding to it. Yet it cannot be suppressed. On the other hand, however, we may resent regarding something's existing as a mere fact, our inability to field the question *why?* leaves us little alternative. Since the fact that something exists is not a feature of that thing, that fact alone supplies no hint whence an explanation might arise.

Yet ironically enough, this is the very reason why the question seems to lead most directly and satisfactorily to God: it promises to assure his existence as principle of all without forcing us to point to any single feature of the world as evidence. What if it turned out, however, that the question leads nowhere? The fact (A) that x exists does not of itself license the fact (B) that God exists as its explanation. For (A) simply does not tell us enough to indicate what might count as an explanation. If God is to explain (contingent) existence, then there must be more to something's existing than facticity. And if this is the case, then we will know something about God: namely what it is about existing which leads us on to him. We will not be able to settle for the mere fact that he exists.[25]

25. Hence John E. Smith can say that a mere "knowledge that" leads in time to skepticism (*Reason and God,* New Haven, 1963, p. 38). The reason, as we have seen, is that it is not a genuine conceptual move at all. Aquinas asserts that things "resemble the primary and universal source of all existence . . . precisely as things possessing existence" (I 4 3). Yet *resemblance* conveys no information here since existence is not a determinate feature.

Reflecting on the argument: Incorporating Kant. The same point might have been made more directly though less dramatically by appealing to Aquinas' own semantics. Even the appropriately extreme statement that "we know of God . . . only *that* He is" cannot dispense us from requiring some meaning for the term God.[26] There will doubtless be as many shades of meaning as there are inquirers, but the family likeness of cognitive connotations—which allow mutual inquiry and communication—may provisionally be summed up under "first cause." The God to whom we are led by demanding a ground for existence bears the imprint of the style of reflection which leads us on: if we can (indeed must) affirm *that* he is, yet cannot say *what* he is, it is because God is proposed as first cause or principle of all. So Aquinas' denial that we cannot know what he is had a purpose—to anticipate the critique of Kant and others of the first-cause formulation. For this expression too must be analogous: " 'to make'," Aquinas says, "is used equivocally of the universal production of all things and of other productions" (In 8 Phy, 2974). Hence the meaning of the term God remains an undetermined one.

Aquinas' move has serious implications, for every subsequent use of language to "describe" God will be justified by reference to causality. Once we are satisfied that 'good', 'just', and 'merciful' can be used of God—even though we recognize that they will be realized in him in a fashion quite beyond our conceiving—we may nonetheless be assured that these terms do refer to something in God, because we mean by God, principle of all.[27] In other words, the justification for analogous usage and the line of argument distinguishing it from the "merely symbolic" theories (of a Maimonides or a Tillich) itself depends on an analogous use of 'cause'. On the credit side,

26. In 2 PA 8, 484; In 1 PA 2, 17; Sum Theol. I 2 2 ad 2; and especially deT 6 3: "de nulla re potest sciri *an est,* nisi quoque modo sciatur de ea *quid est,* vel cognitione perfecta vel saltem cognitione confusa."

27. Cf. my "Aquinas on Naming God," *Theol. Stud.* 24 (1963) 191-92, 203–05; J. C. Murray, *Problem of God* (New Haven, 1964), pp. 70–73.

this shows Aquinas' consistency in declaring analogous usage irreducible to a univocal foundation. On the debit side, Aquinas' views seem to threaten any move to God, for he is apparently acknowledging that any justification for using analogical predicates will be circular, since the meaning of these predicates is secured only through an analogical use of cause.

We can acknowledge the charge of circularity leveled against Aquinas, yet point out, in the spirit of Wittgenstein, that it arises only when we try to justify such usage. So the first step in a contemporary account consistent with Aquinas' analogical usage lies in simply recognizing that we do invoke notions which resist analysis, that we do insist upon using terms that are systematically ambiguous. Even the most austere among us have recourse to expressions like these when referring to our conceptual frameworks and appraising them, say, for simplicity, elegance, or fruitfulness.[28] And to acknowledge that we do speak so is to recognize that we must—that language of this kind is an integral part of inquiry and so native to man as an inquiring animal.[29]

Then if we insist on carrying this inquiry into the reasons for existing, the grounds for there being anything at all, what explains it may be said to be a cause. But as Aquinas recognized, cause will be used in a quite different way here, and a modified form of Kant's critique will help us realize why this must be so. Attention to the form of an inquiry into the grounds for existence will lay bare the logic of the dictum that the "principle of all must be outside every genus." For inquiry gets stuck on existence. We are not used to inquiring why anything exists at all, but rather why x is, or does y. In Aristotle's terms we are taught to ask: Why is it that this predicate may be said of this subject? But '. . . exists' does not behave like an ordinary predicate. So wondering about the grounds of existence is not demanded by the logic of ordinary inquiry. That x exists does not stick out as an unexplained regularity does. Yet on the other

28. Rudolph Carnap, *Meaning and Necessity* (Chicago, 1956), pp. 33, 43, 66, 214, 221.

29. Cf. J. L. Austin's apologia for "ordinary language" as a criterion in *Philosophical Papers* (Oxford, 1959, pp. 130–37).

hand, nothing licenses us to terminate our inquiry short of this point just because its continuation promises to be unusual.

It seems possible to do justice to both aspects of the intellectual movement involved here if we are permitted an interpretation of Aquinas that is inspired by Kant. Aquinas sums up the move to inquiring about God in the idiom of *manuductio:* "as the mind is led on from what the senses apprehend to [what the thing is], so things understood lead it on to some knowledge of the divine." The simile suggests a continuity, but the use of *manuductio* allows for a good deal of difference as well. My proposal is that the move is not necessary but reflective. Just as the recognition of similarities leads to the formation of a common term and functional similarities lead to analogous predication, so reflection on the need to look for similarities, together with the ability to recognize them, points to an inner demand for intelligibility. Defining God as what fulfills this demand, we can also say of him that he would fulfill the cognate demands for justice, magnanimity, and the rest.

What is accomplished by locating the move to a principle of all in a reflective moment of consciousness? A great deal, really, which will only gradually unfold. Reflection opens the category of the cognitive out beyond concept formation to judgment. This extension is already implicit in the way we submit conceptual frameworks to appraisals of simplicity and the like. Attention to reflection acknowledges a specific role for judgment and links observations as initially disparate as Gilson's about analogous judgments with Wittgenstein's on use and usage. Attending to reflection will help us to incorporate the suggestion of some prominent contemporary philosophers and theologians that assent to the statement 'God exists' has a measure of freedom about it incompatible with the conclusions of ordinary inquiry. Assent is free not because logical argument gives way to a willful leap but because the relevant movements of understanding cannot be displayed logically. They rather represent reflections upon the logic we ordinarily employ.[30]

30. Henri deLubac has orchestrated this theme in *Discovery of God* (New York, 1960). Kierkegaard took to the highly sophisticated device

EXTENDING INQUIRY

We return to Aquinas when we insist that the question, "Why does x exist?" reflects a continuity with the original impulse of inquiry. When someone demands an answer to that question, he is certainly asking for too much. Yet it is no less impertinent to suggest that we simply opt for one story or another to stop the questioning. A more sophisticated response recognizes that the question reveals more about us than about the world; it reflects our natural penchant for intelligibility pushed to its outer limits. By recognizing that penchant for what it is, we may at least learn to accept it: to accept that questioning never ends and yet will never be satisfied.

The proposal would sound altogether too pious for the medievals, however; to preach acceptance would strike them as selling out. It offers too abrupt a departure from the rational *élan* of inquiry which allowed the question to emerge. Yet perhaps questioning has met its limits. At that point two strategies present themselves: retreating into the chaste mysticism of silence or appropriating the luxuriant hierarchies and neolgisms of neo-Platonism. Aquinas will tend toward the former, but treat it as a temptation to be held off as long as possible in the name of a responsible continuation of the original impetus of the inquiry.

To forsake language before it is absolutely necessary would betray the very reason that raises questions. Furthermore, language offers the only assistance available at this point. So an inquiry which moves beyond the pale must retain at best linguistic links with its ordinary counterpart. And to continue to

---

of pseudonyms to show what exposition cannot: the reflective quality of an account in this domain. It was his fate, of course, that commentators should have fastened on an expression which one of his pseudonyms took over from Lessing ("the leap") as giving *his* statement on *the* relation between faith and reason. Compare, for example, the treatment of Climacus in the *Fragments* or the *Postscript* with that of the pseudonymous authors of *Either/Or* or its later replica: *Stages on Life's Way*. See the introduction of Paul Sponheim to *Stages* (New York, 1967).

use language means to remain subject to rules. These rules for the medievals were grammatical in form. Logic acknowledged its grammatical roots, and grammar provided a ready and highly developed control when one sought to carry discourse into divine regions. The conditions invoked by philosophical theologians like Albert and Aquinas were principallly two: (A) try to distinguish what is to be signified from the manner of representing it; and (B) cull out all predicates except "perfections." Both rules are simply recalled as common property, but with different emphasis. Aquinas invokes (A) as a lever to transcendent usage, but merely insists upon (B) without adverting to its role in the argument. This provides an excellent example of performance outstripping one's ability to explain one's moves. For we shall see, negatively, that (A), the distinction between *res significata* and *modus significandi* (what is signified/manner of signifying), while necessary, will not do the work Aquinas apparently wants it to do; and positively, that (B) is the crucial stipulation—that all predicates be perfections.

Distinction of Res/Modus

Taken at face value, the distinction of *res* and *modus* not only cannot accomplish what Aquinas wants it to but also leads us directly to a formulation like that of Scotus. Aquinas invokes it without explanation, assuming a tool in common possession. Proposed by Boethius, this distinction was developed by the intervening generations of biblical scholars turned grammarians to meet the problems arising from God's revealing himself in human speech. The time/eternity issue was paramount: How can Scripture (or anyone) speak of eternity when our speech carries an aura of associations linking it so firmly to time? Or how can we make statements about a God who is simple, when the very form of the statement bespeaks a composition of substance/accidents? [31]

The problem of the temporal "consignification" of verbs baffled the grammarians, but Aquinas managed to work out a

31. M. D. Chenu, *Théologie au douzième siècle* (Paris, 1957), pp. 95 ff.

solution rigorously dependent upon a personal and illuminating reading of Aristotle on statements about future contingent events.[32] More immediately relevant to the questions of analogical predication, however, was the structure of predicate terms. These were said to "signify a substance together with its quality." [33] The radical grammatical distinction of subject/object, together with its logicometaphysical counterpart of substance/accident, suggests the distinction. Starting from a frank recognition of the realism of ordinary language, it proposes some relief by offering a certain distance.

To be sure, just in 'John is just' signifies justice, but this need not send us looking for a corresponding thing or substance. It is simply that every term signifies so; what it signifies we call the *res significata*. But the ordinary usage of a term betrays certain grammatical features that provide us with important ontological clues. We never say of anyone, for example, that he is justice, but that he is just. This fact alone undermines the Platonist move, but the tendency remains. 'John is just' (*justus*) and 'Joan is just' (*justa*) may well carry subtly different connotations, but the grammatical philosopher would want to say that both refer to the same thing, viz., justice. The manner of signifying is associated with grammatical inflections, and distinction wants to claim that these may vary without altering the meaning of the word.

The distinction shares with substance/accident its initial plausibility together with many of the subsequent logical puzzles. Thus it is proposed: whenever a term is to be used of God, overlook its peculiar manner of signifying, and neatly affirm what it signifies.[34] But just as we have never come across a quality-less substance, so no name signifies outside of a gram-

32. Cf. my "Aristotle and Future Contingencies" (*Phil. Stud* [Maynooth] 13, 1964, 48–52).

33. M. D. Chenu, "Grammaire et théologie," *Arch. hist. doct. litt. de M-A.* 10 (1935–36) 5–28.

34. I 13 3; 2 ad 2; 9 ad 3; CG I 30; Albertus Magnus, *Sum Theol.* I t 14, q 58, m 1, ad 3 (Borgnet XXXI, 583–84); for Alexander, cf. Lyttkens, pp. 125–26.

matical position without "consignifying" as well. Things are
simply not distinguishable from their manners, nor is *quod
nomen designat* conceivable apart from the *modus quo*. And
what is more, those who used the distinction recognized this.
Albert raises the objection whether merely affirming the thing
signified can mean anything. In responding he admits that
names must designate in a certain manner. He also draws a
strict parallel between thing signified and substance on one side,
and manner of signifying and qualities on the other; yet Albert
would doubtless agree with both Aristotle and Aquinas that the
only way we know a substance is in and through its qualities.[35]

Nevertheless, Albert, and Alexander too, are intent upon
making the distinction work when speaking of God. So they import a special illumination in this case to supply the meaning of
just, for instance, when the term lacks any accompanying mode
—when it stands indifferently for just or justice.[36] This knowledge is, they say, confused, vague, and quite inferior to that of
the blessed; but knowledge it is. That it is knowledge remains
assured by divine illumination or innate ideas belonging to the
soul as the image of God. This last solution is similar, as we
have seen, to that which Scotus will offer. Instead of themselves using the *res/modus* distinction, Albert and Alexander
were rather used *by* it, led on to posit a privileged access to
what the term signified when the manners of signifying failed
to provide the clues.

Now Aquinas, who would rather avoid such an illumination,
inveighs against there being a (necessarily univocal) something which the analogous term signifies. Yet some residual core
of meaning seems to result from a straightforward use of the
res/modus distinction. So Aquinas must insist that the names
we use to attribute something to God signify *in the manner we
understand them:* "as we understand, so we speak." [37] We can-

35. Albertus Magnus, *Sum Theol.* I t 14, q 58, m 1, ad 1; *Decem
Predicamenta* 1, 2 (Borgnet XXXI, 583; I, 151–55).

36. For Alexander, cf. Lyttkens, pp. 125–26; Albertus, *Mystica Theo-
logia* 2, ##1–2 (Borgnet XIV, 839–41).

37. I 13, 2; 1 ad 2; I *Sententiis* 22 1 2 ad 2; *In Liber de Causis* 6; I
50 2 for use regarding the angels; and cf. A. Kenny, "Aquinas and
Wittgenstein," *Downside Rev.* 77 (1958–59) 217–35.

not speak or signify, certainly, in any other way! Besides, when we say that God is just, we mean to say that his manner of achieving it is utterly beyond our conception. Hence even if it made some sense to speak of a *res significata,* we would have to reintroduce a manner of realization when affirming it of God.[38]

Of what use, then, is the distinction if it raises a host of semantic puzzles, if it leads to a "core-of-meaning" doctrine for analogous usage, and if it still cannot tell us *how* God is just? In point of fact, if Aquinas invokes it, he does not rely upon the distinction, for his practice contradicts it. And the *res/ modus* distinction does not lead him to deny his empirical theory of meaning, as it did the others. Aquinas' real recourse is to a peculiar expression: *intendit significare*—"mean to say" —and to the possibility of being led on (*manuductus*) by inquiry to the reason why there is anything at all. The paradigm then is not a distinction reminiscent of substance hidden by accidents, leading quite naturally to some form of intuitionism. Aquinas looks instead at what he is doing, and invites his readers also to allow themselves to be led on from question to question, from one style of question to another, until we ask about questioning itself.

The paradigm is the person inquiring, which recalls the other stipulation about using terms of God—that they denote perfections. Furthemore, Aquinas' recourse to a specifically human model and his effective rejection of the distinction inherited from the grammarians suggest that the issues of analogical discourse cannot be resolved on the level of logic or semantics alone. Or it may be that a semantics closer to the paradigm he actually uses, one whose unit of meaning is the statement and not the word and whose attention is directed to use as well as structure, will provide a satisfactory analysis. We shall return to this question in the final evaluation.

"Perfectio"

'Perfection' is used in many different ways by Aquinas, providing an index to the traditions coursing through his work. It

38. I 13, 5; 8 ad 2; CG I 35; and Lyttkens, pp. 388–89, 471.

is often employed in the classical sense of containing everything and lacking nothing,[39] or in the Aristotelian sense of
prior to what is imperfect "as act is prior to potency" (in 8
Phy 14, 1090; 19, 1134). Yet Aquinas also employs the term
in the neo-Platonic manner of what contains the imperfect (In
2 CM 1, 291), what attains to its source (In 8 Phy 14, 1131;
In 2 CM 4, 334), or what communicates or diffuses itself (In
1 CM 21, 216; 13 DN 1, 957–68). Some of these asspects are
harmonized in a summary statement characteristic of medieval
commentary style (In 10 M 5, 2028):

> Everything is said to be *perfect* in that it attains its end.
> Outside the end there is nothing, for the end is what is
> ultimate for each thing and what contains the thing. Thus
> what is perfect has no need of anything outside itself, for
> under its perfection it contains everything.

This schematic rendering of perfection accents the two characteristics relevant to our inquiry: first, something is perfect
which has what it ought to have, i.e. possesses its nature completely; and second, every nature seeks its perfection as its end
(In 7 Phy 6, 920). Perfection, then, connotes the teleological,
the fulfillment-dimension of things. Accenting this makes any
account of it necessarily schematic, for perfection will be relative to the types involved and variant with the context.

But this is only the initial reason why 'perfection' (or any
particular perfection) resists an accounting. The more germane
reason threads through all the literature against naturalism
from Plato to Moore. No description can capture what we intend to say by good, just, and the like, for such terms look not
to achievements so much as to aspirations. They are open to
use in areas where their specific realization may not be conceivable, but when we encounter these terms we can recognize
them as answering to man's specific yearnings and "deepest
aspirations." By so tying perfection to fulfillment, Aristotle
registers the fact that values must reflect some inner affinity

39. I 3 Phy 11, 385; In 1 CM 20, 206; In 5 M 18, 1934–39.

with man—without attempting to provide an account of how
this is so. For if the proper subject for 'fulfillment" is clearly
man, its meaning when used of him is far from clear. Fulfillment, like perfection, remains open-ended.

All this, however, simply glosses the obvious fact that values
enter the world with man, and that man can know no other
measure than his own response as it becomes progressively un-
biased through increasingly disinterested involvement. That is
to say, logically there can be finally no other measure for man's
fulfillment. And we actually can experience and watch a pro-
gression to greater authenticity through self-criticism. This fact
provides the extra impetus Aquinas needs for a final affirmative
moment in the unusual and invariably negative inquiry into
what-explains-existence. His statements must be negative in
tone, since many finite facets of a predicate must be rejected:
perfection, said of God, for example, does not imply privation,
the preliminary lack which creates in us the need or desire to
achieve (In 2 DN 1, 114). Yet while everything finite may be
denied of God in this way, God is said to be preeminently just,
merciful or good. Why may these predicates apply and not
others? Because they answer in one fashion or another to the
fulfillment-dimension of man; they bear an affinity to Plato's
sincere inquirer.

Toward a "Philosophical Anthropology"

If we recall the schematic psychology available to Aquinas,
we will notice that the use of perfection, fulfillment, and similar
terms opens a door to the will. Closer attention to *willing* was
implicit in his decision to entertain seriously the question of the
intelligibility of existence. For once the issues are existential,
something more than argument is involved. In fact, we can
trace more precisely the manner in which inquiry is extended
to existence itself by noting how the will makes its presence
felt.

Aquinas' hitherto sharp distinction of intellect/will breaks
down as the entire person is engaged in a way unsuspected in
ordinary inquiry. There, we recall, will and emotions were

considered obstacles, something to be kept in control so that the truth might reveal itself more clearly. Here, on the contrary, will is explicitly invoked. It seems to work in tandem with knowledge, taking over where knowledge must leave off, so disposing one to a progressive understanding where the person permits it.[40]

Yet Aquinas' remarks to this effect are scattered and often only asides. The main line of his exposition leaves 'perfection' undeveloped and seems to rely more on the semantic distinction of *res* from *modus,* which we saw would not hold up. We may suspect the reason: Aquinas wanted to keep the inquiry going as long as possible, even though he realized it was a most unusual form of inquiry.[41] But we can recognize what he may not have: what is really operating here is a full-blown "philosophical anthropology." Couched in terms of a faculty psychology, it remarks: as the intellect seeks order and intelligibility as its perfection, so the will seeks after good and finds

40. Thus "mens potest comprehendere voluntatem et intellectum . . . , ut sub 'mente' intelligatur comprehendere omnes illae potentiae quae in suis actibus omnino a materia . . . recedunt" (deV 10 1 ad 2). The context is Augustine's use of *mens* as the image of God in man, which Aquinas pinpoints as the aspect of *mens* whereby man is polarized on God and on himself (deV 10 2 ad 5). But this is realized only by a conspiracy of intellect and will: "where the operation of the intellect terminates, there the will begins." Since the knowledge we can have of God is limited to "knowing what he is not," the will must as it were make up the difference (deV 10 11 ad 6. Cf. also deV 21 1 ad 13; DN 3, 989–93). T. Bonhoeffer agrees that *perfection* is the lever allowing us to speak of God, and in the sense here explicated: terms like *maxime ens* or *causa esse et bonitatis* presuppose some kind of call or invitation from God since they function only with respect to "what all men call God" (*Die Gotteslehre de Thomas von Aquin als Sprachproblem* (Tübingen, 1961, p. 108).

41. "It is therefore said of us that when we come to the end of our knowledge, we acknowledge God as the Unknown, because the mind has made most progress in understanding when it recognizes that God's essence lies beyond anything that the mind in its state of being-on-the-way can comprehend" (deT 1 2 ad 1); cf. J. C. Murray, *Problem of God* (pp. 72–73).

its perfection in consenting to what is good.[42] If these demands are never completely fulfilled, they are nonetheless imperious: nothing can justify truncating inquiry nor explain a refusal to carry out its original impulse.

For Aquinas, to take these demands seriously is to be led on to affirm their source in God, since the demand of intelligence for explanation is all-embracing and the need of the will for motivation tends toward an ultimate goal.[43] But this summary statement overlooks the semantic difficulties in moving from explanations to an all-embracing explanation, from goals to ultimate goal. And since Aquinas himself was aware of the difference, a more careful rendition is in order. The rhetoric of "deepest aspirations" explicitly envisages man's intellect and will. Where aspirations exhibit a certain universality (which is part of their "depth"), this fact alone demands an explanation. If the reason proffered is—as in Aristotle—that man is so constituted, then we may still ask how it is that he is?

But how does one come to grips with a question like that? The crucial step, as Wittgenstein never ceases to recall, is to select an idiom that will not mislead.[44] This is the negative side of Peirce's criterion that our expressions be "suggestive of future development." Peirce's criterion offers us no clear-cut way of deciding in each instance, but it gives more weight to the observation that certain lines of inquiry will prove more successful than others. If one were to compare the idiom I have proposed, for example, with a certain standard antinaturalist style of argument, one would notice my preference of 'aspiration' for 'intuition of value'.[45] This is a deliberate move imply-

42. Cf. F. E. Crowe, "Complacency and Concern in the Thought of St. Thomas" (*Theol. Stud.* 20, 1959, pp. 1–39, 198–230, 343–95) for a comprehensive analysis of the relation between intellect and will in Aquinas.

43. DN 1, 797; 2, 823; deT 6 5 ad 5. Cf. Victor Preller's critical reconstruction in *Divine Science and the Science of God*.

44. *Investigations,* ##103–08; *Foundations,* I, pp. 6–8, 117–25.

45. Thinking, for example, of G. E. Moore's "Is Goodness a Quality?" in his *Philosophical Papers* (London, 1959), or H. A. Prichard's

ing that *value* corresponds in some way to what man is. My
choice is designed to make sympathetic response more internal
to the definition of valuable than 'intuition' can.[46] And what is
more, 'aspiration' is more faithful to Aquinas' usage, though his
idiom is more ontological, whereas the language of aspiration
is more anthropological.

Person as Paradigm for "Nature'

Aquinas tends to speak of all of nature seeking its perfection
—*quaelibet res quaerit perfectionem suam*—but he would be
the first to recognize that seeks is used analogously, with person
as the paradigm. Yet of course not only seeks, but thing and
perfection are analogous as well; and the very *quaelibet . . .
suam* form shows us that this is more a schema or a rubric than
a statement. It states what to look for in examining any kind
of thing. According to McInerny's interpretation of Aquinas,
this schema states a "common intention"—what I would call
a meta-linguistic expression—and gains what meaning it may
have from the presence of a prime analogate falling within it.[47]
Analogues will fall under the common intention only when
they can be shown to bear some relation to the primary usage;
structural similarity, ability to fit the schema, is insufficient.
(Note how Aquinas' account is open to an ongoing inquiry,
and really needs it to forestall triviality. *Some* relation among
usages can always be conceived. The question is whether the
analogy will prove useful, whether the relations required to
sustain it will be illuminating; in this case, whether it is helpful
or misleading to insist that everything, squirrels and electrons
included, seeks its end.)

"Does Moral Philosophy Rest on a Mistake?" in his *Moral Obligation*
(Oxford, 1949).

46. P. H. Howell-Smith, *Ethics* (Harmondsworth, 1954), pp. 224–25,
and "Contextual Implication and Ethical Theory," *Proc Aris. Soc.,
Suppl.,* 36 (1962) 1–18.

47. McInerny, pp. 135, 150–52, and my review article, "Religious
Language and the Logic of Analogy" (*Inter. Phil. Quar.* 2, 1962, 643–
58).

The prime instance of seeking is doubtless man's seeking, so man as the locus of aspirations becomes the prime analogue presupposed to Aquinas' account of "all nature seeking its end." The move is characteristic of Aquinas—to insist on an encompassing ontological formula but to operate with a philosophical anthropology. It is further characteristic that he overlooks calling our attention to the fact. We must attend to the examples he will use—invariably a man to exemplify substance —and note the clearly schematic form of the ontological formulae. That he would not oppose man to nature is indicative of the *Weltanschauung* prevailing in his day; that he should be forced to use man as nature's privileged instance is a sign of Aquinas' keen ear for semantics: 'seeking' is clearly anthropomorphic and analogical in the sense already explained. Nothing can present us with a *res significata* that will provide the core of an encompassing ontological usage, but each one of us provides a paradigm instance.[48]

There is an originality to man, especially in the dimension of value. Indeed, by consensus of psychologists if not by definition, healthy means open to growth, flexible; pathological connotes a confinement to formulae and rigid patterns of behavior. Men experience unlimited aspirations and know multiple realizations, enough at least to be wary of trying to capture recommendations like adjustment or acceptance in a formula. So when the notion of perfection, already context-variant, is used of man, it exhibits an inner dialectic which fast gives rise to paradox: the perfect man is the very one who will be able to accept his own imperfections.[49]

Thus we have a notion peculiarly apt for use in speaking of God, and one which by its originality and fecundity at least suggests a move to God as its explanation, even if it fails to license such a move. Perfection is especially apt because it resists any

48. Cf. especially Yves Simon, "Order in Analogical Sets," *New Scholasticism* 34 (1960) 1–42.

49. Representatively, Karen Horney, *Neurosis and Human Growth* (New York, 1950), and Erik Erikson, *Identity and the Life Cycle* (New York, 1963).

determinate articulation, as we have noted before, and which
the paradox dramatizes. Moreover, the twin notes of originality
and fecundity strike that sympathetic chord in us that spells
kinship with those deepest aspirations (or imperious demands)
of reason and will, which invite (or compel) us to carry inquiry
beyond its reasonable limits.

This fact suffices to open the way for a move to God. (By
a move to God I mean something akin to proposing a hypothesis. Proposing is distinct from confirming, though we can only
responsibly propose what we have some idea how to verify.) I
say open the way for a move because we are not at present
concerned with what warrants this move so much as we are
with its prior plausibility. But certain consequences do follow
from this procedure. The procedure itself intimates that whatever such a move may be, it will not be a proof. This is so
not merely because no unobjectionable one has been proposed,
but specifically because the language here is inextricably inter-
twined with that of willing—'fulfillment', 'aspiration', etc.—
which renders the very notion of proof obscure. It follows, then,
that an adequate description of the "move to God" will exhibit
not only logical and analogical components but also involve
dimensions of the person not patient of logical or semantic
analysis.

The situation is a frankly self-involving one. Yet so are many
others in human life. Expressions reflecting aspiration are
woven into our discourse. The more definite the description of
a human situation, the more engaged our sensibilities, our fears
and aspirations, become.[50] We may try to find an idiom so dis-
engaged as to portray a human situation in terms quite neutral
to these human concerns. And we have, of course, not only
tried but succeeded. What sounds ludicrous as a proposal has
proven sinister when carried out. For the very neutrality of the
new idiom galvanizes our aspirations to offer us a new deal. In the
face of this phenomonon we have come to a renewed appreciation of the resources embedded in natural language itself. It

50. For a persuasive statement, see Julius Kovesi, *Moral Notion*
(London, 1967).

would seem to be a safer and more fruitful tack to explore the logic of the expressions we already possess than try to repress or replace an entire dimension of our language. These expressions do have an open-ended way about them, which suggests a transcendent reach. The more accurately we can understand that open-endedness, however, the more clearly we can discriminate genuine from ersatz transcendence.

Corollary: Aquinas on Actus Essendi

It is worth noting that for Aquinas the move to what-explains-existence—while dramatized by the stark query "Why is there anything at all?"—is actually executed in the more hospitable context of "perfections" or human aspirations, and carried along by the multiple associations these connote.[51] He simply calls to our attention one facet after another of the root demand for order and fulfillment which encourages us to extend inquiry beyond the limits of what can safely be answered. Once we recognize the role of perfections in extending our inquiry to meet the existential question, the decision to continue pursuing the demand for intelligibility might embolden us to consider existence itself a perfection, as an *act*. Aquinas in fact does speak of the act of existing. He regards the expression as an adequate and proper substitute for 'to exist' (*esse*), and contemporary Thomists have made much of this "existential turn" in Aquinas.[52] We have seen a way of making sense of this notion. Now it is time to look somewhat critically at Thomistic enthusiasm.

Act of existing. Actually we seldom speak of the 'act of' anything, and 'act of existing' will prove the oddest expression of all. Act of appears to be largely a solemnity used to signal important events or identify act with agent, as in, "You are witnessing the act of signing the peace treaty with Japan," or, "he

51. Cf. T. Penelhum, "Divine Necessity," *Mind* 69 (1960) 175–86.
52. For Aquinas' use, cf. I 4 1 ad 1 (and index to *Summa Theologiae*); also E. Gilson, *Being and Some Philosophers* (Toronto, 1952), pp. 108–216; and Joseph deFinance, *Etre et agir* (Rome, 1960), pp. 78–120.

saw the act of murder." This usage is closely allied with 'in the act of' which is used to pinpoint temporal connections: "As I came in, he was in the act of pouring a drink." What is interesting about these cases is that act of and in the act of are superfluous. Ordinarily we simply speak of signing, murdering, pouring as themselves denoting action, something we do.

But existing is not exactly something we do. So it is not an act in any ordinary sense of the word: hence the need to explicate 'act of existing'. Nor is it an ability, for existing is said to be an act. Yet it is clearly not the kind of thing I exercise. What does it mean, then, to call existing an act? Whatever else may be involved, it certainly betrays a decision to look upon existing as needing an explanation. It becomes then one of those things that demand to be explained: regular occurrences or acts. Regular occurrences need not be acts, of course, in the sense of something we do, and existing conveys spontaneity as much as regularity. Hence the tendency to assimilate existence-to-be-explained to an act rather than a regularity.

Decision, of course, is a recognized way of introducing usage. It has been proffered to legitimize our recourse to counterfactual conditionals in scientific inquiry.[53] Not that anyone or any group deliberately decides upon an idiom, but rather that a way of speaking recommends itself and is gradually adopted. We will be inclined, in time, to accept the new usage as quite ordinary, patient of all the implications that accrued to the expression in its home context. One might be led, for example, to speak of 'exercising the/my act of existing'.[54] While con-

53. Wilfrid Sellars, "Counterfactuals, Dispositions, and the Causal Modalities," *Minnesota Studies in Philosophy of Science* 2 (Minneapolis, p. 286.

54. As does G. B. Phelan: "every being exercises the act of existence in proportion to its essence" (*St. Thomas and Analogy,* Milwaukee, 1941, p. 39). Existenz-philosophers, of course, do not hesitate to say that existing is what a man does. Hence there would be no impropriety in their speaking of act of existing. By restricting it to man, they assimilate it to a perfection (as we have analyzed them) and in fact sum up all aspiration therein. But existence is also contingent and without reason, so aspiration to order is absurd and inquiry ends in meaninglessness. John Smith calls

tinuing to speak of the contingency of existing, one might be tempted by the act language to treat it as an achievement as well. And since it is a mysterious sort of act, existing becomes the source and font of every act we perform, indeed, of all perfection.[55]

But the radical contingency of existing, which forced the question in the first place, has been overshadowed by the decision to regard existing as an act. In other words, the very expression 'act of existing' embodies the desire to explain why there is anything at all. It offers a relatively smooth way of extending ordinary scientific inquiry, for it suggests a category within which we can locate existing: the category of action. The proposal to extend inquiry to explain existing tends to lose its distinctive character. The semantic peculiarities latent in the proposal are glossed over, and what-explains-existence (God) becomes a super-explainer.

Advocates of Aquinas insist that he does not fall prey to this danger, even though he does speak of existing as a mysterious act. But if Aquinas manages to avoid the pitfall, he does so only because he finds the search for what-explains-existence leading inescapably to a creator. And that conjunction brings other philosophical constraints into play. Act of existing will then be said properly only of the creator, as the one-who-explains-existence; everything we know to exist will participate in this act. Everything created will receive its act of existing from the one whose act is to exist. No lesser scheme could explain existing.[56]

---

this the "dialectic gone mad"; with Wittgenstein we might ask: Is not language idling here? ("Relation of Thought and Being: Some Lessons from Hegel's *Encyclopedia*," *New Scholasticism* 38, 1964, 41).

55. I 4 1 ad 1, and Lyttkens' critique, pp. 448–49.

56. Thus Hayen: the solution of discourse about God entails admitting some sort of proportion between the creature and God, and *esse* is meant to say just that while preserving transcendence (5 DN 2, 660); hence "the Thomist metaphysics of analogy and participation poses as its fundamental thesis that the creative presence of God to his creature is intrinsically constitutive of that creature" (*L'Intentionel selon S. Thomas*, Paris, 1954, pp. 89–90).

The mention of creator forces Aquinas to assert an even greater transcendence, and saves him from pretending to comprehend what it is to exist. Furthermore, since we can know nothing of what it would be like simply to be one act or merely to exist, Aquinas is not tempted to picture creation or to describe participation. What-explains-existence remains an enigma because existing is. And the manner of explaining remains as obscure as the explainer.

To call existing an act rather calls attention to the demand that it be intelligible after all. The demands that give rise to such an expression may well be the best indicators of reality we possess. But nonetheless the expression 'act of existing' reflects our inbuilt need for intelligibility more than it describes a feature of the world. Attending to this fact should help us keep alive to the twin movement involved in using it: (1) from our general puzzlement about things to our concern about their very existence and our attempts to account for it; and (2) from the questioner's awareness of his own existence (as prime analogate) to a derivative use of 'act of existing' for that about ordinary things which escapes ordinary explanation—their coming-to-be.

When Aquinas discovered these intellectual movements leading into the logical terrain of creation, he was able to allow them full scope yet control their pretense to offer a proper explanation. For creation lies beyond the pale of human comprehension, but to possess the notion nonetheless allows one to go on. It allows him to do so, that is, provided he does not proceed as though he were offering an explanation! So creation offered Aquinas a way of responding to our human penchant to continue asking why. And attending to the role creation plays for him allows us to follow his arguments in the spirit in which they were composed. Josef Pieper has made much of Aquinas' use of creation, calling it the hidden element in his philosophy.[57]

57. *Silence of St. Thomas* (New York, 1957, pp. 47–50); corroborated independently by James Anderson, "Bases of Metaphysical Analogy" (*Downside Rev.* 66, 1948, 38–47), and Mark Pontifex (ibid., 67, 1949, 395–405).

It proves central to Aquinas' own program and to our assessment of it.

Conscious Activity. There is another strain of inquiry in Aquinas, however, which shows the limitations of the rather austere analysis we have been following. It examines act in the context of persons, and promises to shed light comparable to our analysis of perfection. To be, for a person, is to be conscious. To exist is to act and be aware of one's actions.[58] If this is the case, to be, for man, will never be equivalent to merely *being there.* Aquinas invokes Aristotle's testimony to show how directly this awareness influences our appraisal of life itself: "so that if we perceive, we perceive that we perceive, and if we think, that we think; and if to perceive that we perceive or think is to perceive that we exist . . . ; and if perceiving that one lives is in itself one of the things that are pleasant . . . , and if life is desirable, and particularly so for good men, because to them existence is good and pleasant . . .—if all this be true, as his own being is desirable for each man, so or almost so, is that of his friend" (EN 1170a31–b8).

However we appraise it, consciousness is a fact. It may become problematic to analysis but the fact is secure. And Aquinas' account comes near to saying just this. He insists that the person is aware of himself only through his acts: "no one perceives that he is understanding except in so far as he is understanding something, because understanding something else is prior to understanding that we are understanding. So the person arrives at actually perceiving himself to exist by the fact that he understands or senses something" (deV 10 8). And lest the use of perceive and understand lead us to suspect a straightforward knowing-that-we-know thesis, Aquinas goes on to explicate this use in terms better served by the more guarded 'awareness'.

The category he employs to describe it is presence: the

---

58. The proposition is argued in the 9 Eth 11, 1902, by analogy with *De Anima* II 4: "In the case of living things their being is to live" (415b13). I am indebted to John S. Dunne for insisting on this aspect of Aquinas' usage of 'act'.

person is present to himself, and in this way can know that he is conscious without being able to analyze consciousness itself. Here again the person will achieve this awareness only in the act of knowing, and of knowing something else: "our mind cannot understand itself in such a way as to immediately apprehend itself; rather it is the case that in apprehending something else, it arrives at a knowledge of itself" (deV 10 8).

Interestingly enough, mere awareness—this sheer *knowing that*—extends no further than the fact of consciousness itself. When it comes to specific abilities, we cannot be sure that we possess them without knowing in what they consist: "I cannot know whether I am charitable without knowing what charity is" (deV 10 9). Such imparity simply betrays what is unique about consciousness. Descartes tried to express it in *"Je pense donc je suis."* But for Aquinas there is no *donc* precisely because simple awareness is not knowledge but presence, not knowing-that but being-present-to: "our mind knows through itself, in so far as it knows concerning itself, *that it is*. Indeed, from the fact that it perceives that it acts it perceives that it is" (CG 3 46).

If this sense of act is paradigmatic—conscious act which acts through itself—then Aquinas' use of act of existing becomes considerably less strange. The additional theorems of a creator with creation sharing variously in his creative act would be required, of course, to lead off any pan-psychism; but act could not simply be identified with regularity. Furthermore, we would have an instance of knowing that something is, which need not entail (or presuppose) any knowledge of what it is, for what "acts through itself knows concerning itself that it is" (CG 3 46). This would suggest the lasting attraction of the more Augustinian approach to God through consciousness. If Aquinas travels by another, more conceptual route where knowing *whether x* is cannot be disassociated from knowing *what* it is, we nonetheless feel Augustine's presence unobtrusively guiding the way. Could it be that Augustine's searching of consciousness supplied Aquinas with a usage of act which Aristotle could merely assert: a category unique and sufficiently paradoxical to suggest the divinity itself and yet internal enough to human experience to keep it from being a wishful or arbitrary extension? [59]

Like perfection, then, the status of act (or act of existing) as a metaphysical category would be considerably illuminated by its roots in a philosophical anthropology. Yet to illuminate a usage is not to justify it *tout court*. Indeed the impropriety of exercising an act of existence is underscored by referring to intentional activity: In knowing that something is the case can I be said to be exercising my knowledge consciously? Or is it simply that to know is to be conscious? The uniqueness of the category must be reflected in these privileged uses of act if we want to use act of existing in a way that will be both warranted and fruitful, leading rather than misleading.

FROM USAGE TO JUDGMENT

Thus far I have spoken in terms of demands. It is time now to illustrate these *in use* by calling attention to that kind of activity where the twin requirements of intelligibility—order and fulfillment—make themselves manifest. I would like to call this activity 'judgment' in order to catch the ordinary connotations of good judgment as well as the term's more sophisticated glosses: appraisal and decision.

Judgment, then, is regarded as engaging both intellect and will, if you wish, and has long been granted privileged status in Thomist tradition. Yet Thomists have not seriously attempted to analyze its workings. Lonergan's choice of the term was doubtless influenced by that tradition, though the recourse to both Kant and Hegel for his formulation makes us wonder whether 'judgment' could be adequately analyzed within the tradition that invoked it. That Lonergan chose to use this term would suffice to explain my choice here and signal the debt owed to him. But a further motive for introducing it in a discussion of analogous usage is Gilson's remark that " 'analogy' for Aquinas refers to our capacity to make the kind

59. Aristotle insists on the uniqueness of mental acts in *De Anima* (417b2–16, 431a6–8), and uses this in his notoriously enigmatic "thinking on thinking" (Meta 1074b34).

of judgments that we do"; it is to be explicated "on the level of judgment," not of concept. This, he insists, is the point of real divergence between Aquinas and Scotus. Gilson's observation that all discussion of analogy of being or of analogous concepts is utterly foreign to Aquinas, who speaks rather of "terms used analogously," not only suggests comparisons with contemporary semantics but also helps uncover a thread of perennial philosophical concern.[60]

Aquinas so explicated can form a pivotal point between Greek fascination with *logos* and contemporary preoccupation with language by offering an illuminating example of language trying to work in quite rarefied regions. The fact that his statements are nearly always couched in the prevailing material mode of speech can easily mislead us. Aquinas' manner of response to objections, however, which so often consists in showing us how he is using his language, manifests his awareness of how he was proceeding. He was equipped, as Carnap would put it, "to avoid the dangers inherent in the material mode of speech." [61]

Some Contemporary Approaches to Judgment

In fact, Carnap's account of the choice of linguistic frameworks offers one avenue for explicating those expressions which supervene any ordinary account. Much as he insists that it is a mere choice—"a practical, not a theoretical question"—the reasons Carnap feels impelled to give for making a choice of frameworks carry us far beyond a mere toss of a coin and well into the cognitive order. For he describes the choices as "expedient, fruitful, conducive to the aim for which the language is intended." [62] Wilfrid Sellars explicitly carries us beyond a simple option to speak of "deciding which conceptual meaning

60. E. Gilson, *Christian Philosophy,* pp. 105–07; *Jean Duns Scot* (Paris, 1952), p. 101; some relevant texts in Aquinas are I 13 5–6; I 13 10 ad 4; CG I 34; II 15.

61. Rudolph Carnap, *Logical Syntax of Language* (London, 1937), pp. 301, 312–13.

62. Carnap, *Meaning and Necessity,* p. 214.

our observation vocabulary is to have." He also accounts for causal modalities entering our language in virtue of a decision, one which sufficiently shifts the meaning of *A* and *B* in '*A* causes *B*'; to entitle us to employ ' . . . causes . . . ' in the counterfactual manner we are accustomed to.[63]

Far from espousing Carnap's dichotomy between practical and theoretical (= ontological) questions, Sellars insists that it is precisely decisions about conceptual frameworks which do imply that the objects presupposed by the accepted framework truly exist. Indeed what else could? At this point Sellars' decision neighbors on a central facet of judgment as it has been traditionally invoked to finalize inquiry and state which conclusions were true. Though no such decision is absolutely final because each is inevitably promissory—"their status can only be understood in the light of the total rationale of the scientific enterprise"—these choices nonetheless do play a kind of finalizing role essential to discourse.[64]

Hence Sellars insists "the important thing is to realize that instead of 'probable hypothesis' or 'mere inductive generalization' being a *terminal* category, it is an interim category." In Sellars' terms, then, the question arises: How can we make decisions which are terminal and yet not terminal? Granted that decisions of this kind are presupposed by discourse as we use it, how are we to explain them? Sellars' apparent response —that they are not something we deliberate about but something we do—succeeds only through its ambiguity.[65] For 'doing' in this case simply blankets the spectrum from carefree toss to responsible decision. But because we insist that it be responsible, *doing* is inevitably more than merely doing—as Peirce came to see.[66]

This brings us to Wittgenstein's metaphor of "playing a role." Here too, of course, more is involved than just doing.

63. W. Sellars, *Science, Perception and Reality* (London, 1963), pp. 356, 357; "Counterfactuals," p. 286.
64. Sellars, *Science,* pp. 118–26, 358; "Counterfactuals," p. 263.
65. Sellars, *Science,* pp. 57 n. 1, 224, 246.
66. C. S. Peirce, *Collected Papers,* 5.429.

Some sense or feeling for the point of the whole play, be it a game or a dramatic piece, is requisite to one's successfully fulfilling one's role.[67] Now this "sense" betrays itself not in what the person performing the role says about it but in the manner in which he acts. So we must describe what the player does in terms of the sense or feeling he has for his part. We can similarly speak of someone's knowing how to dance a reel without being able to tell us how he does it. What is at issue in each case is a certain level of awareness that cannot and need not be rendered explicit. In a similar way, we can know what we want to explain, yet admit to not having found the explanation as yet.[68]

We may then take this way of talking as a warrant for speaking of the "knowledge" such language recognizes and the "awareness" to which I have just alluded. Of both this knowledge and awareness we may say that we have not found an explanation for them though we know what we want to explain. And the sign that there is a kind of knowledge here is our ability to recognize inadequate explanations. What characterizes this sort of knowledge or awareness is precisely that it is not a "*position* in the 'game' of *reasoning*," for it is part of the very process of reasoning itself.[69]

Hare has noted that any intellectual discovery turns up something we could not define but were able to recognize.[70] He himself recognizes of course that this discovery is not novel; Plato saw it clearly. But Plato felt compelled to fill in the paradox which true discovery opens with a mythical account of reminiscence. Now I shall rather focus on the paradox itself

67. Note that the German *Spiel* can be rendered either by *game* or by *play* in the sense of 'drama'. Wittgenstein also speaks of *stagesetting* in *Investigations* (#257).

68. R. M. Hare, "Philosophical Discoveries," *Mind* 69 (1960) 148–52. This is of course the constant thesis of Michael Polanyi, notably in *Personal Knowledge* (New York, 1965).

69. Sellars, *Science,* p. 324. If this be the case, however, Sellars' regress is cut, and he is no longer impelled to the position of page 327, which ill accords with that of page 357, c.

70. R. H. Hare, "Philosophical Discoveries," pp. 155, 162.

and the manner in which recognize differs from know when the latter has the sense of define. And this decision to direct attention to my use reflects yet another aspect of playing a role. It is an aspect somewhat obscured by speaking of decisions: the demands a role makes upon us. Presumably, certain expressions will fit with 'recognize' while others will not, though they may do well with 'define'. And to repeat, recognizing this "fit" is not to take a position in an argument but to surmise something of the shape any argument might take by partially sketching in the boundaries of discourse.[71]

This understanding of recognition is offered as a gloss on Aquinas' "intend to mean" (*intendit significare*). The pregnant Latin expression might also be rendered "mean to say," as if to emphasize that we cannot say what we mean to say except by repeating it—offering (or accepting) alternative statements which we recognize to be what we intended. We may also recognize certain expressions as more adequate than others (even, as in the case of "naming God," within a context where any expression is intrinsically inadequate). And this is the very opening to a discrimination among linguistic frameworks.

"Criteria" for Appraising Accounts

How do we decide that one account is preferable to another? If the question asks for a description of the processes involved, it would be sufficient for our purposes to retort: "We just do, that's all!" But the question can envisage more. It may be asking: What reasons do we give? How do we justify the decision? What do we mean by preferable here?

To begin with the last question, when we say that this account is better than another, we certainly intend that it fit the facts more adequately. There can be no doubt of intent here, but we still may wonder how a set of statements might fit the facts.[72] If the intentions are honorable, they are not altogether clear, and a more promising tack might be to examine the implications of deciding for one account rather than another.

71. Wittgenstein, *Investigations*, p. 218.
72. Cf. J. L. Austin, *Philosophical Papers*, pp. 98, 109.

The very fact of a decision bespeaks a set of values operating in discourse.[73] The principle of sufficient reason, the canons of parsimony and elegance, the so-called laws of continuity and least action in nature—these are the norms, this the style of warrant invoked in favor of a particular account. But they are not laws so much as forms of laws, as Wittgenstein saw so clearly in the *Tractatus* (6.32). They envision not so much the behavior of things as our account thereof. In Wittgenstein's words, they are "about the net and not about what the net describes" (6.35). Yet this warning does not stay our concluding "that we could *describe* the surface more accurately with a coarse triangular mesh than with a fine square mesh [if] the use of a triangular mesh would have made the description simpler" (6.341).

What x is, then, is not independent of an account of it, and any account will be governed by norms like those Wittgenstein alludes to. Now the fact that these norms are not susceptible of precise formulation is no real objection against them: "indeed people even surmised that there must be *a* 'law of least action' before they knew exactly how it went" (6.3211). In fact, one of the cardinal features of these "forms of laws" is an inherent vagueness. But what is the status of these forms of laws? As a first appraisal, they are like Kant's "regulative principles" though more intrinsic to giving an account, since concept formation involves more than simply applying categories. Like his regulative principles, they are certainly not empirical.

For Wittgenstein, "all such propositions as these are a priori insights about the forms in which the propositions of science can be cast" (6.34). Like the axioms of logic, examining them will not teach us anything. Only in applying them do we learn something about the world—"by the fact that it can be described more *simply* with one system of mechanics than with another" (6.342). Unlike the a priori statements of logic,

---

73. I am indebted to Kenneth M. Sayre for calling attention to the manifold differences between 'deciding' and 'choosing', in *Philosophy and Cybernetics* (Notre Dame, 1967). It is worth noting that Carnap ends up using 'decision' or 'decide' where his argument would explicitly call for 'choice', 'choose' or even 'opt' (*Meaning and Necessity*, pp. 43, 214).

however, these own no properly general form. 'Parsimony' means—or ought to mean—different things to the physical and behavioral scientist; 'elegance' invokes different standards in mathematics than in literary criticism; 'least action' would elicit a different set of criteria in biology than in physics.

If the tautologies of logic, then, are firmly established laws of language prior to their application, these norms for forming and appraising theories are not. Their meaning rather lies in the application we make of them. This is but another way of saying that they have no general form of their own. As Wittgenstein expresses it: "If there were a law of causality, it might be put in the following way: there are laws of nature. But of course that cannot be said: it makes itself manifest" (6.36). Why can it not be said? Because "there are laws of nature" tells us nothing—about nature, nor about how to proceed to inquire into it. That is even more "unsayable"—in Tractarian jargon—than the pseudopropositions of logic and mathematics, for the general form of an integer does tell us how to generate one (6, 6.03). These may be manifested "before our eyes," but the principles governing our option of conceptual frameworks can make themselves manifest only through their applications in inquiry.[74]

To speak, however, of principles or laws which are not sus-

74. Attention to the difference between these two kinds of linguistic roles and their relative "unsayability" should prove an illuminating way of characterizing Wittgenstein's shift from the *Tractatus* to the *Investigations*. Certainly the language of the *Tractatus* gives little inkling of a difference; and the emphasis on use of different languages in the *Investigations* indicates a growing awareness of the presence of normative principles other than the formally logical in language. An alternative tack would have been to so define parsimony, elegance, least action, and the rest as to restrict them to their applications in a privileged set of sciences, making these uses paradigmatic for all the rest. This of course would not have succeeded in yielding a decision procedure for, say elegant/inelegant, though the task apparently looked easier to some when so delimited. The fact that Wittgenstein adopted the more latitudinarian view can no doubt be ascribed both to his logical clearsightedness— what would give one method a privileged status?—as well as to his respect for thoughtful people in disciplines other than the mathematical, who claimed to be able to recognize elegance in their domains. (I have been assured that Wittgenstein had great respect for F. R. Leavis.)

ceptible of formulation, whose meaning shifts with each different type of application, is to encroach upon the domain of expressions typed "analogous"—terms used variously in diverse contexts yet short of sheer ambiguity. To say that these laws form the criteria of judgment or appraisal is accurate but misleading, for it is a poor criterion which cannot be formulated. Indeed it must rather be said that anyone who speaks of parsimony, elegance, and the rest in the pluralistic fashion I have adopted is ipso facto committed to something like what we call judgment. For judgment simply names the ability to recognize one account as preferable to another—a procedure justified by recourse to terms like simpler, more elegant, and others. The meaning of such terms, then, is our ability to use them in one or more fields of inquiry. We ought not to try to define them independently of the contexts in which we have to use them. We are left quite simply with an ability to discern or discriminate, which is enough akin to a nose for the relevant to warrant the name of judgment.

Judgment and Awareness

'Judgment' names the ability we have to recognize one account as simpler or more elegant, expedient, or fruitful than the next. Speaking of judgment becomes a way of referring to the presence and function of these expressions in our language. For judgment applies insofar as one term helps to collate the ways in which these expressions are used, to register their resistance to a single formulation, and to account for their privileged and pervasive status. Judgment also succeeds in linking contemporary writing on decision among conceptual frameworks with more classical treatises on truth. The two activities of deciding and assessing are certainly not unrelated to each other.

The measure in which our decision is deliberate, aware, or conscious cannot be expressed in unequivocal criteria, as we have seen, under penalty of regress. But a test remains: our alacrity in recognizing the relevance of an objection. We may reject one because we have explicitly considered it: but more frequently we do so because upon hearing the objection we recognize where we can or have blocked it. Or we see that this objection belongs to another universe of discourse—i.e. that we need not meet it. Or the objection may occasion a modification of a given stance as we recognize its impact on our hypotheses. Or again we might notice how an objection confirms an original view, or shatters it. In every case there is a kind of retrospection testifying to the awareness with which the original judgment was made. That awareness seems to be more like a burden than a light, more akin to committing oneself than to seeing anything.

So awareness is not knowledge, nor is it intuition. It is, as I have described it, a feeling that a particular statement would not be irrseponsible. This feeling is grounded in the satisfaction that we have submitted the proposal to criticism, that its assertions are free from conscious bias, and that we have not knowingly betrayed the demands of inquiry as we met objections. The set of statements is asserted to be true, then, and thereby offered as a contribution to an ongoing inquiry.

The extent to which it is a responsible contribution is not yet settled, however. In offering a proposal, we had to be satisfied that it was not irresponsible. Only in responding to comment and criticism, in our ability to discern what is relevant, to refute or to incorporate, will we be able to show (and to know) *how* responsible a statement it was. This capacity to respond to criticism (our own or others) is the only measure we have of our awareness in making the original assertion. Our performance will never match our intent, of course. Only time and fidelity to the remote condition of inquiry, as well as its ongoing demands, can tell us how close it has come.[75]

75. I am quite conscious here of departing from a strain of interpretation of Aquinas that can only be called intuitionistic in tone, notably that of Jacques Maritain in *Degree of Knowledge* (New York, 1959, pp. 75–90). The historical and systematic groundwork for this departure can be found in B. J. F. Lonergan's *Verbum* (see n. 6 above) and his later *Insight* (London, 1957). The accuracy of Lonergan as an interpreter of Aquinas must be judged in the manner in which his remarks illuminate one's own study of Aquinas (cf. *Verbum,* pp. 180–81). His view of judgment, so reminiscent of C. S. Peirce, is admittedly a development of Aquinas, but certainly in the line of a clearer position.

Where Use Yields Meaning

When we complement the demands of reason with those associated with the will, such as goodness, justice, mercy, or magnanimity, we have a set of terms traditionally used of God. Logically, the terms in both sets share a structure, or lack of structure. None of them can claim to be adequately explicated by a single account. From this point of view, then, appraisal terms like transcendentals must be classed ambiguous or equivocal. But what prevents any account from claiming to be adequate is precisely the fact that we insist on using these same terms in one context after another. And our usage seems to justify a modified form of the *thing signified/manner of signifying* distinction.

Witness that we do claim simplicity for present theories and refuse to be subjected to canons constructed to handle outmoded ones. For instance, we speak of justice in democratic terms which connote a radical deficiency in earlier aristocratic conceptions. Yet to speak in this way amounts to admitting that our present view might well be surpassed, and surpassed in the direction of an ideal simplicity or justice which we cannot now formulate but which we could presumably recognize were we confronted with it. We must acknowledge the ability to recognize future realizations to the extent that we now exercise the right to criticize past achievements. And in the measure that we can recognize one situation to be more just than another, we are entitled to speak of justice as "what we signify." It then enjoys a certain independence from our present experience of it and our ordinary manner of signifying.

But the extent of our knowledge of justice-in-itself lies in our

---

F. Crowe suspects that Aquinas' "regular use of *componere* and *dividere,* terms better suited to grammar and logic than to philosophy, to denote the act of judgment, did much to hinder further development of the position reached so early" ("St Thomas . . . ," in *Sciences ecclésiastiques,* Montreal, 13, 1961, 189 n. 79). My suspicion is that it is *we* who did not appreciate how Aquinas was pressing grammar and logic to serve philosophy.

ability to recognize a better form of justice as we come upon it. No formula can capture the core of justice; any which tries will inevitably be schematic (like the definition of perfection) and so manifest what a strange kind of knowledge it reflects. These radically different senses of knowledge were obscured in the claims of the medieval theologico-grammatical program that we affirm what was signified while denying all manner or signifying. That program laid down in categorical terms what we in fact experience as an ongoing process. Some of its spokesmen went on to present a limiting extrapolation of the process as an operation more rarefied but of one piece with abstraction.

"Negative judgment" and personal fulfillment. We have seen how Aquinas employs the formula distinguishing *res* from *modus,* sharply curtailing its implications. On the one hand, he denies that we can simply operate with the what-is-signified as though it were a "piece of knowledge" on a par with others. On the other, he sketches out the lineaments of the process involved in extrapolating from our recognition of diverse realizations of justice (for example) to affirming its plenitude. By the first warning, he rejects in effect the notion that talk about transcendent realities, or pervasive metaphysical principles, can be explicated as a series of logical moves.

Nor can we have the best of both worlds by insisting that they are analogical moves. For as we have seen, the very notions we invoke to license these moves will not stand up as criteria. The notions give evidence only that we do engage in such discourse. By describing the character of the process carrying us to the threshold of transcendence, Aquinas explicitly brought the will more into focus. He tried to show how such language is not so much a projection as a recognition of needs, indeed of the imperious demands for order and fulfillment. If the decision to inquire into the grounds for there being anything at all is not forced upon us, it nonetheless corresponds to what can only be called the inner structure of the inquirer.

Now the very fact that the inquiry must move into an area where more personal elements of fulfillment and commitment are invoked ought to make us wary of any purely logical or semantic resolution of the linguistic questions raised. I concur with Lyttken's appraisal (p. 475) of the role of the *a:b::c:d* analogy for Aquinas: it is but a "logical aid in stating of God certain properties taken from creation." Yet Aquinas would emphasize that this continues to be an inquiry, even though our ordinary means of concept formation are useless here. He invokes in their place the negative judgment which amounts to the negative side of the recognition sketched above: rejecting any formulation claiming to be adequate.

This is to say that every concept (or representation) we might have of God misses the mark, and so enables us to deny all formulae entailing similarity, in any ordinary sense of that term, between God and creation. Within Aquinas' idiom, the point is dramatized by denying that metaphysical knowledge is the highest (or third) degree of abstraction, and insisting that its proper mode is better called separation than abstraction. I have elaborated elsewhere the systematic implications of this move for Aquinas' metaphysics, and the disastrous consequences for most of his commentators who gloss over it.[76] For the present it should suffice to say that any terms that we then go on to use of God must bear the mark of having been negated. The *res/modus* distinction is at work, as ever, but guided by other criteria.

What allows us to continue to use certain terms and claim to be making statements about God? Nothing, it seems, but the impetus of our original decision to inquire into the intelligibility of existence. Yet this is simply to accede to our inbuilt demands for order and fulfillment as they relate to the nagging question of why there is anything at all. By recalling how the decision to regard *A* as causing *B* can modify the subsequent meaning of *A* and *B,* we can get some idea of how decision gives meaning to subsequent statements about what-explains-existence ($=$ God). These statements must always be referred, as Aquinas insists, to our ordinary usage. In this case, however, we take that usage

76. In "Classification, Mathematics and Metaphysics: A Commentary on Aquinas' Exposition of Boethius' *On the Trinity*" (*Modern Schoolman* 44, 1966, 13–48).

as manifesting a drive to know, a demand for order. So the operating reference is to our desire to know as manifested in restless inquiring, and to the correlative desire for fulfillment displayed in the demands we make of inquiry itself.

A test case: Talk about angels. An interesting consequence of this interpretation of Aquinas is the unique status of God among what he called separables: beings existing in separation from the normal material conditions of existence, and hence more or less outside the pattern of the substance/accident descriptive sentence. Since our language does not enjoy a radical structural correspondence with such entities (so that subject:predicate as substance:accident), any ordinary descriptive expression will prove misleading when used to speak of them.

We need an intervening negative judgment which shows that we are aware of the inadequacy of our normal sentential form, yet not in possession of a language proper to this domain. But if this negative judgment receives its power to affirm through a decision to extend the twin demands for order and fulfillment to the "existential question," then we can use such indirect form of speech only for whatever fulfills these demands. In Aquinas' scheme, this raises serious questions about his treatment of the angels.

All the epistemological theorems remains in force here: what is separated from the conditions of space and time can never be known directly but only indirectly and negatively.[77] In the case of the angels, whatever they may be like, we know they are not bodies, nor are they God. 'Know' is tricky here and raises the question of the place of Aquinas' treatment of angels in his program. He inherited the angels, and with them the tradition that they were spiritual beings. The contemporaries and predecessors of Aquinas had often been content to speak of shadowy beings with rarefied matter. He intends to dispense with imaginaition and employ nothing but a negative logic.

The twin negatives—the angels are not bodies and not God— allow us to say something about their simplicity. Whatever com-

77. I 84 7, 88 2; deT 6 2–3; In 5 M 7, 865; In 10 M 4, 1990; In 3 deA 11, 758; 13, 791.

position bodily structure entails must be denied of angels, but a mode of composition remains. Simple as they may be, angels remain created and hence are subject to the composition of essence and existing (de Ente, 4). This limiting case clearly manifests Aquinas' departure from Aristotle, whose analogues, the heavenly "bodies," must exist *because* they lack bodily composition [M 1073a34]. In fact, the angels often function as limiting cases for Aquinas' speculation. So while we are not sure what it would mean to say that an angel is just, we know that we must put it that way and cannot go on to say, as we do of God, that an angel is justice.

The minimal composition of essence/existing suffices to retain the normal form of an ordinary attributive statement, while God's utter simplicity strains beyond it. Besides this semantic reference to ontological location, however, little more can be said about the angels. Systematic statements can be made, about what position, locomotion, individuality mean here, but they are either negative or metaphorical in tone, and admittedly ambiguous or equivocal.

Angels are "said to be 'in place' equivocally . . . , as it were, containing it" (I 52 1). That is, they are "not in place in a corporeal way through contact of dimensive quantity, but in a spiritual way by a kind of contact of power" (*per quemdam contactum virtutis*) (SS 18). Similarly, an angel "is said to move through place equivocally." The angel's motion is discontinuous, or at least need not be continuous, for his motion is defined from the meaning of being in place, and so means "diverse contacts 'by way of power' of diverse places successively and not simultaneously" (I 53 1, 52, 3). And this gives a kind of time. The angel's time is peculiar no doubt because not necessarily continuous, but time nonetheless because "where there are many *nows* succeeding one another, . . . there is time" (I 53 3). Finally, every angel is a species separate from every other; not however, because we can conceive what this would be like, but rather because an immaterial being by definition has no *matter* to account for individuality (I 50 4).

Early in the discussion Aquinas had defended the metaphorical language of Scripture by admitting that the "properties of intellectual [= immaterial] substances can be understood in sensible figures according to a certain similitude" (I 51 2 ad 1). But how much difference, really, is there between Aquinas' philosophical treatment and the metaphorical expressions of Scripture? Besides saying that the motion, place, time, and individuality of angels is not the same as ours, he can only hint at how they might apply: "as it were . . . , by a *kind of* contact."

One way remains to secure meaningful discourse here: to try to relate these statements to the "existential question." We could consider separated substances as contributing to the intelligibility of the universe (= all there is). Aquinas does invoke this argument but with the limited scope of showing that such beings would befit the universe (I 50 1; CG II 46). Fittingness is no argument, of course: at best it allows us to introduce a hypothesis. And on his own account of the unique semantic status of the existential question, there is no way of testing a hypothesis here. There is no determinate meaning that can be given to 'intelligibility of the whole' to decide whether something contributes to it or not. Neo-Platonism had no trouble picturing formulae like this, but Aquinas *did* have trouble with neo-Platonism. His trouble was epistemological and semantic, much the same as we have with Aquinas' own treatise on the angels.

It may well be that the actual existence of angels is irrelevant to his ontology. On such an interpretation, and it is quite plausible, Aquinas' treatise on angels becomes a systematic exploration of a specific range of possibilities. It will prove useful for him to have a certain command of this region, either as a limiting case for philosophical psychology (as in I 85 5) or as regulative for an ontology of knowledge: allowing introductory statements like "the human intellect holds a middle course between the angelic and the animal" (I 85 1). After such architectonic preludes, however, little more can be said, for our command of this realm of intellectual possibility is professedly tenuous.

Beyond the negative generalities—"an angel is not in place so as to be circumscribed by it"—any further detail is inevitably and at best metaphorical. It must be so on Aquinas' avowed epistemological principle that "the proper object of the human intellect is a nature existing in corporeal matter," while "incorporeal beings are known to us by comparison with sensible bodies" (I 84 7). Thus without the additional element of an interior response to something (or someone) promising personal fulfillment, the claim to knowledge via legitimate analogical usage appears considerably weakened if not nullified.

CONCLUDING REFLECTIONS

The angels offer an unwitting confirmation of my central thesis. Our language contains a set of terms whose syntactic structure leaves them free to be used in ways that outstrip our present settled idiom. These expressions are identifiable: they are generally used to appraise a situation. One suspects that a privileged subset of them would have to belong to any language whatsoever, for they serve as tools for framing what we are up to in using a language. If language is bound up with consciousness, and consciousness with some self-correcting feature, expressions of this sort will prove indispensable, for they reflect into language itself the reflective awareness which a responsible use of language demands.

But nothing appears to be able to provide canons for the correct use of *these* expressions. We are free to employ them in a vague allusive way or to hone them for precise theological assertions. One use is as appropriate as the other; nothing can decide but the context, and the context is shaped to fill the purposes we have in mind.

All that Aquinas' theological treatment demands is that we be able to use them to make true if inadequate assertions about God. By this he meant putting these expressions to more than a metaphorical use, although we are free to exploit their metaphorical resources in trying to suggest what so transcendent an application comes to. His own treatment provides an object lesson for accomplishing what he intends to do. But he nowhere presumes that it is enough merely to have expressions like these in hand. Nor can he offer rules for accurately applying them to God.

The difference between a sensitive application and an insensitive one lies in the execution. What accounts for the difference is not logic but self-awareness. What general rules we possess for discoursing about the source of all are adequately displayed in the strategies Aquinas employs. He exploits the analogous structure of these expressions first to deny what must be denied, and then to intimate what our having recourse to them does intimate. The manner in which one applies these strategies in each case reflects one's level of reflective awareness regarding the realities involved.

One who "hungers and thirsts after justice" will be that much more acutely aware of the ambiguities latent in anyone's using 'just'—of God or of anything else. Finally, his own awareness of that growing feeling for ambiguities in the face of his continuing hunger and thirst sets up the conscious tension ingredient in a transcendent use of just to speak of God. He knows what must be denied, has some glimmer of what might be, and withal feels compelled to assert what he knows must be the case, since it embodies his own good and that of the universe.

It is the final awareness—that the God spoken of is my own good and that of the universe—that makes discourse about God the unique case of transcendent predication. God is separated from angels or anything else that transcends our spatiotemporal language frame by being the source of all. In a more evocative way of speaking, the ground of being is not, cannot be, *a* being. Angels remain things even if much of our thing-language fails to exhibit their manner of being things. God is not a thing. He is beyond even the category of substance, but beyond it in a determinate way, as its *principle* (I 3 6 2). Hence no article, definite or indefinite, befits him. Another way to remark this is to note that he is our good and that of the universe. Aquinas uses the first assertion—that God is principle of all—to set up the logic for transcendent predication. Then he works to awaken our awareness as conscious creatures that our source is our good. Once we have grasped how *good* is latent in *being,* we are in a position to make the kind of affirmation which logic prepared us for.

Logic can set the parameters, but only a person can feel the intellectual demand to make the assertions required. In this sense, then, Aquinas offers no theory of analogy. He does not provide a method whereby one can be sure to speak responsibly of God. He offers strategies based on what he knows of the structure inherent in our language and in certain of its expressions. For the rest, he issues invitations to a quality of self-awareness achieved only in the practice of it.

7. Contrasting Aquinas and Scotus

The kindred concerns of Aquinas and Scotus make the diversity of their methods all the more apparent. We have already seen how different are their ways of doing philosophy; here I would like to show the relevance these differences hold for contemporary philosophical concerns. By approaching these two historical positions in this way, we will be able to appreciate the extent to which analogy remains a perennial concern of philosophy. If my unwillingness to define the issue in too narrow and technical a fashion needs any further justification, this chapter will offer it. In fact, the endless intramural discussions within the systematic parameters of Thomism only reinforce the contention that contemporary philosophy is needed to elucidate what is at stake in analogy and the issues surrounding it. Readers familiar with language analysis may judge whether traditional usage and discussion casts any light in their direction.

This chapter will accordingly be even less concerned than the previous ones with the proper milieux of the philosophers involved. Its aim is dialectical and its purpose better secured the more favorably one is disposed to such a philosophical program. Yet it will suffice if something is conveyed of the manner in which different strands unite to form a single rope called philosophy. In the end, this is all we are asked to recognize in admitting to the existence of perennial philososphical concerns.

For both Scotus and Aquinas the facts are the same: certain terms will inevitably recur, used in ways which are quite diverse yet seem, significantly enough, not unrelated. The task is to account for this usage in a way that recognizes its expediency for our language and its contribution to our way of life. Aquinas and Scotus present us with two different styles of account. The consequences of these differences for a theory of knowledge and a metaphysics show how central these terms are in our general scheme of things. The final section on Ockham will help confirm the analysis and strengthen the comparative judgment of Scotus and Aquinas.

RADICALLY DIVERGENT METHODS

The initial question, of course, following hard on the heels of a recognition that the manifold uses of certain terms are *not unrelated* is: but how are they related? Scotus felt compelled to answer this question and answer it he did; Thomas too, it seems, felt compelled to respond to it, but answer it he did not. Or more accurately, he gave several answers to it, feeling no compulsion to relate these accounts. (*Per prius et posterius,* as we have seen, answers to a different set of concerns than *proportionaliter,* and no evidence suggests that one is to be preferred to the other. And *proportionaliter,* as we shall see, is only deceptively the clearer of the two.)

Thomists of course did feel compelled to relate Aquinas' different responses, and this project accounts for the bulk of their commentary. What they assumed was that Aquinas wanted to answer the question. My contention is that he did not, and that suggesting many answers was an ironic way of saying that the question was wrong-headed. And even if Aquinas had not been able to be so clear about rejecting the question, his practice shows how unimportant he regarded it. Confronted with the facts, it seems that he bypassed the initial question to ask another: "What is the import of such a usage?" At least this last question corresponds more closely to Aquinas' sensitive handling of the issues, and reflects his sense for the semantic traps involved.

The divergence between Aquinas and Scotus is not limited, of course, to accounting for analogous usage. Questions about the one and the many arise in a more straightforward way in relating individual to general terms, formenting the so-called problem of universals. Aquinas' answer to this problem has never been clear; indeed he seemed rather inclined to slide around it. Here again, his erstwhile defenders have rallied to provide his answer, only to come up with a spectrum of replies.[1] I would suggest that

1. The closest Aquinas comes to an explicit treatment are the clarifying remarks of Chap. 2, *De Ente et Essentia.* Cf. also the Introduction to the English edition, *On Being and Essence* (Toronto, 1949, pp. 17–19), by A. Maurer.

he gave no answer because he suspected none could be given; yet the fact of generic usage remains. If he could not explain it, neither did he try to explain it away. Aquinas shifted the inquiry to another more profitable question: "What is the import of this irreducible usage?"

Scotus of course answered the question, responding directly to the problem of universals with his *common nature*.[2] To be a solution, this common nature must be known and known as solving the problems raised by general terms. It will require a special kind of knowledge, different from any ordinary way we know, since the unity of the common nature—what we can know about it—is beyond the ken of our experience. A common nature cannot be numerically one but must be *metaphysically* so. Hence metaphysics must know the common nature and know it as the solution to the metaphysical problem of the one and the many as it arises from our use of general terms.

Scotus' way of responding to the issues latent in the problem of universals reflects a manner quite unlike that of Aquinas, and will serve to pinpoint their differences. For Scotus, metaphysics unravels the deepest issues by eliciting a type of scientific understanding capable of responding to the questions posed. Metaphysics offers an explanation, albeit a metaphysical one. For Aquinas, metaphysics cannot claim the ability to meet such thorny difficulties but only the perspicacity to ask another sort of question. *That John is* is not to be explicated as another fact about him—like the fact that he is white or even that he is rational—yet a deeper, even the deepest fact. Aquinas would probably say that anyone attempting such an explanation shows how little he knows of metaphysics. For he is asking it to perform a contradictory feat: to supply an ordinary type of answer for an extraordinary style of question. Aquinas does not expect the metaphysician to be an answer-man to the toughest of questions, but to recognize which kind of explanation is appropriate when and where. This is for him the upshot of the role metaphysics is

2. For the textual references and the background of Scotus' usage, see Joseph Owens, "Common Nature: A Point of Comparison between Thomistic and Scotistic Metaphysics," *Med. Stud.* 19 (1957), pp. 1–14.

supposed to play in ordering the sciences, as well as a specific effect of the affinity between metaphysics and logic.[3] To ascertain that different explanations may be called for—that 'explains' is an analogous term—is to engage in metaphysical reflection; and faced with the problem of universals, the metaphysician asks not how it is that many individuals may be referred to by one term, but, "What is the import of our making reference in this way?"

The shift is significant in the light of contemporary criticism, for the viability of metaphysics hangs in the balance. In the first case (Scotus) we are led to inquire after something which will explain the facts of thought and discourse so as to unravel its pervasive puzzles. Though vastly more sophisticated, this search is of a piece with that of Columbus for the Indies, or, better, of scientists for a new element. And when further acquaintance with the dimensions of the problem makes it clear that what is needed to solve it bears little resemblance to elements of our acquaintance, a special faculty will be required to know it.

In the second case (closer to Aquinas) we are rather invited to look at the linguistic structures characteristic of these expressions which tend to pervade our discourse, and ask what known and knower must be like in order to demand and to employ such constructions. This is not so much like searching for a definite something as it is an invitation to a greater reach of personal awareness and to a keener recognition of the way in which our discourse about quite ordinary things can veil and reveal some basic philosophical issues. It suggests a style of explanation whose aim would be to elucidate the structures of both knower and known, showing how they complement each other. In the event and to the extent that some basic affinity can be manifested between knower and known—which comes to light precisely in

3. For a fresh discussion of Aquinas' view of the role of logic in metaphysical investigations, see James Doig, "Aquinas on Metaphysical Method" (*Phil. Stud.*, Maynooth, 13, 1964, 20–36, esp. 27 ff.). Aquinas' treatment is to be found in his commentary on Aristotle's *Metaphysics:* In 4 M 4, 574.

the inevitability of our recourse to these forms of speech—we would be in possession of a properly metaphysical account.

But what we mean by explanation and account here will never be quite clear. At least Aquinas thinks not, and nothing seals his difference from Scotus so definitively as his diffidence about metaphysics. The texts are numerous, though they have to be ferreted out. The situation is parallel to that of analogous usage and common natures: without rejecting the straightforward type of question (What relates the diverse uses? What accounts for our use of common terms?) Aquinas simply never gives an answer. He adopts the metaphysical terms but then turns around to stress how tenuous are the assertions which employ them, how vague their meaning, how precarious to accept them as explanations.[4] If we had counted on metaphysics to lay bare essential natures, Aquinas denies that we can ever know them properly except through the ongoing inquiry of science. (The science referred to here is the proper extension of the general functional knowledge of natures with which we begin any inquiry.[5]) Moreover, since metaphysics addresses itself to questions arising from the very structure of language and hence includes knower as well as known, it really lies beyond the human ken. The adequate pursuit of metaphysics would demand a completeness and transparency of reflection we simply do not enjoy.

The strategy of such an approach, then, is to harness the

4. The quality of these reservations can be gleaned from the summary statement in Aquinas' commentary on Boethius' *De Trinitate* (q 6 a 3 n 5), a text that summarizes what is affirmed elsewhere: (1) that the proper metaphysical object is not properly knowable (a) for psychological reasons (In 1 PA 30, 254; in 9 M 11, 1905–07; (b) for semantic reasons (In 7 M 17, 1669–71; In 9 M 11, 1901–04, 1910–16; In 11 M 2, 2189); (2) though at the same time it does not completely exceed the intellect, since *that* it is may be known through a negative judgment (deV 10 11 ad 4–5) which admits of manifold degrees of penetration (deT 1, 2). For a full-length treatment of the status of metaphysical knowledge for Aquinas, see my "Classification, Mathematics and Metaphysics" (*Modern Schoolman* 44, 1966, 13–48).

5. Especially in the introductory section of his commentaries on Aristotle's scientific works, listed below in n. 30.

reflective powers we do have, and gradually to sensitize our awareness of the many ways we come to know something, as well as the criteria whereby we affirm or deny what we do. The clarity we achieve, however, will never match that to which we aspire. And we will always find ourselves yearning to close the gap, to postulate if necessary the structures and kinds of knowledge requisite to answer the questions posed. This marks the temptation to irresponsible metaphysics or ontology.

Similar or Same?

To illustrate the contention that metaphysical methods differ most perspicuously in their sensitivity to the form of the question, two examples will suffice: first, the way that suggests itself for analyzing basic notions like *similar to;* and second, a congenial proposal for handling difficulties which arise in our speaking of God. We seem to have a tendency to explicate 'similar to' or 'like' ('*x* is similar to/like *y*') on the model of 'identical with'. Similarity appears as a weak or deficient form of sameness. If we accept a naive congruence notion of identity, it might initially be suggested that:

(A) '*x* is like *y*' means that *x* shares a sufficient number of matching characteristics with *y*.
But this soon is forced into:
(B) *x* has a sufficient number of characteristics *sufficiently* matching those of *y*.
Which before long takes the final form:
(C) *x* has a sufficient number of *relevant* characteristics sufficiently matching those of *y*.[6]

Now to mention relevance is to remind us that similar to must be explicated in context. So any attempt to give a context-invariant definition or to find some one characteristic which *x* and *y* must possess to be similar to each other is doomed to fail. The search for definitions or characteristics assumes that similarity is a weak form of identity, and of course that identity is

6. Cf. W. V. O. Quine, *From a Logical Point of View* (Cambridge, Mass., 1953), pp. 60–64.

patent of unequivocal definition. But the added note of relevance does not simply make 'similar to' weaker than 'same as'—whatever weaker might mean here. Rather it reminds us that similar to expresses a different kind of notion, equipped for a quite different role. (In much the same vein, a mathematician has suggested "approximate isomorphy" to illuminate the role of models in physical theory. But the kind of clarity promised by the formal notion of isomorphism is vitiated by its pragmatic modifier 'approximate'.[7])

Wittgenstein has elucidated this in a more phenomenological vein by calling attention to our ability to recognize likenesses without reference to constituent characteristics.[8] Either way, the template method of gauging similarity on the model of congruence is thoroughly discredited. We are reminded rather of Aristotle's remark that recognition of similarity in dissimilarity requires a peculiar genius and exercises a skill which cannot be taught (*Poetics* 1459a5). The roles of identical with and similar to are diverse as is logic from poetry.

But if a lowest-common-denominator univocal feature theory (reminiscent of Scotus) cannot account for our use of similar to, what can? What more can be said? We may direct our attention to relevance, and note that the aspects relevant to our use of similar to (or like, or synonymous with) are decided by their fruitfulness in furthering the inquiry at stake. Which ones these are may be evident immediately from a working familiarity with the context, or may take time and involve eliminating dead ends, as in original research. But the similarities worth recognizing, the aspects functioning as relevant, are those expedient in bringing the inquiry to a successful issue. So 'relevance' invites appraisal terms like fruitful or successful, and these we have seen function analogously. (In works of art, the similarities—metaphors and other figures of speech—employed are judged by their contribution to the unity of form of the whole work.) What is significant

7. Leo Apostel, "Towards the Formal Study of Models in Non-Formal Sciences," *Synthèse* 12 (1960) 125–61, esp. 142–52.
8. *Philosophical Investigations*, ##285, 378; pp. 197–98, 203. Cf. also J. O. Urmson, "Recognition," *Proc. Aris. Soc.* 56 (1955–56) 259–80.

here is not simply that an explication of 'like' via 'relevant' issues in ambiguous or equivocal terms, but that these terms (such as relevant and like) for the most part *give us little or no trouble in practice.*

This remarkable fact certainly must be calculated in any final appraisal of analogous usage. To the Greeks it was a sure sign that something unique was operating here, something presupposed to the entire procedure. We might call it "intentionality"; they called it *nous.* For Plato, it referred primarily to the capacity to discuss and to grow therefrom, a capacity which could be disciplined into the only adequate watchdog for error: a habit of sincere inquiry through dialogue.[9] For Aristotle, it is the inborn capacity "to grasp the analogy," operative in forming general terms as well.[10]

But whatever we may call it, the capacity to recognize similarities involves at least implicitly the ability to employ terms analogously. Since *identity* does not succeed in clarifying our usage, we might query whether identity is simply assumed to be more available, more easily grasped than similarity. Would it not be as accurate to conceive identity as a severely restricted similarity as to assume that similar to is an extension of identical with? It seems that the ubiquity of metaphor in ordinary speech, together with our propensity to subtle similarities and unobvious comparisons in common conversation, amply testifies to an ability to operate without difficulty with terms whose syntax carries us away from univocal into analogical usage.

The Res/Modus *Distinction*

Another way of pinpointing metaphysical differences is to ask about the ways we speak of God, and see what manner of account is proffered.

I have already sketched the different uses to which Scotus and

9. *Phaedrus* 265–78; *Gorgias* 454–58, 487, 495–500; *Sophist* 230, 246; also R. L. Nettleship, *Lectures on the* Republic *of Plato* (London, 1910), pp. 278–82; and I. M. Crombie, *Examination of Plato's Doctrines,* vol. 2 (New York, 1963), pp. 562–67.

10. Compare *Metaphysics* 1048a35 with *Post. Analytics* 99b30–100b5.

Aquinas put the *res significata/modus significandi* distinction. Perhaps we can see more clearly now why the distinction seemed more at home with Scotus. For the 'what is signified' formulation leads us to look for something common to account for similarity and relate analogous uses. And Scotus invariably scouts in that direction: *being* is what is most common to all things, for it underlies any statement one might make about a thing and so links every statement together. "Taken in its absolute commonness, 'being' is said in some sense of everything," and so can be considered as an indeterminate—indeed the most indeterminate —*what* or essence.[11] This is of course the thesis of the univocity of being, and Gilson's hypothesis that it represents a transposition to being of Avicenna's doctrine of common nature sounds quite plausible.[12] The linkage is supplied by treating 'is' as a predicate, a maneuver coherent with Scotus' hyperrealistic demand that words denote things.[13] Just as the unity of the common nature is one that remains indifferent to every ulterior determination (i.e. "it" is neither singular nor universal *in se*), so the univocity of being attaches to its utter communality.[14] And just as such a peculiar mode of unity demands a special form of knowledge—metaphysics—so what is most common and hence epitomizes this unity beyond every determination (i.e. being) forms the primary and adequate object of the intellect, our properly metaphyscial faculty.[15]

And if this is the case with *being,* the same explanation can certainly be given of other attributes applied to God. What is known in each case is the nature of the attribute in question: it is known in a metaphysical manner as yet indifferent to the way the predicate will be used or the subject of which it will be

11. E. Gilson, *Jean Duns Scot* (Paris, 1952), p. 99; T. Barth, "De fundamento univocationis apud Joannem Duns Scotum," *Antonianum* 14 (1939) 204.

12. Gilson, *Scot,* p. 88; Barth, "De fundamento," pp. 288–97.

13. Barth, ibid., pp. 284–85, 297.

14. Barth, ibid., p. 187; Scotus, Oxon 1, d 3, q 3, n 8; IX, 108; n 12; IX, 111; Wolter, *Duns Scotus: Philosophical Writings* (London, 1962), pp. 4–8.

15. Gilson, *Scot,* pp. 89–91, 517–22; Barth, "De fundamento," pp. 185, 206, 288–97.

predicated.[16] This is the *res significata,* the element common to every use of the term. To apply it to God, in Scotus' view, all we need do is conceive the attribute as infinite and perfect. Without stopping to ask how we might conceive something as infinite, let us inquire about conceiving it as perfect. Scotus would doubtless postulate a notion of perfection at work—like that of infinite—which allows that we may conceive something as perfect.[17] And we may presume that the ability to do so with any particular attribute acts as a necessary condition for employing it of God.

Scotus apparently feels that 'perfect' can function well enough on its own, without any intrinsic link to the subject it modifies, whereas for Aquinas predicates like perfect, and any specifications of them) shift their meaning with the subject of which they are said. Aquinas takes this semantic shift to indicate a structure appropriate for use in speaking of God. That is why he insists that any term which may properly be used of God must be a "perfection." The difference in viewpoint originates in Scotus' conception of common nature as the something that accounts for our use of general terms, and in the metaphysical type of apprehension which alone can grasp these natures.[18]

Once we have postulated *common natures* along with the intellectual ability to ferret them out, there is no need for analogy since there is no longer a problem in analogous usage nor a difficulty in naming God. The usage has thus been explained as variations on a univocal theme, and God can be named by those predicates convertible with 'is' or conceivable as infinite and perfect. Gilson speaks of a "vehemence—or passion—for the abstract" in Scotus.[19] This is certainly in evidence but is motivated, it seems, by a passion for certitude. It is this passion that led Scotus to employ the paradigm of the *Posterior Analytics* everywhere—ignoring both the practice of Aristotle and the warnings of Aquinas.[20]

16. Gilson, *Scot,* p. 537.
17. E. Gilson, *Scot,* pp. 101, 224, 240.
18. Barth, "De fundamento," 293–97; Gilson, *Scot,* pp. 108–14.
19. Gilson, *Scot,* p. 241.
20. Cf. the methodological introductions to the *Physics* (I 1, II 1, II 9), *De Anima* (I 1), *Ethics* (I 3), and Aquinas' observations that only

Role of Posterior Analytics

We have already noted how Scotus relied upon two fundamental models: the complex-out-of-simples picture of concept
formation and the paradigm of a deductive system. Although we
remarked how one complemented the other in his employ, the
fact remains that they represent two opposed traditions: em-
piricist and rationalist. Scotus appears to have borrowed indiscriminately from one tradition or the other, employing whichever
model he needed in an attempt to have all the necessary philosophical tools at his disposal. So *being,* which is the most general
of all notions, is altogether the most simple and hence the first
object distinctly known by the intellect.[21] There is, to be sure, a
distinction of *de jure* and *de facto:* the intellect in itself has
being as its intuitive object but in its present condition arrives at
being only as the ultimate abstraction from sensible things. But
this bow to psychology does not affect the role which being will
play: abstracted or intended, it remains the "first and most common object of our intellect." [22]

By identifying common with simple, Scotus was able to claim
extraordinary certitude for metaphysics, and also anticipate
Descartes's reconstruction of Aristotle's ideal of a deductive
science. But the combination common/simple is unstable, as
might have been expected, and nothing exhibits its instability
better than Scotus' doctrine of "modes."

Let us recall for a moment how Aristotle used his scheme for
scientific knowledge laid down in the *Posterior Analytics.* Since
his aim was to demonstrate attributes of a nature—to show that
certain characteristics belong to a thing—the scheme could
function optimally only in mathematics, where natures can be
defined with a transparency that allows us to identify which
features are necessary.[23] In physical science, the more material
subject matter makes definition elusive and strict demonstration

---

mathematics can fulfill all the requirements of the *Posterior Analytics'*
paradigm for science: In PA 4, 43 bis; In 2 PA 12.
21. Barth, "De fundamento," pp. 206, 200–01; Gilson, *Scot,* pp. 93–94.
22. Barth, ibid., p. 195; Scotus, Oxon 1, d 3 q, n 20; IX 145.
23. Cf. Aquinas, In 1 PA 4, 43 bis.

impossible. We must settle for a knowledge of what happens "for the most part" as the best kind of necessity available to us here. (This is the place where a more hypothetical conception of garnering initial definitions, together with the correlative techniques of verification, might have supplemented Aristotle's sensitivity to diverse subject matters. Such a move could have helped lead us to a more viable conception of natural science. But Aristotle's very conception of natural science as falling off from the deductive ideal realized in geometry would suffice to block the move to an independent method.) Metaphysics, however, can have nothing to do with the scheme at all, because the logic of genus with difference and essence with attribute is endemic to the deductive paradigm, and being is not a genus. The most we can say of being is that it is said in many (but not unrelated) ways. Any attempt to explain its multiple uses by the logic of genus with difference fails because no difference can fall outside of *being* (Meta 998b20).

This is Aristotle's classical argument leading away from univocity to analogy to set up the root problematics of metaphysics. Scotus accepts it but plans to stop short of analogy by introducing "intrinsic modes." Being is not a genus for him, not because it must reflect analogous usage, but because it is too common. Nor do the transcendentals (one, good, true) specify being. Rather they refer to "formal entities determinable from within by their proper modality." [24] But why is being not specified by the transcendentals? Because for Scotus being "virtually includes" its transcendentals without their bringing anything extraneous to it; as *rationality* does to *animal,* being is specified "from within." [25]

Now what is this but to say that modes act like specific differences but are not differences? They act indeed from within because this is what Scotus needs to avoid a dilemma arising from the logic of genus and difference. So introducing modes amounts to inventing a logic for this rarefied domain, but a

24. Gilson, *Scot,* pp. 239–40.
25. Barth, "De fundamento," pp. 373–78, 382 ff.; Scotus, Oxon 1, d 8, q 3, n 26; IX, 626.

logic constructed ad hoc and based on metaphors—spatial: "from within"; biological: "virtually include." Finally, modalities (and their cousins, formalities) are needed "to separate what univocity unites"—in other words, to duplicate analogical usage.[26] Once again we detect the need to explain by postulating something that will account for the facts of usage. If his motivation was to stay within the Aristotelian methodology for science in the *Posterior Analytics,* Scotus' tactics are quite similar to those of contemporary science which postulates entities of the necessary variety via selected models of the phenomena. The crucial difference, however, is that modern science has devised methods of falsification to assist ongoing inquiry; Scotus' modes are postulated as ultimate explainers and said to form the base of any inquiry. No amount of further inquiry can unseat them.

But we can show—as I have tried to do—that the ultimate explainers explain nothing because they presume to function without any ties with our familiar usage and logic. Hence they can be no more than an idiosyncratic way of referring to the original problematic, a new name for an old question. And the reason why Scotus' modes do not explain is that they presume a kind of explanation continuous with that of physical science but in a higher order: they result from looking for *something* that explains. Scotus separates radically from Aquinas at this point, as we have seen. And we cannot help but see something of this hyperrealism and desire for certitude motivating the divergence: *"What* explains the fact that. . . ? If I cannot find *it,* I cannot explain that. . . ; if I cannot *name* it, there is no explanation."

These twin demands for realism and certitude are best satisfied by as close an adherence as possible to the paradigm of science in the *Posterior Analytics.* It is a pattern carefully designed to yield a maximum of certitude, although the requirements were so stringent that Aristotle himself saw how few inquiries could hope to conform to them. But Scotus seems to have imbibed little of Aristotle's feeling for diverse subject matter. Metaphysics must yield knowledge because metaphysics treats of being. And being "must be known before anything

26. Barth, ibid., p. 377; Gilson, *Scot,* p. 629.

else can be known distinctly, since *being* is part of every concept." [27] On this model of concept formation, if the knowledge of being is jeopardized, widespread skepticism will inevitably follow. Hence metaphysics must lead to certain knowledge; it must be a science in the sense epitomized in the *Posterior Analytics*. And 'science' of course must be univocal. So Scotus presents us with a first philosophy which acts as a foundation science, elucidating the elementary component of every other kind of knowledge. The component is the most common notion of all hence the ground of all predication; it is the most simple and hence the most certain notion; and by rights it is the first-known of all: *being*.[28]

Such a recursive application of the *Posterior Analytics* schema to the different kinds of knowledge is tempting, especially for one with such a passion for the abstract as Scotus. It is not Aristotle, of course; but there is no doubt that many a person's view of Aristotle and his program as outlined in *Posterior Analytics* has been deeply influenced by this novel application due to Scotus. Aristotle's own procedure in his ethical, political, biological, and especially his metaphysical inquires argues against such a comprehensive application of the demonstrative schema; and his methodological introductions to these inquiries explicitly modify the schema to fit the subject matter at hand.[29] But Aristotle exhibits a dominantly architectonic strain as well, and it is this strain that came to pervade the writings of Scotus.

A similar ambiguity prevails when it comes to interpreting the schema Aristotle offers to clarify analogous usage: *a:b::c:d*. To most of us and to many scholastic commentators, the very structural simplicity of the schema, together with its striking similarity to mathematical ratio, suggests a paradigm of formal logic. Here lies a criterion for a successful analogy, and like the

27. Barth ibid., p. 201.

28. Barth, ibid., pp. 200–06; Gilson, *Scot*, pp. 93–94; Scotus, Oxon 1, d 3, q 2, n 6; IX, 18; q 3, n 9; IX, 338; n 12; IX, 340.

29. Aquinas' commentaries are lucid on this point, especially *In 1 Physica 1, In de Sensu et Sensato 1, In Proemio Metaphysica, In Proemio Meteorologica*.

ordered couples of mathematics, a method for arriving at new knowledge: knowing three terms, we can derive the fourth.

On closer inspection, however, this view proves quite false to Aristotle's intentions. He used the schema to call attention to the kind of "perception of similarity in dissimilarity" characteristic of metaphors and woven into the fabric of ordinary speech. So another interpretation can be proposed. Instead of regarding a mathematical ratio as a paradigmatic instance of the schema, we can just as easily think of it as a degenerate form of proportionality. For in a mathematical ratio the relationship is nothing more than equality; therefore the sense of the four-termed relation may be adequately expressed by either one of the ordered couples or by its appropriate equivalent. Since $2:4 = 3:6$, the relationship expressed is simply $1:2$.

Such an interpretation allows us to recall the kinship of analogy with metaphor, as well as Plato's insistence that there is no technique nor algorithm available to find the "real joints," to assure that we make an appropriate division and hit upon the relevant differences in seeking to account for a general usage (Plt 263a, 286d). So once again, as Wittgenstein saw so well, the recognition of similarities and differences preliminary to definition is not unrelated to the attention we give to analogous discourse, and both are closely akin to the common yet baffling phenomenon of metaphor.

OCKHAM'S CONTRIBUTION

Before we bring these observations to a focus, however, a brief look at Ockham may help to corroborate the comparative judgment of Aquinas and Scotus.[30] Contrary to what we might

30. The sources for my discussion of William of Ockham include his *Commentary on the Sentences* (or *Reportatio*) and the *Summa totius logicae*. These are abbreviated as Rep and Sum log respectively, and the page references to P. Boehner's translation, *Ockham: Philosophical Writings* (London, 1957), follows, preceded by a B. Besides the works referred to in the notes below, Philotheus Boehner's *Collected Articles on Ockham* (St. Bonaventure, N.Y., 1958) were of particular assistance, and Jean Paulus, *Henri de Gand: Essai sur les tendances de sa métaphysique* (Paris, 1938, esp. pp. 321–25, 376–81, 387–94), provided an illuminating

have expected, little new is forthcoming from William of Ockham. His touted nominalist tendencies reflect a certain ontological preference, but the epistemology and semantics are basically Scotist. We shall note some interesting anomalies, however, which this union of nominalism with extreme realism begets.

"Being" is the most general answer to the question, "What is *x?*"; namely, *something* (Sum log I 38, B 90). So 'a being' functions like 'an animal', betraying utmost generality (ibid., B 91). On this position, of course, the *res significata/modus significandi* distinction may be employed without question, and we shall see that Ockham does not hesitate to do so. Thus far, there is no appreciable difference from Scotus. It might be thought, however, that Ockham's nominalistic preference for similarity over sameness as the criterion for general usage would favor our program. For this preference suggests that the formation of general concepts is not so automatic an affair as some accounts have suggested, and a more flexible treatment of concept formation could open the way to a more viable treatment of analogous usage. But Ockham's recourse to *similarity,* it turns out, is inspired less by semantics than by his nominalist ontology. *Sameness* is avoided to the extent that it connotes a common nature or feature, yet all the puzzles about general terms return under the rubric of similarity.

Ockham offers three degrees of univocity or generality, all explicated in terms of similarity. Most stringently,

> 'univocal' denotes a concept common to things which are perfectly alike in all essentials without any dissimilarity [*habentibus perfectam similitudinem in omnibus essentialibus sine omni similitudine*]. If 'univocal' is understood in this sense, then only the concept of the lowest species is univocal. since in individuals of the same species there is nothing to be found which differs in kind in the one and the other.

---

insight into the period. Cf. also J. Paulus, "Sur les Origines du nominalisme," *Rev. de Phil.* 37 (1937) 313–30.

More liberally,

> 'univocal' denotes a concept common to things which are not absolutely similar and not absolutely dissimilar, but in certain respects similar and in certain others dissimilar [*in aliquibus similia et in aliquibus dissimilia*], either intrinsically or extrinsically. In this manner, man and donkey agree in the concept *animal* as a univocal concept; though their specific forms are difference, yet the matter in both is of the same kind. Thus they agree in something essential and in something else they differ. In this manner also man and angel agree in the concept of *substance* as a univocal concept . . . , because they have accidents of the same kind, viz. intellection and volition. . . . It is of 'univocal' in this sense that the Philosopher says in the seventh book of the Physics: "Many equivocations are implicit in a genus." For if we understand 'equivocation' in contradistinction to perfect similitude or to univocation as between things which are perfectly similar, then neither the concept of the subordinate nor that of the highest genus is univocal; but rather there is equivocation in the genus [Rep III 8, B 106–07].[31]

This prepares us for the most liberal sense in which,

> 'univocal' denotes a concept common to many things which have no likeness [*non habentibus aliquam similitudinem*], either substantial or accidental. In this manner, every concept which applies to God and to creatures is univocal to them; for in God and in creatures there is nothing at all, intrinsic or extrinsic, which is of the same kind [ibid., B 107].

It should be clear from the use of likeness (*similitudo*) here that similarity is functioning no differently from sameness. The

31. Cf. Armand Maurer, "St. Thomas and the Analogy of Genus" (*New Scholasticism* 29, 1955) where natural genus would not seem to be so univocal for Aquinas either, but rather "conceived through a judgment of proportionality" (p. 144).

central problem for a thoroughgoing nominalist—which features are essential?—receives no recognition in Ockham's "perfectly alike in all essentials." And perfectly alike, of course, is equivalent to the use of same in the phrase 'same features', since no one has ever intended that the features be numerically the same. So *similarity* serves no distinct semantic purpose. Indeed Ockham's use of it merits Austin's full astonishment. For *"it is not in the least true* that all the things which I 'call by the same name' *are* in general 'similar', in any ordinary sense of that much abused word. . . . All that 'similarity' theorists manage is to say that all things called by some one name are similar to some one pattern, or are all more similar to each other than any of them is to anything else; which is *obviously* untrue. . . . It is a most strange thing that 'nominalists' should rest content with this answer." [32]

All this corroborates the general feeling that Ockham's nominalistic ontology is simply grafted onto Scotus' epistemology. Where general terms served to denote a common nature for Scotus, Ockham would have them designate individuals. It is interesting that the relation of signification is reduced in either case to denotation or reference. The ontological generality of the common nature or feature lent a *sense* to Scotus' referring relation, but with Ockham any distinction between sense and reference collapses. This fact illustrates, however, how precarious a status already obtained for any distinction between *sense* and *reference*. Scotus had already detached the sense of a term from its use, for when terms simply denote, their use is irrelevant. The sense of a term was assured only by the ontological status of the referent, the *common nature*. Hence any distinction simply vanished when Ockham substituted an individual referent. It was not necessary to change the description of concept formation or alter any semantic relations. All that Ockham need do was to postulate an object of different ontological type.

The difficulties which arise when one fails to acknowledge any distinction between sense and reference are now notorious.[33]

32. J. L. Austin, *Philosophical Papers* (Oxford, 1961), pp. 37, 42, 38.
33. Ockham's criterion for truth is a case in point: "For the truth of a singular proposition it is not required that the subject and the predicate

Yet they cannot detain us here. I merely wish to signal how easy the transition can be from Scotus to Ockham. It is more relevant for our present inquiry to note that Ockham's tripartite division of univocal terms speaks always of concepts. We might cite the medieval predilection for concepts and propose that this expression is being used in a sense vague enough to be interchangeable with 'term'. Yet Ockham does distinguish between word and concept in speaking of one form of analogous usage: " 'Healthy' primarily signifies the health of an animal, and it also signifies a diet and urine, but in such a way that it always connotes the health of an animal. . . . Therefore, formally speaking, 'health' [as applied to 'animal', 'food', and 'urine'] is only one and the

---

be really the same, nor that the predicate be really in the subject, or really inhere in the subject, nor that it be really united with the subject outside the mind. It is sufficient and necessary that subject and predicate should stand for [*supponant pro*] the same thing" (Sum log II 2, B 76). As Boehner illustrates, "the proposition 'Socrates is white' is true if there really is one individual signified by the term 'Socrates' and also by the term 'white' " (B xxxvi). According to this criterion, 'the evening star was shining brilliantly this morning before dawn' would be true if faithfully reported. Now Boehner insists that Ockham "is merely stating the same things as Aristotle but with greater precision" (ibid.), yet acknowledges elsewhere that the theory of signification reflected in this criterion is an interpretation quite diverse from that of Aquinas. Although Boehner's discussion suffers from ambiguity because of a failure to distinguish sense from reference, the meaning seems to be this: Ockham follows Scotus in rejecting what Boehner calls the "indirect signification of words" and interprets as "meaning that the word signifies the concept and through the concept the thing." Scotus and Ockham, on the other hand, "decide in favor of direct signification of the thing by the word with which a certain meaning is connected" (p. 194). So far the conflict could well be verbal. In clarification he says, "According to Ockham the word, for instance 'homo', and the corresponding concept of man, immediately signify everything which is a man or has been a man or will be a man or is possibly a man. Hence both signs, the natural, which is the concept, and the artificial, which is the noun, are parallel in their signification" (p. 219). This would seem to corroborate my reading and confirm my case against both Scotus and Ockham: signification is primarily designation. When they say 'words signify' they tend to mean exclusively 'words refer'. Sooner or later one must ask: If the function of term and concept is parallel, what does one do that the other does not?

same word; [as expressing the health of an animal,] it is one and the same concept" (Rep III 8, B 109).

Cajetan will call this type "analogy of attribution" and relegate it to an inferior position because the extended usage denotes something extrinsic to the subject. This is apparently what Ockham wishes to convey by insisting that these uses of health, while clearly related, can claim nothing more than verbal unity. The point seems to be that what is being referred to is always the health of an animal; this is the only bona fide present. We might indicate this in another way by remarking that while we may speak of a healthy diet or the food's being healthy, only of an animal may we inquire into its health. This grammatical difference seems to indicate relatedness yet diversity in function. It marks a separate class for Aristotle of paronyms or "things said to be named 'derivatively', which derive their name from some other name, but differ from it in termination. Thus the grammarian derives his name from the word 'grammar', and the courageous man from the word 'courage' " (Cat 1a12). The structural difference is apparently enough for Aristotle to classify this usage differently from the equivocal where the same name answers to different definitions. It is noteworthy that Ockham, preoccupied with concepts, overlooks the linguistic facts remarked by Aristotle and, relying on the adjectival use alone, acknowledges a verbal sameness but denies conceptual unity.

His intent becomes clearer when Ockham describes another sense of analogy, presumably the more significant of the two meanings he will countenance. In this sense,

> it is taken for a univocal concept of the third kind, which is neither purely equivocal nor purely univocal. For it is one concept and not many; but neither is it purely univocal by having the most perfect univocation, viz, the first type, nor by having the second type. For that reason, it is said that it is midway between pure univocation and equivocation [Rep III 8, B 108].

Analogy, then, coincides with his third degree of univocity: "a concept common to many things which have no likeness, either substantial or accidental." By remarking that it is "said [to be] midway between pure univocation and equivocation," Ockham clearly intends this to be the type of analogy traditionally associated with metaphysical and theological discourse. But it is also clear, by his insistence that "it is one concept and not many," that the adversary is Henry of Ghent and his "vague concept" uniting into one what is really two. Once again, Ockham shares both problematic and polemic with Scotus. Whatever a concept may be, there is enough association with Aristotle's requirement of a definition (or formula) for Ockham to demand that it be determinately one.[34] Ockham does not pretend to give an account of analogous usage, any more than Scotus did. He knows how to work only with concepts, and a concept cannot but be univocal.[35]

But does not Ockham leave us with a solution every bit as implausible as an "analogous concept?" How can we countenance a concept that answers to no likeness whatsoever? Only by associating it with 'being', which designates no distinguishing feature yet can be said of all things, Creator as well as creature. Yet precisely because being in so common one might ask what we find out about a thing by saying it is being. To say that being may be predicated of all things since any individual can be conceived as a being begs the entire question by assuming this to be a legitimate procedure. We have already indentified this maneuver in Scotus, and Ockham sees no need of modifying it.

34. For Ockham, "a conceptual term is a mental content or impression which naturally possesses signification or consignification, and which is suited to be part of a mental proposition and to stand for [*supponere*] that which it signifies" (Sum log I 1, B 47). Since his universe is made up of determinate individuals and concepts stand for these, they must needs be determinate. His nominalistic ontology reinforces the residual Aristotelian demands for "one formula."

35. It is telling that M. C. Menges' contemporary study of univocity in Ockham speaks freely of "predicating concepts" and sympathetically develops Ockham's defense of univocity against those who propose analogous concepts (*The Concept of the Univocity of Being Regarding the Predication of God and Creatures According to William Ockham*, St. Bonaventure, N.Y., 1958, pp. 125–26, 142–43).

Yet his nominalist ontology succeeds in hobbling him here, apparently unwittingly, for being, like man and substance, can signify only the individual.

If we found it reprehensible for Scotus to say of anything that it was a being, and intend thereby to state something about it, it turns out to be impossible for Ockham. For 'x is a being' means the same as 'x is a thing', 'x is an individual', etc., and these forms of expression cannot be countenanced except as tautologies (B xlii). If being simply serves as a token referring to any individual, then it is equivalent to the variable x; 'x is a being' says that x is x. So even if we could recognize a viable process of "abstracting the concept of a being (*ens*) which does not refer more to this accident than to substance, nor more to creature than to God" (B 111), Ockham could not use the notion. It could not signify except tautologically, which would make the notion meaningless on his own account.[36]

Satisfied that Ockham fails to present a viable alternative to analogous usage, we might attempt a more sympathetic reading in terms of intent. Should that be done, we would discover what we have already come across in reading both Aquinas and Scotus: the operating notion is not *being* but *perfection;* or if you will, being as a perfection. We can say that God is wise but not that he is a stone, yet one is as dependent upon him as the other. The difference, while couched in terms of "abstracting a common concept," actually turns on the demands made by perfection. Ockham, parroting Scotus, speaks of

> removing imperfection from the wisdom of a creature and attributing to it what belongs to perfection. This must mean abstracting from created wisdom a concept of wisdom which does not mention either a created or an uncreated thing, since mention of a created thing brings in imperfection. For that reason, to abstract from the imperfection in

36. Signification is radically incomplete for Ockham without reference, since the "primary object of our knowledge is not a common nature but an individual thing." Hence "universal terms . . . signify individual things," which leaves statements without reference devoid of meaning as well (Armand Mauer, *Medieval Philosophy,* New York, 1962, p. 279).

the wisdom of a creature is nothing else than to abstract from an imperfect creature a concept of wisdom which does not refer more to creatures than to what is not a creature, and then the result is attributable to God by way of predication [Rep III q. 8, B 112].

Now for some reason this will work for 'wise' and not for 'stone':

notwithstanding the fact that the distinction between the wisdom of a creature and the wisdom of God is as great as the distinction between God and a stone, and though in neither case do we have things of the same kind, nevertheless from created wisdom we can get by abstraction a concept common (to God and creature), but not from a stone [ibid].

But why does wisdom yield a "concept common to God and creature" while stone does not? Presumably because of the epistemological peculiarities of notions like wisdom. Yet to speak of the presence or absence of a common concept which refers no more to the created than to the uncreated and prescinds from both chokes further inquiry by postulating a highly questionable procedure.[37] What is more, our attention is diverted from the indications we do possess that something special is associated with terms like wisdom; viz., the idiosyncrasies they might exhibit in use. I have already suggested one: the fact that perfection expressions like wise seem to defy restrictions and find one context as hospitable as another, while stone demands a quite determinate ecological niche. We shall examine this peculiarity and some of its implications in the succeeding chapters.

37. As Menges acknowledges, "Again and again, we have seen that the point of departure occurs at the question: Is it possible to conceive God and creature without implicitly considering their intrinsic modes? Ockham answers in the affirmative. If his answer is denied, then his concept is inadequate and false" (pp. 162–64). This in another way of casting our discussion of the *res/modus* distinction in Scotus, and the issues remain the same. Ockham exhibits no originality here.

8. Review of Philosophical Usage

The threads of my historical investigations have already suggested the direction an adequate account of analogous uses of language must take: it must incorporate the role reserved to expressions generally characterized as perfections. This role is executed by any evaluative term and by the more exalted transcendental predicates. Before proposing a systematic account of the role called analogy, it will prove useful to review the positions taken by Plato, Aristotle, Aquinas, and Scotus, and then to examine some contemporary ways of accounting to help position my own.

Plato: Search for a Method

Plato, we recall, was struck by the formidable peculiarities accompanying any inquiry into the principle of all, the *good*. He insisted that this inquiry be structured and pursued unlike any other. If it surpasses logic, it must be all the better versed in logical technique; if it is to carry man beyond language, it must so master language as to make it come alive, sing, and dramatize this predicament. In pursuing the principle of all, man's very reason for being is called into question so radically that he cannot afford to stand apart from it. In the questioning which inquires into the sources of questions, the questioner himself is inescapably involved. It is probably easier for us to appreciate the cogency of this self-referential program than it was for Plato and his Academy. Certainly the program required unparalleled skill with logic as well as an appreciation of the distinction between proposition and statement, and a capacity to put that distinction to work. Plato gradually seemed to lose his nerve in carrying out this program, however, and came to rely more on a simple juxtaposition of a rigorous logical procedure with the mystical model of knowing as direct vision.

Aristotle: Language and Its Limits

Aristotle managed to avoid the problems associated with self-reference and to discredit the analogy of knowing with seeing by directing his attention to language. Language and its rules of use became the key to right knowing. By focusing on language, Aristotle hoped to incorporate Plato's sophisticated appreciation of the self-reflexive character of ground-level inquiries, while avoiding some of the stylistic complications. For as man's most intimate creation and expression, language can yield a privileged access to human aspiration; yet its intersubjective character provides language with the desired objectivity and makes it available for analysis. This care for language and attention to its idiosyncrasies helped Aristotle pose the issues handed on to him in an illuminating way. He was able, as we have seen, to shift the pressing question about *being* into a discussion of the myriad uses of to be. And by showing that to be does not function like an ordinary predicate, he was in a position to suggest that 'being' deserves a pattern of elucidation all its own.

But the very aspect of language which clarifies—its quasi-objectivity—can mislead in turn, as the fate of Aristotle and his successors illustrates so well. The given, matter-of-fact character of statements as they are set down invites treating every use of language as material to be organized and accounted for in a systematic way. This temptation is reinforced by the fact that language does prove amenable to scientific inquiry. And for a master of logic, especially the one who first developed a systematic way of exhibiting the key logical relations, the temptation to domesticate every linguistic usage into a predicatable pattern will certainly be overpowering.

We have already seen with Plato how the expressions that would give rise in Aristotle to the rubric of "analogy" were the very ones which defined a logical account. The test is simple: all we need to do is observe that whenever we try to offer an expression in lieu of an analogous term, that expression itself will invariably contain other terms which are apt to function in diverse contexts. And these terms will in turn demand a different account of each context. All such terms, then, will be marked by a predilection to use them matched only by the facility with which we do employ them. In short, any analysis of an analogous term yields analogous terms in turn. So no logical account will succeed in tethering them down more accurately since every logic requires a set universe of discourse, an invariant context. The demand that analogous usage be subsumed under logic is no doubt indigenous to a linguistic approach. We have seen that demand assert itself in Aristotle and recur with the advent of a mathematical ordering procedure in logic. And we have noted how misleading that tendency can be. The other way in which Aristotle proved misleading, however, stems rather from his followers' failure to advert explicity to the linguistic character of his analysis. Without constant vigilance, coupled with the logical and semantic techniques necessary to sustain it, we seem to lapse quite naturally into the material mode of speech. Analogous uses of being too easily become the *analogy of being*.

This is a delicate point of difference. There is no doubt that the peculiar uses of being (either in '*x* is a being' or in '*x* is', where *x* may refer to anything at all) manifest something about things. These uses especially show something about our attempts to characterize the range of *x*, namely that it extends over everything that is. So facts about usage manifest more than usage. But this observation does not license us to talk about being and guarantee we are saying anything. Indeed, closer scrutiny of the facts of language ought to discourage any direct reference to being, for the same appreciation of language corroborates that *being* is not a characteristic nor marked off by any set of characteristics. Hence being presents no normal subject of discourse. In short, an examination of analogous usage tells us that we dare not assume that these peculiar expressions refer in a straightforward manner. Thus we cannot go on as though we were speaking of some ordinary referent. Our best and only clue to the unity indicated by the use of one term lies rather in what the usage itself suggests. The shape of the linguistic structure manifests whatever we can know of its subject matter.

Aquinas: Use Versus Formulation

This crucial distinction between what we can *say* and what is *shown* in discourse would seem to be the fruit of careful attention to the difference between formal and material modes of speech. Yet the tendency was rather to blur them, moving easily from one to the other, from analogous usage to analogy, from 'being' to being. The medievals were conscious of the distinction between use and mention, however, and were normally quite astute in employing it.[1] It is true that they did not break through to a systematic discrimination between what language could say and what it could only show. Not even the most acute of them, Thomas Aquinas, was able to do that. Yet it must be said that his formulation of the key issues leaned rather in this direction than toward the more unabashedly ontological penchant of his commentators and more contemporary followers.

Aquinas' treatment of issues basic to metaphysics reveals, as we have seen, a keen semantic sophistication. He does not shrink from the consequences of the impredicative character of '. . . is,' '. . . is good', and the rest. He does not demand an occult account where the logic of ordinary explanation fails. This is particularly evident in his treatment of the "names of God," where the tendency of the reasonable believer to find *a* similarity is so strong. Aquinas was not afraid to espouse a semantics leading apparently to agnosticism; he would not be coerced into postulating an underlying property, a deep-seated univocal core, when none was forthcoming on his analysis.[2] The tie to reason was not to be found in a gratuitous extension of the ordinary logic of

1. Note how Aquinas discusses the problem of showing that God exists, in opposition to Anselm (*Sum. Theol.* I 2 1). He notes that it is the proposition 'God exists' which must be shown to be true, and that this cannot be accomplished simply by invoking the understanding that everyone possesses the name God (ad 2), though this same meaning of the name God will be used as the middle term in the constructed proofs (2 ad 2). Cf. also E. Moody, *Truth and Consequences in Medieval Logic* (Amsterdam, 1953), pp. 19–20.

2. Cf. E. Gilson, *Christian Philosophy of Saint Thomas* (New York, 1956), pp. 107–10, esp. n. 51 and the reference there to Sertillanges.

attributes but in the fulfillment-dimension of human understanding. As I have tried to show, it was not the *res significata/ modus significandi* distinction that ended up doing Aquinas' work for him, but rather the stipulation that the predicates applicable to God must represent perfections.

Aquinas left no coherent statement about analogous usage. The variety of his explicit remarks, however, taken together with his lack of concern to draw them into a systematic unity, should intimate that he thought a unified theory of analogous usage impossible or useless, or both. Arguments from silence are notoriously weak, but in this case Thomas' own intensely systematic bent lends some added support. One cannot help but feel that he would have wrapped up the issue if he thought that could be, or needed to be, done. The weightiest challenge to this hermeneutical point comes not from the writings of Aquinas but from the subsequent and voluminous efforts of disciples to supply the order he failed to elicit. The confusion ensuing upon this enterprise can only reinforce a line of reasoning which begins from the opposite assumption. There is no need to provide a missing theory; Aquinas' omission is not a sign of incompleteness but a premonition of where the truth lies.

The other difficulty bequeathed us by Aquinas *is* a failing, however, and explains why two accounts so diverse as this one and Professor Anderson's could both claim to be in the spirit of Aquinas, and each appeal to his writings for support. The reason lies in Aquinas' failure to program the distinction between formal and material modes of speech throughout his work, however conscious he showed himself to be of its usefulness.[3] As a failing, this one is quite comprehensible: to turn it into an accusation would court anachronism. Furthermore, there are important philosophical points to be secured by insisting on an easy flow between speech and things. No one would be tempted to call Aquinas' pursuits merely linguistic or dream of defending his metaphysics because it quietly confined itself to language. Yet in sealing off this flank, another was left open and inviting:

3. For example, *Sum Theol.* I 13 1 ad 2, where abstract and concrete roles are a deciding factor in how terms are to be used of God.

naive realism. So Aquinas' followers have nearly all found it necessary to defend a "realistic metaphysics," meaning thereby the legitimacy of talk about *being*. It is left ambiguous whether, in talking about being, we *say* important things about it or *show* them. This ambiguity would seem to go hand-in-glove with a certain disregard for the language we must use, and a consequent failure to attend to the different levels at which we are inevitably discoursing.

Scotus: Ontology over Language

As a result of neglecting the finer points of philosophical usage, many interpreters were able to hand on to us an Aquinas who was not that much different from Scotus. In fact, it became easy to collapse their differences under the rubric of scholasticism. Yet nothing, as I have tried to show, could be further from the truth—both historical and philosophical. Scotus was as naive a realist as any historian of philosophy could hope for: 'being denotes a property at once underlying and transcendent, since it can be predicated both of God and of creatures." For him there is no fear of agnosticism in naming God. The common characteristic is securely known as the thing signified (*res significata*) in (or under) the various modes of signifying.

Although skilled in logic, Scotus cared little about distinguishing the formal mode of speech from the material mode, for language was not really important except as it subserved a realist ontology. Since words inevitably named things, none of the vagaries of discourse was worth serious attention. Any linguistic variation could be explained as one of the many ways of apprehending an underlying similarity. Common-sense semantics has always tended to view similarity of meaning as possession of a common property. Here it draws Scotus away from a more empirical attention to discourse, and what it might manifest of reality, to a prearranged metaphysical explanation of its operation. Such an a priori style of accounting must finally be anchored in something like an intuition, and one is well advised to strengthen this tie by an appeal to introspection. Scotus, we have seen, lives up to these expectations. The most positive

recommendation one can glean from examining his approach
signals the need for a semantics born of an attention to language
so careful that no prior demands can flout the evidence of usage.

METAPHYSICAL ACCOUNTS

The revival of scholarly and systematic reflection on medieval
philosophy over the past century has produced some pointed
work in the area of analogy. Nearly universally, this work
offers a rigorous account of analogy, though with a rigor
that does not pretend to be linguistic so much as it purports to
be metaphysical. It is the mark of this school to propose analogy
as the only adequate key to metaphysics, while the accounting
it offers for analogy is frankly metaphysical.

Now, to speak of a "school" borders on the tendentious. Yet I
am pressed to this expression by the language of those who
freely refer to a doctrine of analogy. So these at least conceive
of themselves as forming a school. The recent rash of studies on
Aquinas makes it increasingly difficult to identify the school as
Thomist however. And the fact that others who sympathetically
identify with Aquinas offer different if not conflicting accounts
of analogy further complicates the issue. Yet it is not difficult to
locate contemporary spokesmen. James F. Anderson is doubtless the clearest and certainly among the ablest of these. A
review of the requirements he lays down for properly analogous
discourse should give an adequate picture of the doctrine defining the school.[4] Voice to a dissenting view by Yves Simon
can then be allowed.

Anderson: Proportional Similarity

Anderson feels it necessary to defend two propositions:

> (A) that analogy is not a logical procedure but a meta-
> physical principle—or indeed *the* metaphysical principle
> (pp. 320, 288 n.);
> (B) that "analogy of proportionality" is the only form that

4. Notably *Bond of Being* (St. Louis, 1949).

can preserve that principle intact against the perennial and connatural temptation to univocity (pp. 232–40, 251–54).

Although Anderson gives these theses equal weight, it seems clear that (B) is ancillary to (A). At any rate, we may consider (A) first. As a metaphysical principle, analogy refers not to any common concept but to a "proportional sharing in the act of existing" (p. 279). But to speak of the act of existing, Anderson admits, is to make implicit reference to creation—the divine act bestowing existence upon all that is (pp. 309–10). We have seen why this is so: to refer to existence as an act bespeaks its intelligibility. And only a Creator can assure that what presents itself to us as mere fact enjoys a meaning, an intelligible structure. Thus the status of analogy as a metaphysical principle ultimately rests on a decision, a reasonable and critical decision, but a decision nonetheless: to regard the universe as intelligible.

The defense of (B), the form analogous statements must assume, purports to be formal. It rests on a distinction between the nature of a notion and the use to which it is put and depends on there being certain notions by their very nature analogous, independent of usage (pp. 226, 233, 248–51). This assertion is required for Anderson to distinguish analogy proper from metaphor, which rather "employs a concept . . . univocal in itself . . . in an analogical manner" (p. 181).

But how do we discern those notions which are naturally analogous? Presumably we may test them on the proportionality paradigm (a:b::c:d) to see if each usage may be said properly of its subject. Hence both the judge and his decision may be just, while strictly speaking only a corporation and not a professor (qua teacher) can be bankrupt. But so far Anderson has proposed no argument. All we have is an indication that there is a difference among kinds of terms, together with a decision in favor of just and against those like bankrupt. Reasons are given to support the decision, of course, notably that just can be said properly both of a man and of an act, while bankrupt demands an active comparison of the state of a teacher's preparedness with that of a corporation's negotiable assets. But Anderson's reason's do not compel. It may be that we simply become more accustomed to using just of a man, for the term does seem to apply more directly to his acts. Is not a just man someone who acts justly? What Anderson regards as properly analogous may well be a degenerate metaphorical usage, or one so vague and abstract that the internal reference to a paradigm case has been obscured.

Anderson's intent is clear: to account for likeness without demanding that a common property be present (pp. 278–83). But "proportional likeness" of itself says nothing and offers no more clarity than the alternative "focal meaning" or "reference to a paradigm case" account, which Anderson opposes (pp. 248–51). Indeed proportion is used in so extended (analogous or metaphorical?) a way here that Anderson must bolster it up by reference to the basis of proportional likeness in the metaphysical division of being by potency and act. This recourse sets the stage for the essence/act-of-existing distinction.[5] But to rely on this distinction is to admit that (B) simply restates (A), and that proportionality can cast no independent light on analogy as a metaphysical principle. So the entire account must remain irremediably obscure. For Anderson to fail to give an account on a formal level means that we are offered a metaphysical justification of the conceptual device which was designed to show us how we can use certain expressions to make a metaphysical point.

Simon: Ordered Usage

Most Thomist writing adopts Anderson's restrictions and is subject to the same criticism.[6] The common inspiration is of

5. Anderson, "Mathematical and Metaphysical Analogy in St. Thomas," *Thomist* 3 (1941) 564–79, esp. 571.

6. Although it is difficult to testify for the range of Thomist writing on this subject, a random sampling which would include J. Maritain and G. B. Phelan corroborates my judgment. Both seem to rely uniquely on proportionality as validating analogous usage (cf. Maritain, *Degrees of Knowledge*, New York, 1959, 418–21; Phelan, *St. Thomas and Analogy,*

course Cajetan. Yet there has been a significant if subdued alternative proposal dating from Sylvester of Ferrara, a younger contemporary of Cajetan, and represented in our day by Yves Simon and Ralph McInerny.[7] No less metaphysical in intent, these men have resisted the subtle attraction of proportionality as a kind of normal form. In metaphysical usage, Simon insists, "proportional resemblance . . . is irreducible; in other words, no analysis, abstraction or manipulation ever can reduce it to a resemblance that is not proportional." Even though our use of terms like wise or good can be made to "look very much like the expression $\frac{2}{4} = \frac{3}{6}$, the difference is that whereas the unity of the latter proportion is reducible to the concept of half, it is forever impossible to do away with proportionality in the former case" (p. 33).

But Simon does not rest content with insisting that the unity be proportional and hence intrinsic to the notion in question. For him the irreducible "form of proportionality . . . stubbornly expresses difference together with resemblance, negation together with assertion, . . . by associating, in diverse degrees, the negation of the common ground with its assertion" (p. 33). Words Hegelian in overtone, but not so in effect, for assertion (= affirmation) and negation in Thomist writing makes specific reference to judgment rather than to apprehension. And while this distinction is a simple enough one to recognize, Hegel

---

Milwaukee, 1941). The same can be said for G. Klubertanz (*Saint Thomas Aquinas on Analogy,* Chicago, 1960, pp. 111–56), who also provides a working bibliography for Thomistic writings on analogy (pp. 303–13). The oft-cited study of M. Penido, *Le Rôle de l'analogie en théologie dogmatique* (Paris, 1931), while sensitive to theological concerns, does not grapple directly with the difficulties we have raised.

7. It is significant that Simon's "Order in Analogical Sets" (*New Scholasticism* 34, 1960, 1–42) is among the last of his written works and may be taken as representing a lifetime of critical reflection on this subject. McInerny's critical study of Aquinas and the tradition of his commentators established the groundwork for a study such as this one by noting the linguistic character of Aquinas' discussion of analogy. Simon explicitly acknowledges his mentor, F. A. Blanche, especially "Une Théorie de l'analogie" (*Rev. de phil.* n.s. 3, 1932, 37–78).

seems to have been unable to acknowledge it.[8] We are reminded of Gilson's remark that the Thomistic "doctrine of analogy is above all one of a judgment of analogous uses." [9] Yet while this observation has proven to be a fruitful guide, it is hardly illuminating in isolation. Simon's specific way of articulating analogous uses will help give us a clearer grasp of the issues at stake.

Analogous terms are distinguished according to Simon, by the order their use displays, even though we can use them without reflecting on any order. When we do use an analogous expression without adverting to any order or priority in meaning, the situation resembles our use of a dead metaphor: "many people who know that 'crocodile tears' stand for demonstrations of feigned sadness do not know why such demonstrations are called crocodile tears" (p. 37). But dead metaphors are intelligible only by reference to live ones, and a full-blooded metaphorical role seems to demand active comparison: " 'cheerful' as predicated of an apartment is meaningless except in reference to a cheerful mood" (p. 5). Moreover for Simon this element of conscious comparison would seem to be the difference between metaphorical and analogous usage, if one can sustain any difference at all. Simon acknowledges that there is a difference, admitting:

> It would be absurd to say that 'good' as predicated of a physical condition is intelligible only by reference to 'good' as predicated of a human action, or vice versa. This is expressed, in common teaching, by saying that no first analogate needs to be included in the definition of secondary analogates [p. 5].
>
> To the question 'Why is a healthy condition counted among the things that are good?' the answer is that a healthy condition *is* good, that is, possessed of goodness intrinsically and in its own way, whereas expressions of feigned sadness

8. Frege remarks it quite clearly: "A judgment is not merely the apprehension of a thought or proposition but the acknowledgement of its truth" ("On Sense and Nominatim," n. 7, in H. Feigl and W. Sellars (eds.), *Readings in Philosophical Analysis,* New York, 1949, p. 91).

9. *Jean Duns Scot* (Paris, 1952), p. 101.

are not crocodile tears. To understand why 'good', as predicable of a healthy condition, is included in the set of the goods, I do not need to mention any first analogate, such as pleasure or moral excellence. In proper proportionality, a meaning can be understood to *be in* a definite set without any consideration of the first analogate [p. 38].

Yet he insists that the "problem of order in proper proportionality is not settled by these . . . remarks" (p. 5). Simon, then, accepts the traditional distinction between analogous usage and metaphor but feels that more must be said. Even though one can use an analogous term properly without acknowledging any relation with its other uses, even should this sort of flexibility be the distinguishing characteristic of an analogous usage, nonetheless "the set of which we speak is an ordered one" (p. 38).

What makes Simon insist upon an order inherent to this usage? What constitutes the order? If we can use a term without remarking any order and use it properly, what indicates to us that the set is in fact ordered? Simon's answer, given through examples, amounts to saying that while one *can* use the terms without doing so, a more discriminating and sensitive use will include an awareness of more common and hence more original uses. Without this discrimination, "something *that cannot be done by abstraction, but can be done by order, is left undone*" (p. 39).

Consider for example our use of 'life'. We do not study life but living things; we speak of many different kinds of life, and some even extend the notion to include immaterial realities. (In *Summa Theologiae*. I 18 2, Aquinas introduces the notion and carefully extends it.) A definition of life, then, such as 'what has the capacity to move itself' is not meant to denote some minimal characteristic present in each—as Aristotle saw so clearly (*De Anima* 413a20). What it rather provides is a rule by which one might decide whether one could talk about something, say a computer, being alive or not. The meta-linguistic rule describes a pattern and nothing more. It glosses over the fact that our sensitive usage of the words, living, alive, life, depends upon

our accepting a primary sense for the term in question as well
as our realizing *that* the present way we are using the term is
somehow related to that sense, even though we may not be able
to trace exactly *how* it is related.

But to be aware of an order is not to assert it. And to speak
of uses being ordered is vague and potentially ambiguous since
whatever is ordered is ordered to a purpose. We cannot speak of
order without a specific ordering principle. (Which meaning of
life, for example, is more primary: that akin to our proper
experience or that making reference to same minimal organic
structure?) So we can wonder whether the use of a term, say
act, for act of existence, is appropriate or not. We are asking
whether the order this use exhibits to other uses of act—notably
intentional acts—will prove illuminating or not. Similarly with
predicates used of God: none is adequate yet some seem more
appropriate than others. The deciding factor would seem to lie
in their ability to point beyond themselves, a factor already
evident from ordinary use. Thsee semantic pointers are all we
have to direct us to a more exalted domain in a way that also
promises to lead us to some understanding of God.

In speaking of an order among their uses, Simon has hit upon
a characteristic that will prove useful in understanding the role
these analogous expressions play. Since the notion of order is
itself analogous, however, it is not quite a characteristic. I can,
however, suggest some properties this ordered usage would have
to have, taking care to leave them suffcently schematic.

Negatively, ordered usage can refer to the fact that no single
use is canonized. An ordered set of uses bears upon that usage
designated as primary by the ordering principle, yet every use
remains proper. More positively, the order is reflected in a certain facility in moving from one context to another. It may be
a long way from the wise owl to the wise counselor, or from the
canny mongrel to the canny politician, but understanding the
use of wise in one context facilitates our using it in quite different ones. We do not need to be able to come up with a scale
and plot relative positions to speak of uses being ordered. The
essential fact seems to be that one leads on to another.

If we add our ability to use the terms without specifying an order or even insisting that there be *one* such order, the account takes on a certain shape. In the place of an unfulfilled promise of a formal pattern, we have an account that accents the developing and self-regulating character of our knowledge. Whatever order may be present becomes manifest as we find it useful to employ the term in different situations. This note of progressive discernment bodies forth Simon's intimation that "order" accomplishes something "that cannot be done by abstraction." In our terms, it shows what judgment adds to the mere schematic rule or pseudodefinition of an analogous term. That is why Simon insisted that one could use these terms without adverting to any ordered usage. It is not a simple question of the use of a term according to a rule—if one means by that the mere application of a rule. We are concerned rather with a discriminating use, which entails a progressively sensitive awareness of the conditions for an appropriate use. And to speak of two kinds of use presupposes that certain notions do in fact exhibit a hiatus between mere use and discerning use.

Once again, the obvious candidates are evaluating terms and those expressing perfections of one kind or another. The reason these can be used analogously also accounts for our inability to exhaustively characterize them and warrants Simon's observation that contemplating the range of application of "absolute perfections . . . paradoxically implies a never-ending movement" (p. 42). For these expressions embody our efforts to communicate the richness of our aspirations; even though their descriptive side is tied to our achievements, we insist upon using the same expressions in passing judgment on those achievements. Any discussion of a just law will borrow some elements from our experience but also project toward a more ideal situation as yet not realized. But that ideal or even utopian situation would have to be subjected in turn to a criticism that would employ the very same expressions, though functioning now on another level.

By emphasizing that our discerning usage of analogous terms exhibits an actual order, Simon is able to respect the traditional concern that the diverse uses be properly predicated and yet introduce the more active criterion of a progressively discriminating sense for their propriety. And once again we notice that what accounts for our growing realization of this order among the uses, and the ability of one usage to lead us on to another, flows from the role they share as perfection-expressions. Proper proportionality designates the semantic peculiarity of these terms, which is their ability to be at home in diverse contexts. Far from explaining their use, however, the schema merely serves as a criterion, a way of filtering out candidates.

The more important feature, introduced by Simon in terms of order, lies in the fact that we use these terms to appraise as well as to describe, an activity requiring us to develop keen and discerning judgment. Remarks about order and judgment carry us well beyond the mere observation that we can use these expressions properly in diverse situations. We have recourse to judgment to account for the fact that our use of analogous terms always admits of greater nuance and sensitivity as we become aware of how different the connotations are from one context to another. The proposal of an ordered set represents an effort to reconcile this diversity with our original predilection for using the same term.

It seems that the different ways of accounting for analogous usage in part reflect different conceptions of its role. We have noted the breakdown of the more formal accounts, and Simon's analysis suggests a reason why: analogous usage, like metaphorical, demands the active presence of judgment. Precisely because the more typical metaphysical statements exemplified by Anderson pay little or no attention to this role of discriminating usage, they run the risk of circularity.

In this essay I have focused throughout on usage, and have succeeded in isolating certain styles of analogous expressions. McInerny has shown that this approach is not so novel as one might suspect. By driving a critical wedge between Aquinas and later commentators, he has indicated the relative novelty of the "analogous concept" and uncovered Aquinas' working concern for usage. Taken together with Simon's reflections, the very fruitfulness of this approach suggests that we try aligning a quite traditional discussion with the more contemporary treatment exemplified at the outset by John Wisdom and Dorothy Emmet. The guiding hand for my analysis as well as theirs will be Wittgenstein of the *Investigations*.

LINGUISTIC ACCOUNTS

The leading edge of my historical analysis of key figures, as well as many other attempts to elucidate analogous discourse, keeps turning up affinities with evaluative language. It seems quite clear that all terms of evaluation are analogous; it is not certain whether every term we should want to use analogously would be playing an evaluative role as well. A decision here will rest in part upon our ability to distinguish a properly analogous usage from the metaphorical, but that is not all. Indeed the question may well be formally undecidable, given the obscurities surrounding the evaluative/nonevaluative distinction. One writer has remarked that we simply assume that "nonevaluative" usages exist, yet no one has succeeded in delivering one.[10] To this difficulty of classifying, add the bevy of attempts to explain what constitutes an evaluative role, and the result is certainly a poor choice to serve as a model for yet another form of discourse. But it would be misleading to say that I am seeking to explain analogous usage on the model of evaluative terms. It is rather that the two kinds of usage display important structural similarities, and the discovery that language is freighted with evaluative expressions seems not unrelated to recognizing the ubiquity of analogous terms in our discourse.

There is a growing consensus that evaluative terms function irreducibly at the very heart of our language.[11] Focusing

10. Mary Warnock, *Ethics since 1900* (Oxford, 1960), pp. 138–40.

11. The inspiration is of course Wittgenstein, but the testimony of Noam Chomsky, that "whatever the antiquity of this insight may be, it is clear that a theory of language that neglects this 'creative' aspect of language is of only marginal insight," is useful ("Current Issues in Linguistic Theory," in J. Fodor and J. Katz (eds.), *Structure of Language* (Englewood Cliffs, N.J., 1964, p. 51). He also comments with respect to the proposal of a "context-free grammar," which would

on their analogous character makes all the more tenuous any proposal to assimilate linguistic rules to programmed moves. For the proposal to shape an ideal language to a canonical system means eliminating all consideration of relevance; yet it is precisely judgments of relevance that find expression in evaluative language. Once we see how notions like similiarty expand into irreducibly analogous expressions, the project of finding a sure formal base for working notions like similar to and synonymous with appears misguided and vain. We will no doubt continue to be fascinated by template models and other proposals to secure a clear and unequivocal basis for our various language uses, but we hope the dream will no longer be able to bewitch us.

Sellars: A Common Decision

This attempt to account for analogous expressions by the role they play in language owes a great deal to Wilfrid Sellars. Invariably Sellars invokes the notion of linguistic role to supply what we sense to be lacking to those accounts inspired by a formal logical paradigm. What distinguishes common nouns from any proposed disjunctive analysis of them is precisely the role they play, the function they subserve in discourse. This role betrays an intent—not yours or mine but the community's decision to employ general terms so. It is a "decision"— and not simply a decision—because it precedes our individual choice

---

amount to an "arbitrary Turing machine," that the "apparent gain in flexibility . . . is quite illusory, since it merely shifts the problem of specifying the formal features that make natural language distinctive" ("On the Notion 'Rule of Grammar', " in ibid., p. 130, n. 26). At least one of these features has been remarked by Rulon Wells: "In order to pronounce the German 'sterben' and English 'starve' cognates, comparative linguistics must judge that they are *sufficiently similar"* ("Is a Structural Treatment of Meaning Possible?" *Proc. VIII International Congress of Linguists,* Oslo, 1958, p. 664). The use of these terms in the context of programs of transformational analysis and of structural linguistics is telling. For a more directly philosophical testimony, see Julius Kovesi, *Moral Notions* (London, 1967).

and represents a kind of inevitable move as well, corresponding to a style of question "which will not down." [12]

Again, meaning may be described as use provided we recognize the interposition, indeed the prior presence of the community.[13] Use, then cannot simply amount to the way *I* want to use an expression but represents the weight of community sanction. We noted in the discussion of Aquinas the misconception which seemed to have motivated Sellars' attempt to explain linguistic behavior in stimulus-response terms. His early article ("Some Reflections on Language Games") which attempted this, already foreshadowed its inadequacy, and Sellars' subsequent attention to *action* as constitutive of meaning demands a more subtle and supple base.[14] For the kind of language we invoke in justifying different courses of action is evaluative in intent and analogous in structure.

Carnap: Option or Decision?

This suggests another look at Carnap, whose positions often serve as a base line for Sellars' development. We have already noted how the terms he uses to describe mere (= noncognitive) options for or against competing conceptual schemes reflect an analogous structure. That is, these very terms are not susceptible of an adequate account in any one of the languages in question, yet we nonetheless freely and inevitably employ them to describe our preference for one language over another. We are free to use these analogous terms not just once but (in principle at least) any number of times, for adopting any language$_j$ over any language$_i$. And since we make these comparisons in a language—our ordinary language—that language must be said

12. W. Sellars, "Substance and Form in Aristotle," *J. Phil.* 54 (1957) 694 and n. 11.

13. Sellars, *Science, Perception and Reality* (London, 1963), pp. 38–40, 316.

14. Cf. n. 69, Chap. 6. Sellars' position in *Science,* p. 327, ill accords with the demand stated at 357, c. Cf, my review in *Philosophical Studies,* Maynooth, 13, 1964, pp. 218–23.

to contain these terms which function quite mysteriously—so unlike the way Carnap thinks linguistic expressions ought to function.

Moreover, what gives these terms their specific role is their plainly evaluative intent. Hence Carnap provides further evidence for linking analogous terms with terms of appraisal. And if expressions like these must be employed to describe decisions in favor of conceptual frameworks, these and similar expressions will certainly crop up in our decisions about a course of action. Nothing is adequate to describe a decision except a language that can reflect the intent, the purpose, the *weighing* implicit therein.[15] So for my purposes at least, Sellars' insistence that the deep questions raised by Carnap's option-talk be resolved in action comes full round to raise again the issue of evaluative language—an issue we have recognized to be closely connected with the traditional one of analogous usage.

15. Cf. R. M. Hare, *Language of Morals* (Oxford, 1952), pp. 51–55, 64–69, 102–06. Braithwaite's apologia for his use of Carnap's idiom in speaking of the choice of an alternative theory is illustrative. He means a "choice which though not arbitrary in the sense that no *good reasons* can be given for it, is an 'arbitrary choice' in the sense that another choice would have been equally consistent with the demands of pure logic and of experience" (*Scientific Explanation,* Cambridge, 1953, p. 111; italics added).

Part Four

A Proposed Account

9. A Proposed Account

As one might suspect, my own attempt to elucidate analogy will be more in the spirit of Aquinas than of Scotus. Some ways of speaking defy ready domestication, but the most evident fact of usage is the ubiquity and the utility of figures of speech. Of these, metaphor is easily the most prominent. It permeates our ordinary discourse more than we suspect, working for the lawyer and the scientist as well as the poet. In law metaphor helps make a technical tool into a social instrument; in science it functions in framing models which suggest useful hypothesis; in poetry, it is subject to a severely controlling context.[1] To be aware of the role of metaphor in language generally and of models in more technical discourse is to discover a certain texture to our language, and this very texture betrays something more than the traceable patterns of logic. But since it is logic that brings clarity and promises to make the language we employ into a more effective and responsible tool, we naturally look for some kind of logic to order our language. The suggestion for the uses we have been examining is *analogic:* something like logic, only different.

That suggestion is too vague, but it indicates the way analogy is rooted in a desire to bring to the idiosyncratic. Yet a schematic type of order—like the proportionality paradigm—comes too soon and seems to explain more than it does. On the other hand, the field of models and metaphors is too vast; their uses are too sinuous to classify. Hence I have settled for the narrower

1. For a useful general survey of the literature and look at the issues, see Douglas Berggren, "Use and Abuse of Metaphor" (*Rev. Meta.* 16, 1962–63, 237–58, 450–72). For an insightful discussion of the inescapability of metaphorical construction, see Owen Barfield, "Poetic Diction and Legal Fiction" in D. Sayers (ed.), *Essays Presented to Charles Williams* (Oxford, 1947, reprinted in Max Black ed., *Importance of Language,* Englewood Cliffs, N.J., 1962); and for its role in scientific inquiry, Mary Hesse, *Science and the Human Imagination* (New York, 1955).

range of terms traditionally considered to be analogous, and by examining these in the light of contemporary concerns for linguistic clarity, hope to manifest a perennial strain in philosophic inquiry. Perhaps we can discover by reflected light more about the role that models and metaphors play in the language we put to everyday and to technical use.

The language uses examined here have been recognized as unique. To state that '. . . is' and '. . . exists' do not function like characterizing predicates (and hence are not illuminated by a scheme that offers to explain them on a parallel with descriptive statements) is just a more explicitly linguistic way of putting the medieval observation that 'being' is not to be elucidated by a logic of genus and difference.[2] Similarly, the fact that my use of good overflows the boundaries of any proffered account is evidence enough of its kinship with 'exists'. Traditionally 'exists' and 'is good' were grouped together with 'is one' and 'is true' as transcendentals. Finally, this quality of defying definition is also shared by appraisal terms, whose use cannot be circumscribed by a set of descriptive (and presumably univocal) statements.[3]

Appraisal terms, moreover, are employed not only in assessing conduct but in judging the adequacy of accounts as well. Remarking their role in assessing conceptual frameworks highlights the cognitive function of appraising expressions. Perhaps I might offer a conviction here which would delay us to defend: the statements we make invariably presuppose an orientation freighted with appraisals, and this feature of discourse is reflected in the semantic structure of the expressions employed. The fact that Austin found it difficult to turn up a "flat constative" bespeaks not only our intent but also something about the

2. The now classical paper is G. E. Moore, "Is existence a Predicate?" (*Aristotelian Society Supplementary Volume* 15, 1936, reprinted in *Philosophical Papers,* London, 1959, pp. 114–25). Aquinas' argument is found in commenting Aristotle's text (*Metaphysics* 998b20–27; In 3 Meta 8 #433).

3. This is a commonplace observation of moral philosophers; its most general application is offered by J. O. Urmson, "On Grading" (*Mind 59,* 1950, reprinted in A. Flew, ed., *Language and Logic,* 2nd ser. Oxford, 1953, pp. 159–87.)

structure of language in use.[4] Without the structural characteristics of analogous terms, imperative, emotive, or other harmonics would be impossible. Thus the move from *is* to *ought* should
be a quite natural one, involving the simple recognition that the
way we have been using our language betokens a set of concerns.[5]

The peculiarity of appraisal terms most germane to our discussion is the way they have of suggesting (or of presupposing)
a standard, whereas we employ them without alluding to any
standard at all. This curious fact cannot simply be written off
as a feature of unreflective usage. Any attempt to uncover the
standard for all other uses quickly becomes lost in generality and
can be salvaged only by recourse to some version of Augustine's
theory of illumination. So long as the theory remains a reflection
about usage, however, and does not claim introspective certainty,
it succeeds only in restating the problem: appraisal terms seem
to presuppose a standard, so if we use them we must possess a
standard—whether we are conscious of it or not. Yet the fact
remains that we do appraise and make judgments, employing
these terms without the benefit of any standard. Indeed we use
them all the time without adverting to the semantic embarrass-
ments they can engender. And the fact we use them so freely and
find them indispensable encourages any illumination we can
bring to their use.

4. J. L. Austin, *How to Do Things with Words* (Cambridge, Mass.,
1962), pp. 132–50.

5. P. H. Nowell-Smith, "Contextual Implication and Ethical Theory,"
Aristotelian Society Supplementary Volume 36 (1962), pp. 1–18; and
his *Ethics* (Baltimore, 1954): "The great philosophers do not seem to
have been mistaken in this basic assumption that the language of obligation is intelligible only in connection with the language of purpose and
choice, that men choose to do what they do because they are what they
are, and that moral theories which attempt to exclude all consideration
of human nature as it is do not even begin to be moral theories" (p.
182). Also Iris Murdoch, "Metaphysics and Ethics" (in D. F. Pears, ed.,
Nature of Metaphysics, London, 1960, pp. 99–123) and, more recently,
Julius Kovesi, *Moral Notions* (London, 1969).

PRELIMINARY DISTINCTIONS

The account offered here will have to meet the linguistic facts and nuances we have noted, as well as marshal the utility and power of the accounts we have examined. Presumably some intimation of a more adequate picture has been guiding my evaluation of both traditional and modern accounts and I will propose the distinctions requisite for framing that account and sketch out its main features.

Univocal, Equivocal, and Ordinary

Aristotle's observations about univocal and equivocal terms (at the outset of *De Interpretatione*) offer a useful preliminary division of the field. It will be necessary to distinguish equivocal-by-design from chance-equivocals, as the scholastics did; but even before that, some remarks about univocal or common terms will be required to offset a certain inevitable misunderstanding. It is now commonplace to observe that even univocal terms occur in a context of usage which defies complete accounting. Outside of stipulated and artificial usage, any definition proffered remains vulnerable to counterexamples and knows gray areas of application. This is simply to remark that any account is couched in a language and functions within the background of human concerns as they reflected in ordinary usage. Yet it becomes important to recognize these "facts" explicitly in the face of philosophers' tendency to isolate the presence of an account (or definition) as the distinguishing feature of univocity.[6]

Wittgenstein is a wary guide here—almost too wary—for his markedly pluralistic rendering of general terms threatens our initial division into univocal and equivocal. In the *Investigations* he denies that any account can be given, say of 'game', at least that would be useful in picking out members of the class. The careful attention to features necessary to recognize instances and

6. I am indebted to Edy Zemach for this notion of linguistic "fact": "Wittgenstein's Philosophy of the Mystical" (*Rev. Meta.* 18, 1964, 38–57, esp. 40; reprinted in I. M. Copi and R. W. Beard, *Essays on Wittgenstein's Tractatus*, New York, 1966, esp. p. 362).

to distinguish one from another while relating it to kindred cases is constantly undermining the generality required to garner every case.[7] As we are taught to use common nouns by being supplied with instances of how they are used and examples of the kinds of context in which they are normally employed, so we grasp this usage in a flash, recognizing that these contexts are of a kind by seeing the point of uniting them so.[8] But we may never be able to hit upon an adequate formulation of this point or specify the kind of contexts involved. Furthermore, to recognize terms as functioning within a language in this way suggests that language itself is more dramatic than a simple background. For Wittgenstein the diverse usage of language are better linked to roles in a play.[9] So understood, the way is opened to interpreting

7. L. Wittgenstein, *Philosophical Investigations* (Oxford, 1953) ##66–67, 75, 85–87.

8. "But can't the meaning of a word that I understand fit the sense of a sentence that I understand? Or the meaning of one word fit the meaning of another?—or course, if the meaning is the *use* we make of the word, it makes no sense to speak of such 'fitting'. But we *understand* the meaning of a word when we hear or say it; we grasp it in a flash, and what we grasp in this way is surely something different from the 'use' which is extended in time" (#138). "'B understands the principle of the series' surely doesn't mean simply: the formula '$a_p = \ldots$' occurs to B. For it is perfectly imaginable that the formula should occur to him and that he should nevertheless not understand" (#152). "I can see or understand a whole thought in a flash in exactly the sense in which I can make a note of it in a few words or a few pencilled dashes" (#319)— *Philosophical Investigations* (Oxford, 1953).

9. A *standard* is so denominated from its role: "We can put it like this: this sample is an instrument of the language used in ascriptions of color. In this language-game, it is not something that is represented but is a means of representation" (*Investigations* #50). Similarly, "'*descriptions*' are instruments for particular uses. . . . Thinking of a description as a word-picture of the facts has something misleading about it; one tends to think only of such pictures as hang on our walls: which seem to portray how a thing looks, what it is like. (These pictures are as it were idle.)" (#291). Finally, "the criteria which we accept for 'fitting', 'being able to', 'understand' are much more complicated than might appear at first sight. That is, the game with these words, their employment in the linguistic intercourse that is carried on by their means, is more involved—the role of these words in our language—other

the script and altering the roles to make a personal and pertinent point; thus we have the extensions of ordinary usage associated with more literate, poetic, and technical speech.

From this perspective, "ordinary usage" seems to stand in for Aristotle's "univocal," with an added proviso that the common ability to use the term correctly may not be susceptible of formulation. Ordinary then shares the weakness of univocal, in that it is difficult to distinguish ordinary from "extended" usage. Nothing is perhaps more characteristic of human conversion than metaphorical allusion, nothing quite so indicative of that *wit* Aristotle associated with the language-user. And metaphor succeeds so admirably in making the points we wish to make by deliberately "crossing sorts" and forcing the association of apparently disparate kinds. Yet if we succumb to the temptation to characterize ordinary usage in terms of a set of accepted roles for common nouns, then mixing these roles becomes extended usage. The temptation is inevitable, since we want to be able to invoke "ordinary usage" in a normative and not merely a descriptive way. And there seems to be no other handy way to set it off from the rest of discourse.

We might opt for disassociating ordinary from univocal discourse, but this association comes naturally, so the damage is done. Once we acknowledge the freedom with which ordinary language employs allusion and exploits ambiguity, we dare not continue to claim a perfectly adequate division between univocal and analogous usage. Yet by a reversal quite characteristic of Wittgenstein, it seems the very instruments of destruction are the best tools for reconstruction. Is not one of the most salient features of a univocal term its quite accustomed usage? Is it not this more settled aspect which allows us to give a definition that is reasonably adequate? We are able to define the term because enough of its uses have become sufficiently common to precipitate into an accustomed groove. And does not metaphor count

---

than we are tempted to think. (This role is what we need to understand in order to resolve philosophical paradoxes. And hence definitions usually fail to resolve them; and so *a fortiori* does the assertion that a word is 'indefinable')" (#182).

on this very background of domesticated usage to make its point? We could not "cross kinds" to advantage were such crossing the usual thing—for them we could neither call it crossing nor would we have any kinds to cross.[10]

That it is quite ordinary to do this, however, testifies more to the ability of language users to master a language and so to make it serve their ends than it undermines the fact of more settled linguistic habits. Indeed the command of any instrument demands an extensive undergirding of habitual skills learned through hours of practice. And it is notorious how the unskilled underestimate the extent of a virtuoso's dependence upon these quite ordinary abilities, now so unobtrusively his. We can, then, speak of an ordinary or univocal usage so long as we neither insist on its fixity nor count on it as our final norm. For accustomed usage can shift within limits to meet changing conceptual demands, and no one can hold anything against unusual (or "queer") usage if it succeeds in making its point.

Metaphorical constructions, on the other hand, have become embedded in much of our present usage to the point where they have lost their "crossing" function. Thus are univocal terms often born. The metaphor, domesticated, settles into accustomed usage. Once established, the new univocal usage should, on our account, provide a base for further metaphorical extensions. So 'apprehend', like most cognitive terms which are at root metaphorical, might be adopted to describe computer behavior. But this looks more like a stipulative and hypothetical extension than a suggestive metaphorical one. It seems that these terms born of metaphors tend to serve too abstract a purpose to freely propose themselves for further metaphorical use. We may feel the need, however, to remind language-users of the origins of such terms, in an effort either to animate or to neutralize the associations subtly conveyed into our everyday speech by this sedimented metaphorical usage.

10. See W. Wimsatt's review of Martin Foss, *Symbols and Metaphor in Human Experience* (Princeton, 1949, in *Rev. Meta.* 4, 1950, 279–90), where he accuses Foss of "celebrating the bonfire to the ultimate negation of the fuel" (p. 283).

The fact, then, that we can and must speak of an accustomed usage in established areas of discourse shows that Aristotle's observations about univocal terms can be helpful. That accustomed usage is often at root metaphorical only reinforces the warning against trying to assimilate similarity to identity, and further exposes our temptation to liken the formation of common nouns to a template process. It is rather misleading to speak of this basal usage as ordinary. We find it just as ordinary to mix established kinds for the more dramatic purposes of description—like "disk-jockey" or "girl Friday." We would not call descriptions like these technical, for they are quite ordinary. They succeed, certainly, in providing univocal reference, but only to someone who catches the allusion or succeeds in fixing the expression in context.

This point is crucial. If we were simply to identify ordinary language with univocal usage, we might completely overlook the ease with which we mix established uses. And this oversight would divert our attention from a signal way in which using language testifies to our ability to command a language: to use it to serve our ends by molding accustomed usage to meet novel demands. Now if this ability can be shown to operate on the level of ordinary discourse, then the hope of explaining analogous usage looks more promising. Wittgenstein has encouraged the direction of this study by pointing up so appositely the complexities of semantics and of human purpose already at work in the process in forming and using general terms. But once we have recognized these facts, the question remains: How does more properly analogous usage differ from the ordinary ways in which we mold language to serve our purposes? Or does it?

Transcategorical Terms

The time-honored candidates for properly analogous usage are those terms that appear to be equally at home in every category and mode of discourse. Hence their appellation as transcendentals: standing outside of the normal presuppositions of usage which restrict expressions within a certain range designating their proper subject matter. The penalty for so transcending the normal limitations of discourse, however, is to lose claim on any definite meaning. "Being "(x is a . . .) reflects no answer in particular but simply notes that the *question:* "What is (the nature of) x?" is a question that will not down. To assert that p is true is simply gratuitous unless the context supplies some clues to the method of verification, to the kinds of statements that could count as evidence. And to say of anything that is *one* (a unity, an individual) suggests little more than the viewpoint from which someone is regarding it and the general character of his intellectual concern about it.

But to recall that the meaning of these terms is relative to the inquiry in which they occur is no novel observation. It is simply the logical inverse of their transcategorical qualities: a term useful in every mode of discourse must be characterized in each. What is most startling about the terms, then, is not that they possess no "carry-over" meaning of their own, but the fact that we find it useful, even necessary, to employ them. The proportionality schema $a{:}b{::}c{:}d$ conveys well enough the pluralism inherent in their use. But it explains nothing about our need to use these expressions. Yet this inherent need may well be the only meaning proper to them, as the instance of 'being' suggests. The answers to "What is x?" vary with x; and the shape of the question is not very illuminating for it countenances only what Plato called "the safe but stupid answer" (Phd 105c). So what is left is the fact that this style of question "will not down." And this is as much a fact about the questioner as about the world— about everyone, whoever it may be, who engages in inquiry.

We can express this propensity of analogous terms to include the language user in another way, a way that also signals their unique role in discourse—that is to regard these terms as expressions within discourse which function in a reflexive manner as well as in a straightforward intrasystematic way. In their reflexive role they allow us to make reference to the manner in which we use language itself to successfully refer (. . . exists, that p is true), to appraise (. . . is a good . . .), to fix an object for inquiry (a . . . is a (type of) . . .).[11]

11. Victor Preller argues in greater detail for this interpretation of transcendental expressions in *Divine Science and the Science of God* (Princeton, 1967, pp. 64–69, 153–54). See my discussion of this seminal

These all seem to be functions of language which are pre-supposed to anything else one would want to do with it. If, for example, I want to say something in the case, I need to be able to fix the subject matter into an object ("unity"). And since that effort may or may not be successful, I should be able to appraise it ("good"). Finally, I want to be able to indicate whether or not I am stating what is the case ("true"). It is interesting to note that successful reference includes both the . . . exists scheme and the that p is true scheme, for we refer with expressions having a sense, and we successfully refer in the event such expressions are true.

Analogous expressions, then, come into play precisely at those points where one wishes to speak of language itself or of the relation between language and the world, and yet realizes that one must have recourse to a language. At these points we need expressions that function within our language but whose serviceability is not restricted to their role within the language. They must function within the language so that we can get our bearings in using them; but they cannot be restricted to that intrasystematic function if we want to be able to use them in speaking of what we can do with the language as a whole.

The fact that these expressions own a proper use within each language framework and yet are also used in every framework is what suggested their identification as transcendentals. It would be more proper, then, to refer to the expressions as expression-schemes or more simply as schemes.[12] What is being claimed for this privileged set of expressions is a role proper to each language within which they function, as well as a role in every language which we are not content simply to put on display but want to use. Thus, for example, we know what makes a good musician

---

work of interpretation in "Religious Life and Understanding" (*Rev. Meta.* 22, 1969, 681–90).

12. I am consciously borrowing and adapting two notions here: that of W. V. O. Quine on the role of logical schemata (*Methods of Logic,* rev. ed., New York, 1957, pp. 22, 91–92) and Wilfried Sellars' dot-quotes, whose use is introduced in "Abstract Entities" (*Rev Meta.* 16, 1963, n. 3), and justified throughout the article.

and what counts as verifying a statement in a particular context; and we also want to be able to speak of good ballplayers and test our assertions in a framework appropriate to another sort of inquiry. Moreover, this very account presupposes some capacity to single out distinct "languages" and so employs the scheme of *unity*.

What does it mean, then, to be in possession of such a scheme? How can we be sure we are using these expressions properly? We use them properly when we respect these "facts" about the roles they play. Thus I cannot pretend to know what '. . . exists' means *in general,* for it has no generic use. I can, however, understand how it may be used within the framework of material objects, and also understand its being used in other frameworks. I can further appreciate that the expression also reflects within a framework the "fact" that we use that framework to refer to things. So, for example, if I am listing the requisites for a political candidate, I need not demand that he exist. That is presupposed to the enterprise of making a list.

The way in which we are in possession of an expression-scheme, as well as an expression within a particular language when we employ a transcendental term, was expressed by the scholastics as a *ratio communis*.[13] One could speak of the *ratio communis* of good, for example, without pretending to possess an overarching set of criteria that would allow one to pick out good musicians, ballplayers, and automobiles. The *ratio communis* turns out to be the "fact" (reflected upon and adverted to) that we use an expression like good in a schematic way. One can reflect upon how these terms function and come up with a scheme (a *ratio communis*) without thereby claiming that we can formulate what is common to their different intra-systematic uses.

Offering an account of transcendental terms does not mean, of course, that these terms themselves will be useful in providing an account. In fact, transcendental terms both indicate and

13. For a careful discussion of scholastic linguistic usage, see Ralph McInerny, *The Logic of Analogy* (The Hague, 1961); *ratio communis* is discussed on pp. 150–52 and passim.

exercise our capacity to reflect on what we are trying to do with the language we use. That is so even though we are unable to formulate our intent in straightforward terms. Here we touch upon the affinity between this privileged set of terms—transcendentals—and metaphysical inquiry. To understand the logic of the use of these terms will also help to place in relief the unique character of that inquiry. One would not be so tempted to consider the relation between language and the world as something susceptible to description or explanation if one understood that only an analogous language would be appropriate to state that relationship. For the presence of analogous terms is itself a sign that something other than describing or accounting is going on.[14]

Appraisal Terms

The transcategorical characteristic of analogous terms is especially evident in the transcendental scheme 'good'. On the usual paradigm, x is good means x is fulfilling its nature. In this context fulfillment is a markedly anthropomorphic notion. But since we are using the scheme good to articulate the decidedly human activity of appraising, it is quite unexceptionable to offer an irreducibly anthropomorphic analysis of its meaning. That

14. My discussion of analogous terms has been a conscious attempt to respond to Wittgenstein's observation in a central passage in the *Tractatus:* "In a certain sense we can talk about formal properties of objects and states of affairs, or in the case of facts, about structural properties: and in the same sense about formal relations and structural relations. . . . It is impossible, however, to assert by means of propositions that such internal properties and relations exist: rather, they make themselves manifest in the propositions that represent the relevant states of affairs and are concerned with the relevant objects" (4.122). And further: "It would be just as nonsensical to assert that a proposition had a formal property as to deny it" (4.124); trans. D. F. Pears and B. F. McGuinness, London, 1961. My contention is that the presence of analogous terms ipso facto shifts the form of a statement to an elucidation. Hence the meaning of the analogous expressions must be exhibited in the context, and the presence of the expression itself announces this fact to the initiated.

good or fulfillment is an anthropomorphic notion, however, has been denied, even in this unobjectionable sense of that term. And this denial is relevant to our analysis for it signals the fact that good, and indeed every appraisal term (elegant, expedient, plausible, simple, . . .) functions as though reflecting a standard.

Once we move beyond the utilitarian identification of good with good for, and recognize our propensity to use it assimilated to "fulfillment," then the pluralistic features of good become embarrassing. We begin to look for a standard. (Here lie the roots of the manner called Augustinian or Platonic.) The difficulty, of course, is that the very mode of analysis that sundered good from good for showed the impossibility of formulating any such standard. In other words it showed that *good* could not be calculated or measured because 'good' functions analogously. And we have already noted that liability of analogous terms: they may be replaced only by schematic accounts. So for good we were offered fulfills its nature. But such a variable scheme cannot very well serve as a standard. The standard meter, or any ruler, would have to be made of rubber to fit the needs of the object measured.[15]

To say that good functions analogously or is susceptible of none but a schematic account, however, explains only one facet of its use. Like the proportionality paradigm, this fact reflects only the structural peculiarities of the usage. It says nothing of the further fact that we cannot help comparing, judging and appraising. However vulnerable may be the status of the terms we use to convey these judgments, it is nonetheless true that we *do* appraise. And we can learn to do so increasingly well even though we may not be able to formulate the standards we appear to be using.[16] Yet that we do appear to be using standards is the other prong of the argument against assimilating

15. L. Wittgenstein, *Remarks on the Foundations of Mathematics* (Oxford, 1965), pp. 3–4.
16. Cf. J. O. Urmson, "On Grading" (*Mind*, 59, 1950), and R. M. Hare, *Language of Morals* (Oxford, 1952), pp. 96–106.

good to good for. It remains true that appraising as we do it is more like applying a standard measure than calculating an advantage, or at least it can be so.

What then can we say? That the use of appraisal terms betrays the role of the language-user in discourse. As we noted in reviewing Aquinas on judgment, the use of terms which bespeak criteria in the absence of any criteria simply reflects the fact that we can judge so. Considering the ease and the flexibility with which we use these terms, the mere absence of criteria is but a fraction of the story. Suppose we were to follow the twin leads of the grammar of the words (which apparently presupposes a standard), together with a normal rationalistic temper to postulate a criterion or set of criteria operating. (Whether we were conscious of this or not would be irrelevant, for we are no more conscious of what leads us to form general terms.) The demands of reason would then seem to be satisfied—or would they? How would these criteria be applied? Like a measure to a block of wood? How would the mere existence of criteria help if their application reflects a subtlety, a discrimination and judgment quite ill served by the image of a congruent fit?

Again it proves illuminating to apply what we have seen regarding transcendental expressions to appraisal terms. Why not consider appraisal terms as reflecting the ways we wish to direct our language to the sensitive task which appraising often is? The rich supply of appraisal terms argues for language as a multipurpose instrument. We normally do not draw upon this rich store of terms unless we have a particularly delicate job to do, but the expressions are there should we need them. We employ them, for instance, in trying to help a person unravel his emotional turmoil in a counseling session, or when we attempt to let someone know that his work is below par without adversely judging him as a person.

To do one of the many jobs we call appraising—commending, criticizing, approving, canceling, etc.—appraisal terms presuppose a working linguistic framework. This is notably evident where the conditions for overt employment of a language are reduced to a minimum. Think of a recorded message or of the frames in a teaching machine. Flashing "good job" or "well done" comes across as silly and inappropriate precisely in the measure that the recording or the computer is not an agent. We do not hold them responsible to carry through with what those expressions imply, for appraisal terms do imply a consequential way of acting.

For our part, we must appraise in the course of inquiring, and in doing so we invariably have recourse to terms like expedient, simple, and plausible. The meaning of such terms remains vague even while we learn to use them with facility. In fact, to decide to use them in diverse situations is to discover the criteria for their proper use.[17] Such a procedure, reflected in the peculiar structure of these terms, must then be native to the human person, the inquiring subject.

This conclusion is indirectly supported by the need of thinkers like Augustine to posit a divine illumination to cope with the dilemma posed in the *Meno*. Aquinas, on the other hand, assimilated Augustine's response to the problem by shifting illumination from the status of an event to whatever it is that specifies and characterizes the very structure of a knowing and discriminating subject.[18] Augustine followed the bent of grammar suggesting a standard and succumbed to the influence of a neo-Platonic rationalism which demanded one. Then the whole procedure was crowned with a theological warrant. Aquinas, desiring the same warrant, located it rather in the structure of the inquiring subject. In that way, the need to postulate intuitive illumination was obviated and attention shifted to the peculiar grammar of terms like recognize, understand, see the point. These and others like them deflect the *Meno* inquiry from extrinsic validation to the inner constitution of the knowing subject.[19]

17. Hare, *Language,* pp. 49–67.
18. Note Aquinas' recasting of Augustine in *De Veritate* 10 11 ad 12. (ed. Spiazzi, Turin, 1949).
19. For the texts from Aquinas, see B. J. F. Lonergan, *Verbum: Word and Idea in Aquinas* (Notre Dame, 1967, pp. 25–33). For a more systematic development, see Lonergan, *Insight* (London, 1957, pp. 3–32);

I have focused on appraisal terms of the sort which even Carnap must invoke to describe our opting for one language rather than another. Recourse to these terms, I have tried to show, indicates that his option is more akin to judgment or discrimination than to a mere flip of a coin. And I have singled out appraisal terms only because judgment and discrimination function more obviously and dramatically in appraising than in instances of knowing that something is the case. A tactical weakness in relying on Carnap would be to imply that the formation and application of common nouns functioning within any particular linguistic framwork is an affair quite independent of discrimination and easily assimilated to a congruence or template model. The merit of Wittgenstein is to have shown how naive and oversimplified a supposition that is. Wittgenstein calls our attention to the subtleties of usage present already in general terms. He sensitizes us to our manner of communicating those general terms by adducing examples and to the peculiar nonlogical way in which these instances culminate in a common usage.[20]

Here the grammar of words like recognize is relevant. To recognize something as an instance of a type is often not clear-cut and is never susceptible of an adequate list of criteria. Never, at least, outside of languages designed to be unequivocal. Of course, such languages remain restricted to their constructed domains. In ordinary situations, then, to recognize that an x is a y involves a decision regarding relevant features. If we were pressed further to explain how these relevant features could warrant our making the classification we did, we would invariably have recourse to some essentially analogous phrase like sufficiently similar.

THEOLOGICAL USAGE

Theological language represents a limit of discourse and so provides an interesting if not crucial test. On the account I am

and for a lucid resumé, see his "Cognitional Structure" (*Continuum* 2, 1964, pp. 530–42).

20. *Philosophical Investigations,* ##71–73, 127, 201, 208.

proposing, transcendentals and appraisal terms form a set open to use in characterizing a God who must remain uncharacterizable. Transcendentals claim membership most obviously, because they cannot be constrained to any single intracategorical use. But appraisal terms qualify more appositely and effectively because they directly engage the subject. Specifically they bear on his dimensions of aspiration and fulfillment. This observation simply reflects Aquinas' stipulation that only perfection be used in speaking of God. It also embodies Peirce's unabashed avowal that the limits of discourse are anthropomorphic, though in the unexceptionable and inevitable sense in which there simply is no further bar of judgment than man's aspirations as manifested in the regulative principles of inquiry.[21]

My discussion of analogous term and the logic of their use suggests two ways of characterizing the logical space in which language about God might function. The first is more straightforwardly ontological and the other perhaps best termed semantic. One of the harmonics of this study is that classical writers like Aquinas may be interpreted in either of these ways. To speak of these writers as classical need not invite the interpretation of their work which we are tempted to make: classical, hence ontological.[22] This, I take it, is what Heidegger is getting at when he speaks of recovering a classical author.

Ontological Interpretation

Aquinas introduces his treatment of God with the descriptive formula: " 'God' is [means] 'the beginning and end of all things, and especially of rational creatures.' " [23] He does not argue for this formula but simply offers it as a summary description of what men mean by God. Hence it is a schematic formula, admitting of a fair degree of plasticity. One might well substitute

21. C. S. Peirce, *Collected Papers* (Cambridge, Mass, 1931), 5.121, 5.212, 5.46–5.47, 5.536.

22. I have argued agaist this prejudical use of 'classical' in "Religious Life and Understanding" (*Rev. Meta.* 22, 1969, 690).

23. Introduction to I 2: ". . . Dei cognitionem . . . secundum quod est principium rerum et finis earum et specialiter rationalis creaturae."

more evocative English expressions like source and goal, or origin and aim, or whatever. Yet certain logical "facts" hold for Aquinas' scheme, however we might improve upon its associative reach. So, for example, God is not one of the class of everything. This means that he is not a thing. Of course, this fact cannot be asserted because it sets God (or discourse about him) in opposition to one of the "facts" of discourse (more about this in the semantic interpretation). If we name the class of everything "the universe," God is then conceived as originating the universe but is not himself a part of it. Thus it is formally inappropriate to ask whence God originated, for the synthetic a priori contention that every event has a cause ranges over the universe. It is one of the formal features of the system we employ to explain things that happen "in" the universe.[24]

Normally, of course, there is no use for the particular "in". That we are constrained to use it here displays the decisive feature of an ontological interpretation of God-language. Philosophical discoursing about God is logically equivalent to discoursing about the universe. To be in a position to speak about the universe—its origin, its sense, its features—is to employ the same "categories" with which one could properly speak of God. (Whether one could ever get oneself into such a position is not at issue here; these are grammatical remarks.) So in the same measure as I am able to speak of the cause of the world (universe), I am able to make a statement about God that would be syntactically correct: God is the cause of the world.

This is the sort of statement that suggests a straightforward ontological interpetation. Before looking at that, however, we ought not pass over the semantic sophistication involved in framing the statement. The ontological assertion God is the cause of the world is not equivalent to the earlier summary description of men's usage: 'God' [means] 'the beginning and end of all things.' In fact, Aquinas offers the summary description in introducing question two, the very question containing those ways

24. This account is argued by Wilfrid Sellars in "Counterfactuals, Dispositions and Causal Modalities" (*Minnesota Studies in the Philosophy of Science* 2, Minneapolis, 1958, pp. 225–308.

designed to help people reach the point of entertaining propositions so outrageously ontological as "God is the cause of the world [all things]."

The difference between the two statements (A) 'God' is [means] 'the beginning and end of all things,' and (B) God is the cause of the world, was signaled by an early scholastic like Anselm as the difference between (A') understanding "the word signifying [the object]", and (B') understanding "the very entity which the object is." [25] Later scholastics formulated the difference in terms of *nominal* and *real* definitions. The device of quotation marks used in (A) helps to make this distinction with negligible epistemological distractions. It is not two sorts of realism, Aristotelian or Platonic, that are at stake, but two ways of understanding. The difference lies in the presence or absence of an overarching framework.

Statement (A) and (B) may be considered as associating a subject term with a predicate formula. The association is diversely accomplished, however, depending whether or not we are in possession of a framework that allows us to draw implications using the subject term. This is an awkward yet sophisticated way of saying what Anselm recognized. His formulation is less awkward, though more misleading, in distinguishing between knowing the thing and merely knowing its formula. To assert that God is the cause of the world is to pretend to understand God—that is, what God is. The form of direct predication ipso facto announces either substantive or accidental information. In this case it is clearly substantive. And from such substantive facts about a thing, other things follow. That is how we come to know, or as Aristotle would say, what knowing is all about. In the terms I am suggesting, direct predication signals that we are in possession of a framework within which these implications may be drawn. In that sense, we understand "the very entity which the object is."

So long as we consider predication in these terms, it is irrele-

25. Anselm, *Basic Writings* (LaSalle, Ill., 1962): *Proslogion* (Chap. IV); cf. also M. J. Charlesworth, *St. Anselm's Proslogion* (Oxford, 1965), pp. 119–21.

vant whether or not we translate the 'is' into 'means'. But it is not irrelevant in the case where 'is' links two expressions conspicuously placed within quotation marks. Here 'is' *must* be construed as 'means', for the use of quotes calls attention to the fact that we can use each expression without yet being clear as to its implications. In that sense, then, we are doing something more like associating two names, as though the predicate expression should be construed "beginning-and-end-of-all-things." This is not completely accurate, of course, for it was this formula that allowed us to go on in the initial stages of the inquiry. Understanding some of the implications of such a formula suggested the framework which was introduced for using 'God.' And we had to grasp something of what the formula means for it to influence us so. Nonetheless the formula intends to summarize common usage. We can of course quite properly use any of the formula's many variants—in imprecations, in worship—without having to be all that clear about its implications.

Is it not something like this that Anselm was groping for when he distinguished understanding the word signifying the object from understanding the very thing itself? What seems to be at stake is a common phenomenon of growth in understanding. Anselm's way of stating it puts us off because of intervening philosophical controversies. But we could say, and he would surely agree, that to really understand the word or formula is one thing, and to use it without understanding it is another. I have tried to mark that difference by speaking of one's possession of a framework within which implications can be drawn. I am speaking here of a working possession, and to that extent a conscious one, though one may understand little about frameworks or what it is to possess one.

It is significant that Aquinas uses the first way of defining God as a means for setting up the framework within which we can assert the second statement about God, i.e. the ontological one. The so-called nominal definition, then, functions like reasons offered for adopting a certain framework or way of thinking and speaking, while the real definition turns out to be one of the theorems of that system. By calling attention to the difference in this way, we can mark a genuine difference without driving any ontological wedges between language and the world. A real definition differs from a nominal one in that we *really* understand the expressions we are using, because we are in possession of a framework within which a consistent and fruitful set of implications may be drawn.[26]

Let us return to our proposed ontological interpretation of philosophical discoursing about God. We have already noted that speaking of God as the cause of the world suggests that statements which take God as a subject are in the same logical space as those that seek to explain or to describe the universe. The reason, of course, is not that God is the universe, but that the only vantage point from which statements might be made about everything is precisely and uniquely that of the origin of everything: God. We can direct our attention either to God or to the universe. That shift in attention will be indicated by the subject of the sentence, but the laws governing the structure of the propositions involved will be the same. Pantheism and creationism, then, would be different ways of organizing the same logical space.

An identifying feature of such discourse would seem to be the ubiquity of analogous expressions. So, for example, one is at a loss to think of how to assign any feature to the universe, but one can risk an appraisal of it: it is good, it is governed by laws, it forms a system. No one is in a position to say what the entire picture is like, so logically no one can state *how* the universe is lawful or systematic. In that sense, then, these predicates do not describe a feature of the universe so much as they announce our expectations. Statements like these function much as Kant insisted that "regulative principles" function: they do not organize our experience into patterns (or features) but serve to guide our organizing that experience. It is difficult to say what one might mean when one insists that the universe is lawlike. Kant invoked a pre-Kantian notion of "subjective" to underscore this fact. Yet

26. I am indebted to Victor Preller, *Divine Science and the Science of God* (pp. 135–40), for breaking ground on this interpretation of real/ nominal definitions.

the fact remains that we can and need to use expressions such as lawlike in this way. We do apply them to the universe, and the relevant fact for this inquiry is that any such expression will inevitably prove analogous..

If a pantheist insists that God informs the world, his manner of informing the world will not be like any other form making something what it is. This would be so precisely because his informing the world is compatible with each thing being what it is, while ordinary forms are incompatible. Similarly, for Aquinas, if God is the cause of the world, he is *not* a cause in any ordinary sense. He can be said to be a cause of the world precisely because his causing is compatible with other causes acting in their own right. In point of logical "fact," Aquinas will insist that God is the cause of each thing being a cause, as well as of the thing's being itself. He is the cause of its being at all, yet without coercing the thing into doing what it is doing.[27] This is to assert that God is a trancendent cause; and the only way such an assertion could be possible would be where cause was being used analogously.

So the semantic fact of analogous expressions (or of the capacity certain expressions possess to be used analogously) is a prerequisite to forming those statements offered as examples of straightforward ontological statements. The structural feature of analogous expressions that makes them amenable to such use seems to be this: they possess an intrasystematic use together with a capacity to refer from within any system to what we wish to make the system do. This allows one to experience the difference between understanding and really understanding, as one becomes more adept to shifting from one use to another. It will also allow someone to use them in situations when he literally does not know what he means by the application but judges that it is an appropriate one. Insisting that the world is lawlike is one such example.

27. What B. J. Lonergan has called the "theorem of universal instrumentality" is formulated thus by Aquinas: "agens divinum, quod influit esse sine motu, est causa non solum in fieri sed etiam etiam in esse" (In 7 Meta 17, 1661; M. R. Cathala and R. Spiazzi, eds., Turin, 1950).

I have singled out the Socratic formula as the paradigm case of this feature of analogous terms: Socrates is the wisest man in the world in realizing that he is not wise. In relating this feature of language to straightforwardly ontological statements, one is reminded of a requirement pressed upon philosophic discourse by Hegel and reiterated in Heidegger: the ontological difference.[28] It is only a suspicion, but I do wonder whether we might profitably locate the "difference" that can give rise to ontological, in contrast to an ontic, consideration, in this semantic feature of analogous terms. In any case, what is germane to an ontological interpretation (either in Heidegger's terms or in those more congenial to classical philosophy) is a language that allows one to make such statements. The semantic structure of analogous terms alone, of course, could never warrant the statements. But that structure does serve as a necessary condition for our being able to make assertions like God is the cause of the world.

A Semantic Interpretation

"The universe" does not play so prominent a part in what I wish to call a semantic interpretation of the logical space in which one uses language to speak about God. The primary tenet of the ontological interpretation made philosophical discoursing about God equivalent to speaking about the universe. A more semantic interpretation will not deny that feature of God-language but rather focus on the manner in which whatever is said can be cast so as not to mislead.

I have already mentioned that the introductory formula, " 'God' is [means] 'the source and goal of all things, and notably of rational creatures'," implies that God is not a thing. A state-

28. Cf. John E. Smith, "The Relation of Thought and Being: Some Lessons from Hegel's *Encyclopedia*" (New Scholasticism 38, 1964, 22–43; and M. Heidegger, *An Introduction to Metaphysics* (New York, 1961, pp. 73–74): "being is not an essent and not an essent component of the essent. . . . No; in the word 'being', in its meaning, we pass through word and meaning and aim at being itself, except that it is not a thing, if by thing we mean something that is in any way essent."

ment like that gives untold logical grief, and the reason is clear
to one who has learned the lessons Wittgenstein was teaching in
the *Tractatus*. For language is simply not constructed in such a
way that we can say of anything that it is not a thing. Nor is
anything asserted when we say of something that it *is* a thing.
The reasons are suggested by the indispensable role of 'anything,' 'something', and 'thing' in my last two observations. Being
a thing is presupposed to whatever it is we are talking about;
yet this "fact" cannot be asserted nor need it be, for it is shown
in the structure of our discourse.

Aquinas illustrates this "fact" in terms appropriate to Aristotelian semantics. He sets up what cannot be said about God
once we accept the summary formula: beginning and end of all
things. God is not composed of matter and form, nor does he
belong to any genus—not even the genus of substance. Nor can
God be spoken of in substance/accident terms.[29] What this adds
up to is a strict and literal rendition of the implications of something's not being a thing. In fact, by blocking every conceivable
way to speak of God, Aquinas shows that he understands the
implications of the original formula as well as the curious logical
status of something's not being a thing.

In fact, there is only one way in which one might speak
properly of God, and one is at a loss to convey what one means
in so speaking. We can say that *to be God is to be*. This assertion
is not the same as stating that God exists; it simply translates
Aquinas' systematic observation that the real distinction in
everything else between *what* it is and *that* it is cannot be countenanced in the source of all things.[30] As might be expected, the
form of the assertion fractures a normal form for substantive
predication: *to be x is to be y* or *to be (a) x is to be (a) y*. Thus,
to be animal is to be sentient, to be blue is to be extended, to be
canny is to be quick-witted. Now in the case of God, we have
already seen that we must leave the *y*-place blank, for whatever
might fill that place would be a genus or a property of sorts.

29. This is the burden of the articles in q 3 of the *Summa:* On the
Simplicity of God.
30. *Summa Theologiae* I 3 4.

Hence one can say nothing about him—which is a way of saying what cannot be said: that he is not a thing. At this point Aquinas makes a virtue out of this apparent deprivation, and says that, in the case of God, the truncated and hence improper formula is the only proper affirmation that we can make: *to be God is to be.*

To try in any way to attentuate the scandal of this manner of speaking is to blunt the point of Aquinas' theology. The temptation proper to ontology at this point is to go on to speak of being as a superproperty, as one of those things which fills (to overflowing) the *y*-place. Such is not Aquinas' way, however. He sticks by his earlier insistence about what cannot be said about God. Aquinas allows the stark impropriety of this formula to announce a transcendence which cannot be spoken of without betraying it.[31] He understood when to be silent, yet also seemed to grasp that what could not be said might still be shown.

What does it mean to say that to be God is to be? That, obviously, is not for me or for anyone to try to say. What does it mean that this is all that we can properly say? It means that God is not a thing; it means that he transcends any human way of consideration. It means further that anything we might want to say about him will be said improperly. Yet we may be allowed relative improprieties if not absolute ones. Relative improprieties occur when we fill in the *y*-place with an analogous term in the line of human aspiration. Such a predication, while improper, will nevertheless not be wrong. This sort of relative impropriety can be termed inadequacy.

It is difficult to give a precise sense to discourse being inade-

31. Ibid., I 13 8. My suspicion is that this formula 'to be God is to be' is the only acceptable rendering of the touted "necessary existence" of God. In other words, Aquinas sees that affirming God's existence to be necessary neither implies nor is equivalent to asserting that God "exists necessarily." Our use of 'exists' is simply such that the term cannot be modified by necessarily. Aquinas' way of putting this is to remark that God's existence would be undisputed were one to know it as it is, but that such knowledge is beyond our ken and hence we can dispute it. In other words, there is no way in which we can use the predicate 'exists' so that it cannot but apply (I 2 3 ad 1).

quate. To assert it sounds a bit like announcing noise in a transmission channel. That is news only to one who does not realize that noise-free channels are mathematical abstractions. Yet in this case a precise sense can be gleaned from the logic of the account given and from a remark Aquinas makes. He notes that when one says that God is just, one must be prepared to say as well that he is justice. This is of course another grammatical impropriety, but justified in that we recognize it to be so. Thus we deliberately fracture syntax in an effort to show the transcendence of this object.[32] This grammatical prescription presumes that one normally says that something or other is just with respect to a norm which is properly expressed in the abstract term: justice. In reminding us that with respect to God we must be ready to assert as well that he is justice, Aquinas is noting that the normal situation displayed in the ordinary grammatical matrix for using the term just does not obtain in the case of God. And we can announce this "fact" by being ready to assert that he is the norm as well: justice.

Obeying this rule, however, does not assure that we are using 'just' with complete propriety in asserting that God is just. For, strictly speaking, we do not know what we are saying when we use the abstract term that expresses a norm as the predicate of a sentence. Put in another way, we might try to say what justice is and fail, but we could not begin to try to say what (thing) is justice. To fracture syntax, even deliberately, does not assure that we know what we are saying, even if we know that such is the way we have to put it. So one may use normative terms like 'just' of God not improperly, only when one realizes that one must by the same token be prepared to assert of him the expression for the norm itself. But since one must alter the grammar of the expressions to obey this rule, we must also say that the original predication will be inadequate, though not improper.

Need I belabor the obvious point that only certain expressions allow us to attempt predicating the norm as well as the normative term? What would it mean, for example, with a phrase like six-feet tall? or a word like blue? Once again, the obvious candidates are the transcendentals and that subset of them that fills

32. *Summa Theologiae* I 3 2 ad 1.

out the schema 'good': appraisal terms. Again, the expressions themselves do not suffice to make the subtle semantic points that Aquinas has been able to make regarding our use of them in trying to talk about God. But their systematically ambiguous structure makes those subtle moves possible.

DECISION AND JUDGMENT

If calling attention to the structural features of analogous expressions does not explain why we use them as we do, what does? This question is central to my thesis about analogous usage. The question is fundamental precisely because I have been contending that one cannot speak of analogous expressions except as a shorthand for "typical ways in which we find ourselves using certain expressions analagously." Hence the semantic or structural features of the expressions offer a necessary condition for using them as we do. But looking at expressions qua expressions in this way remains abstract, for we have yet to locate sufficient conditions for our use of them.

Yet the facility with which we can speak of the expressions as a shorthand for the expressions-in-use indicates that the explanation for our using them the way we do will be more like a set of reasons than a series of causes. What an expression is useful for seems to be inscribed in some mysterious manner in what we have been calling (with no less mystery) its semantic structure. Ways of speaking reflect and give coherence to ways of living. So it seems appropriate to locate the sufficient reason for employing language analogously among that set of activities summarily called decisions. Moreover, it appears to explain specific analogous uses of terms by reference to specific decisions.

This will not be explanation of a causal type, as we have seen, since the activity of deciding is itself very much bound up with using language analogously. Explaining or offering sufficient conditions in this case will be more like elucidating what is in fact going on. Or it may be like offering reminders designed to detect formal features common to our acting and speaking in this way. It is somewhat fashionable to speak of decisions warranting a particular form of discourse. I must make more precise the sense in which I am using this strategy, and also show why it can be offered as a summary of the accounts surveyed and the previous critiques offered in this study.[33] We have already observed what recommends this tack initially: decisions will not thereby be counted irrational even though they cannot be given a completely systematic warrant. This fact of life and of discourse encapsulates a recurring theme of this study of analogous uses of language: there is no method for assuring proper analogous use. Every ana-logic offered to regularize these uses by assimilating them to unambiguous ones has been found wanting.

From Logic to Language User

The temptation to ana-logic is always present, however, for an explanation seems to gain respectability by its affinity with logic. The very word analogy suggests a "super-logic" operating here. But the repeated failures to discover or construct such a support have been exposed, and my account has taken the opposite tack. It has been concerned with facts about life and language which reach beyond logic to reveal something more of the shape and texture of our language.

The first of these is a capacity to recognize similarities in dissimilarities. That capacity is shared by poets, scientists, some philosophers, and nearly all ordinary men. Another is the indispensability of models, examples, and instances in communicating a point and laying a base for using more general or technical terms. Any particular model or single example is normally dispensable, but recourse to them generally is not. This of course presupposes that we know how to use such models and examples and can grasp the point of them.[34]

33. I have noted (n. 24 above) how Wilfrid Sellars invokes decision in warranting counterfactual conditional expressions. Victor Preller finds that Aquinas' manner of " 'taking' [the world] is not forced on us; it would be a *decision*" (*Divine Science*, p. 172); and Michael Novak, in his closely reasoned *Belief and Unbelief* (New York, 1967), concludes that "the real as intelligible is the product of a decision: a decision to accept as sufficient the reasons which support one's claim to know" (p. 120).

34. L. Wittgenstein, *Investigations*, ## 71, 73, 201, 208; also Lonergan, *Insight*, pp. 7-12, and Paul Holmer, "Kierkegaard and Philosophy,"

Not far removed from this fact about language and language-users is the dramatic dimension of our usage. We clearly need to break out of accustomed usage to describe the unfamiliar or reveal forgotten facets of the too familiar. Correlatively there is the usage that seems to be oblivious of category distinctions yet needs to be explicated afresh in each context: the frankly transcendental expressions. What strikes us more and more about this unusual language is simply the demand to use it. Similarly, what impresses us about evaluative language is our ability to appraise and to make judgments in the absence of any operating standard.

And all these facts of language: the grammar of words like recognition, the peculiar role of analogies in shaping general usage, the deliberate and dramatic crossing of kinds, the unabashed employ of transcendentals, as well as our facility with appraisal terms—all of these point from language to the language user. Or rather they speak of language as emanating from a person with aims and purposes.

And of course this *is* the context of language—human life and life's concerns. It is the language arising therefrom which forms the matrix for logic. To call attention, then, to those aspects of our linguistic comportment which are neither susceptible of a rigorous account nor in need of logical justification is not to spurn logic. It is to preserve its integrity. Indeed it is not logic so much as an excessive demand for clarity which stands in the way of the proposed account. To require that 'similar to' be explicated by way of 'identical with,' for example, reflects an attitude, not a theory.

My strategy has been to expose the attitudes and convictions embedded in our ordinary usage, including the uncanny sense for similarity-in-dissimilarity we display in our frequent recourse to metaphor. That strategy has aimed to create a climate in which our use of analogies in many domains may be considered a respectable as well as an accepted fact. By focusing especially

---

in R. McInerny (ed.) *New Themes in Christian Philosophy* (Notre Dame, 1968), pp. 13–36.

upon transcategorical and appraisal terms, the link of language with language-user came more and more to the fore. This suggests that the justification for analogous usage, which failed to supply, lies rather in the structure of those decisions which are presented to every inquiring person, shaping both his inquiry and his life.

Putting language to a systematic use, for example, demands certain prior decisions. Fastening upon a certain type of account as appropriate to a domain demands that quality of reflection which can express itself only in analogous terms. One style of account is said to be more fitting or congruent, less strained than another. Framing an assessment like this one requires that we take a stand. And if stands are taken *on* a spot, they must also be taken *in* terms which try to exhibit the quality of judgment shaping the assessment.

More simply, we must appreciate that the taking of a stand itself will be an indispensable ingredient in any assessment. Otherwise we are expressing belief in a self-warranting matrix for evaluations, a matrix reminiscent of Newtonian space. But if we reject such a conception, then we recognize that we are in no position (speaking both strictly and metaphorically!) to justify standing where we do. Nonetheless, we can offer reasons for taking the stand. These reasons tend to function more like elucidations than theorems; they will be framed in analogous terms.

Nothing shows quite so clearly that "language is a form of life" as does our recourse to analogous expressions.

From Decision to Judgment

Clues present within the logic of the expressions employed have led us from analogous usage to decision. Yet unless decision be a mere option, analysis cannot end here. Decisions cannot very well be true or false, nor can they be arbitrary. We demand above all that they be responsible, for any decision purposes to shape a whole set of actions. We have seen this requirement that action be responsible undercut the neat pragmatic stipulation that inquiry culminate in action.[35] And if action cannot be the last word, neither can decision. Indeed 'decision' seems to mediate between 'choice' and 'judgment,' demanding at once the reflective acumen of judgment and the optative thrust of choice. On the one hand there is Gilson's testimony that for Aquinas, analogy is to be explicated "on the level of judgment," and on the other, Wisdom's observation that paradoxical usage represents a deliberate choice.[36]

I have largely assumed a distinction between decision and choice. The linguistic differences are manifold. Kenneth Sayre has carefully discriminated many of them.[37] To mention a few: one may decide upon a course of action without ever being faced with the actual choice—as with the old maid who long ago decided what qualities her husband would have to possess, or the defeated candidate who had decided to divide the spoils with his manager. Further, one may decide in private, but choice requires a public performance. Hence we may decide which of the candidates is better qualified, but the choice awaits the actual moment of voting and may even be foiled by an accidental flick of the wrong lever.

Finally, there is a distinction that Sayre sees as more fundamental yet: "the expression 'I choose' frequently is used in a performative sense. The expression 'I decide', on the other hand,

35. And Peirce's own testimony: "If pragmatism really made Doing to be the Be-all and the End-all of life, that would be its death. For to say that we live for the mere sake of action, as action, regardless of the thought it carries out, would be to say that there is no such thing as rational purport" (*Collected Papers*, 5.429).

36. E. Gilson, *Christian Philosophy of Saint Thomas* (New York, 1956), p. 105; J. O. Wisdom, *Philosophy and Psychoanalysis,* Oxford, 1953), pp. 38, 50.

37. K. M. Sayre, "Choice, Decision and the Origin of Information," in K. M. Sayre and F. J. Crosson (eds.), *Philosophy and Cybernetics* (Notre Dame, 1967). I am indebted to Sayre for the development of this point, including most of the examples. We must also note that 'choose' *can* certainly be used at times in a manner nearly equivalent to 'decide'. The presence of differences as well, however, suggests that this use need not be considered paradigmatic.

is seldom used in any sense whatsoever. . . . In short, the act of saying 'I choose (so and so)', given appropriate circumstances, in itself constitutes the act of choice. This is what is meant by saying that 'to choose' is a performative verb. By contrast, . . . to say 'I decide (so and so)', apart from being downright odd in any save very special circumstances, at best could be construed as the report of a decision; . . . it does not in itself constitute an act of decision." [38] Related to this difference is a peculiar orientation toward the past tense exhibited by the verb 'to decide'. The performative use of 'to choose', of course, is limited to the first person present tense, even though it may be used in other tenses to report or predict a fact or state an intention. But 'decide' eschews the present tense. It adopts quite spontaneously the 'have decided' form or at most the "present of policy": 'I (always) decide those matters' or 'I (only) decide things like that after consultation'.[39] Much more could be said, but what we have seen will suffice for prima facie evidence that enough conceptual disparity exists to ground a genuine distinction between choice and decision.

On the other hand, decision seems more akin to judgment than distinct from it. This is so probably because some kind of judgment appears to be the major component separating decisions from mere choices. Hence one decides to study philosophy because one judges it to be worthwhile even though most consider it a waste of time. Underpinning a decision or a series of decisions one will find some kind of weighing, appraisal, or

38. See Sayre and Crosson, *Philosophy and Cybernetics*, 82–83. For "performative utterance," see J. L. Austin, *Philosophical Papers* (Oxford, 1961), pp. 220–40, or *How to Do Things with Words* (Cambridge, Mass., 1962), passim.

39. Sayre and Crosson, p. 84. Much work remains to be done here, and doubtless will be under the pressure of the mind-computer analogy. Sayre notes the paucity of work on the subject. To cite the major contributions, J. L. Evans. "Choice," *Phil. Quar.* (1955) 303–15; W. D. Glasgow, "On Choosing," *Analysis* 17 (1956); T. F. Devaney, "Choosing," *Mind* 73 (1964) 515–26; K. T. Gallagher, "On Choosing to Choose," ibid., 480–96; P. H. Nowell-Smith, "Choosing, Deciding and Doing," *Analysis* 18 (1957).

judgment. And that is because decisions themselves are up for appraisal as responsible or irresponsible.

Peirce: Decision in inquiry. C. S. Peirce affords an interesting testimony at this point. If action is inadequate justification for converting a hypothesis into an assertion, the dimension which naturally suggests itself is volition.[40] For espousing a certain form of expression serves to announce our intent to commit ourselves to a particular direction for the future. Since one form of expression necessarily excludes others, adopting this particular one cannot help but exercise a certain directive force over the remainder of our inquiry. Yet how can we justify so deliberate an intervention? We cannot claim to know where the inquiry ought to go from here without rendering it superfluous—for if we knew already, why continue to inquire? Nor can the choice be arbitrary, for the inquiry process is carried out under an ethical mandate: search for the truth. The suggestion lies in the neighborhood of volition, for where we cannot expect foreknowledge we can ask for responsible behavior. And this seems to be the peculiar twist volition gives to action.

Hence Peirce insists that "to assert a proposition is to make oneself responsible for it." Assert here is taken explicitly in the sense of judgment as "an assertion to oneself" whereby one personally assumes responsibility for the truth of what one says: "the *volitional element* is quite extraneous to the substance or 'meaning' of a concept. . . . For it is no pragmaticistic doctrine that responsibility attaches to a concept; but the argument is that the predication of a concept is capable of becoming the subject of responsibility, since it actually does become so in the act of asserting that predication." [41] In the idiom I have adopted this amounts to assimilating judgment to decision, for it is above all in decisions that we ask for responsibility.

But decision presupposes deliberation. So the roots of responsibility go deeper than volition itself, striking into the reflective,

---

40. For the development of Peirce's thought on this question, see my "C. S. Peirce: Pragmatism as a Theory of Judgment" (*Inter. Phil. Quar.* 5, (1965), 521–40).

41. Peirce, *Collected Papers,* 5.29, 5.543, 5.547.

self-critical capacity of human consciousness. Peirce sees this, and recognizes that a responsible decision about usage can no more rest on mere willing than it could on the need to launch into action. What is required is the ability to sketch out *ab initio* the purposes our inquiry would serve, and in our effort to meet that purpose, progressively to discriminate apt from inept expression. This allows us to speak of assessing without recourse to an obvious standard, since it focuses on the actual inquirer intent upon a purpose. We look to encyclopedists for knowledge, but for evaluation turn to someone with a working familiarity in a field. Peirce expresses this by noting that the deliberately formed habit of inquiry is "self-analyzing because formed by the aid of analysis of the exercises that nourished it." But even further, reasoning for Peirce "not only corrects its conclusions, it even corrects its premises." [42] In the immediate context, this would mean that a progressively discerning eye for an inquiry's serving or failing to serve its purpose would also confirm, modify, or alter our original outline of that purpose. For it was largely our conception of the purpose which led to adopting the language we did.

Judgment and standards. Such a model for inquiry would not only call attention to a progressive refinement of our conceptual tools for achieving certain ends; it would also provide a set of converging indications useful in appraising the ends themselves. This activity employs one of the most exalted uses of 'decision' and 'decide': the sense in which one may be said to decide upon

42. ibid., 5.491, 5.575. We are quite naturally reminded of Plato's description of "dialectic as the only process of inquiry that advances in this manner, doing away with hypotheses, up to the first principle itself in order to find confirmation there. And it is literally true that when the eye of the soul is sunk in the barbaric slough of the Orphic myth, dialectic gently draws it forth and leads it up, employing as helpers and cooperators in this conversion the studies and sciences which we enumerated." (Rep 533d); and Wilfrid Sellars' more contemporary observation that "empirical knowledge, like its sophisticated extension, science, is rational, not because it has a *foundation,* but because it is a self-correcting enterprise which can put *any* claim in jeopardy, though not all at once" (*Science, Perception and Reality,* (London, 1963, p. 170).

ends while one deliberates about means.[43] Certainly this is the sense in which the proposal to speak about God represents a decision regarding the role of human aspirations in inquiry.[44] And if the character of the terms we employ in speaking about God clearly demands some such decision for their responsible employ, the use of evaluative terms generally also tends to presuppose an aim or purpose which reflects certain decisions.[45] As with transcendental expressions, so with evaluating terms: we cannot characterize that purpose without having recourse to vague and ambiguous expressions. But we can, in both cases I would maintain, refine, modify, or alter our conception of that purpose and our warrants for the decision. This can be done by monitoring our use of these evaluating terms and our understanding of those aspirations to fulfillment which led to our proposing to speak of God.

So for example, evaluating a person as authentic or a situation as unjust is open to confirmation or revision as experience re-

43. While it is admittedly novel to introduce the term 'decision' into the Aristotelian framework we have adopted here, something like it seems to be operating in Aristotle's apparently circular definition of actions as "just and temperate when they are such as the just or temperate man would do" (*Nichomachean Ethics* 1105b5). Aristotle was too acute to have missed the obvious circularity. He must have considered it only an apparent one. Such a man is said to possess "practical wisdom," which gives him a "true apprehension of the end" (1142b33). This is first distinguished from "deliberation . . . which regards what is conducive to the end" and then said to be intimately related to it, for "it is thought to be the mark of a man of practical wisdom to be able to deliberate well about . . . what sorts of things conduce to the good life in general" (1140a25). If neither deliberation nor intuition can supply a view of the end, "the good life in general," something like a decision must intervene. This decision will become more or less comprehensible, be considered more or less warranted, as the consequences it is seen to entail, the means one observes to be conducive to realizing it, be judged helpful or inimical to human development.

44. See the references to Novak and to Preller in n. 33.

45. P. H. Nowell-Smith, in "Contextual Implication and Ethical Theory," (n. 5 above), concludes by observing that "Aristotle was right, both in commending those who said that 'good' means 'what things aim at' and in refusing to commit himself to this definition of 'good' " (p. 18).

veals to us the ambiguities latent in these terms. For the terms themselves reflect in turn the strength or inadequacy of the original standards we had felt it necessary to adopt. By assimilating standard to the aims or purposes of an inquiry, we are no longer quite so tempted to require that anyone using evaluative language display his standards on demand.

In fact, once we distinguish 'decision' from 'choice', any activity worthy of being called a decision also amounts to what Hare calls "decisions of principle." [46] In these activities we mold the standard prescription to fit the relevant features of a situation, thus making the standard over into a working standard of principle. This activity may also be described as applying a principle, though this way of describing it presumes that the principle can be such prior to any application. Hare's point is that moral principles become principles of activity only through those decisions which give them a definite sense by molding their meaning to fit the relevant features of different situations.

Hence we teach a moral principle not simply by enunciating it, but we also feel it necessary to show what it means by illustrating how it might give shape to our activity in typical situations. That process of shaping, however, involves making a decision; and a decision of this sort helps us understand the principle-in-use. So teaching a principle involves teaching what it is to be a principle. Part of understanding a principle is understanding how to apply it. So the locution "applying principles" proves to be misleading in much the same way that talk about standards usually does.

We are invited to look for, to formulate the standard, and then to use it as a common measure. But standards resist unambiguous formulation and take refuge in analogous expression. This frustrates the initial leads of grammar, for we expect a standard to function like an ordinary rule and to be a straightforward measure easily applied to the thing to be measured. I have tried throughout this essay to distinguish depth from surface grammar in the ways we speak of passing judgment. By remarking the ways in which analogous terms help make us more aware of what we are doing in assessing as well as shunting aside our expectations about a standard, that task has been

46. *Language and Morals*, pp. 56–78.

provisionally accomplished. The epistemologically astute will notice an affinity with characteristic moves designed to divert similar pressure for a foundational view of human knowing.

It is this ability to monitor our use of analogous terms that I have called judgment. Such monitoring brings us to appreciate the many ways we can use analogous expressions as well as our need to use them. For we do use such expressions, and we can recognize that both their utility and their ambiguity lies in their capacity to be employed with an ever-increasing degree of finesse and discernment. This fact is the testimony offered here in favor of my use of 'judgment.' Finally we have seen how 'decision' carries us far along the path toward delineating this notion of judgment. 'Decision' demands further analysis, however, if it is to do the work proposed for it.

There is little doubt that my own usage needs a great deal more clarification as well. But that is beyond the scope of this present work. It must content itself with having analyzed the major traditional claims of analogy with the proposal to substantiate them. I have sought to isolate the requirement that terms so employed represent perfections, and have attempted an analysis of the two dominant types of analogical usage—transcendentals and evaluative terms. That this analysis has taken positions on issues currently disputed but not within the scope of its intent (for instance, the relation of evaluative language to purpose) is yet further testimony of the central role played by analogy.[47] Some further distinctions and comparisons of that usage remain. They should provide something of a test of these proposals.

47. That the main lines of this present solution in terms of "judgment" were anticipated in Chap. 6 on Aquinas only testifies to his semantic acumen in refusing to be satisfied with the standard medieval solution in terms of *res significata* and *modus significandi*. The fact that Aquinas continued to override the terms of this distinction explicitly as well as in the use he made of it—even while ostensibly having recourse to it—forced a direct critique of the distinction itself. It led me to attempt a more direct description of the actual linguistic characteristics of analogous terms. And this, under the guidance of such contemporary interpreters of Aquinas as Gilson and Longergan, led to the proposal of judgment.

10. Analogy, Metaphor, and Models

In an attempt to distinguish analogy from metaphor, and analogy proper from argument-by-analogy or from the role exercised by models in scientific theory, and to recreate a linguistic climate sufficiently varied and concrete to support analogous uses of language, I have focused on affinities among them and left possible dividing lines vague. Attention to models will reflect the same strategy of recalling us to awareness of the actual context of our inquiry. Moreover, if metaphorical constructions can be detected in an area where the premium on precision renders ambiguity anathema, analogous discourse gains in respectability.

The recent challenge to a hypothetico-deductive account of scientific theory in the name of models parallels that of confronting ideal language accounts with the complexities of ordinary usage. Yet each of these attempts has more the ring of a protestation than an alternative account. Clarity, it is charged, has been won or promised in too cheap and procrustean a manner. The critique of a deductive account in science as well as that of ideal language accounts would call attention to the context in which our theories or constructed languages are expected to operate. For if the actual operation of these frameworks presupposes features of that larger context which the theories or constructed language cannot clarify, their pretentions to clarity and explanatory power are considerably trimmed. It is not the power of language or of science that is in question so much as the accuracy and explanatory power of certain accounts proposed to explain their function.[1]

1. Notably W. Sellars, "Language of Theories," in H. Feigl and G. Maxwell (eds.), *Current Issues in Philosophy of Science* (New York, 1962), pp. 57–89; but also N. R. Hanson, *Patterns of Discovery* (Cambridge, 1958) and "Is there a Logic of Discovery?" in Feigl and Maxwell, *Current Issues*, pp. 20–42; S. Toulmin, *Philosophy of Science* (London, 1953) and *Foresight and Understanding* (Bloomington, 1961); and Mary Hesse, "Models in Physics," *Brit. J. Phil. of Sci.* 4 (1954) 198–214 and *Science and the Human Imagination* (New York, 1955).

TESTING THE DIFFERENCES

But how do these general remarks about the fiber and texture of language, including scientific language, bear upon the question of analogous usage? To note that ordinary usage is quite spontaneously metaphorical (even though not every metaphor is felicitous) and to observe the prevalence of models in scientific discourse (though specific ones are always being revised) would hardly satisfy the claims made for analogy. Traditionally, metaphorical usage and argument by analogy have been dubbed improper, and contrasted pejoratively with analogy proper. Yet as one most sympathetic critic has noted, the very schematism that signaled this distinction has no adequate criteria to distinguish the two. Catejan's demand that analogy proper satisfy the proportionality paradigm merely recalls that one of the grounds Aristotle lists for metaphor is analogy: "Whenever there are four terms so related that the second (B) is to the first (A), as the fourth (D) to the third (C), one may then metaphorically put B in lieu of D." [2]

Modern exponents like Anderson are adamant in opposing metaphorical analogy—which "employs a concept univocal in itself and is merely used by the intellect in an analogical manner"—with analogy proper, that of "proper proportionality." [3] Yet as we have seen, Professor Anderson offers no criteria for distinguishing properly metaphysical notions other than their use in metaphysical statements, which must certainly exceed the univocal and metaphorical. But this excess he never succeeds in explaining independently of a move to a "metaphysical order."

One is tempted simply to reject any attempt to distinguish between terms or concepts intrinsically analogous and those merely submitted to an analogous employ, and be satisfied to catalogue analogy as a subspecies of metaphorical usage. And a quite harmless, domesticated variety it would appear. 'Good,' 'just', and simple' would be barely expressive, though they enjoy

2. Ralph McInerny, *The Logic of Analogy* (The Hague, 1961), p. 22; Aristotle, *Poetics* 1457b16.
3. J. Anderson, *Bond of Being* (St. Louis, 1949), p. 181.

a venerable position and a frequency of occurrence which defy replacement.

But to react so hastily to an overly systematic account would itself be untrue to the full facts of usage for we would be left unable to explain the very presence of a distinct subspecies, much less its prestige and the ubiquity of its members. Using the distinctions already drawn between general terms, transcendentals, and appraisal or evaluative terms, I hope to elucidate those features dear to Anderson by finding room for a distinction between analogical and metaphorical usage that runs faithful to the contours of our language as we use it.

Generic Usage

A division of terms into generic, transcendental, and appraisal will often prove to be inadequate, but that counts in our favor. For one can nonetheless recognize terms as appropriate to one class or another and so employ the distinctions without being required to trace out the dividing lines. Wittgenstein's reflections on the formation of general terms show that categories are not so much given as they are established through interlocking common nouns. Intracategorical usage, then, tends to presuppose a set of general terms whose use intertwines so as to meet successfully a certain coherent set of human needs.[4] Thus a game involves player(s), a certain attitude befitting play (which may be variously defined), a context of social conventions (assuring that an innocent interpretation be placed on otherwise menacing moves), and so on and on, to the despair of a complete contextual account.

That a bounded context can be assumed without prejudicing the range of its usage allows us to speak of game as a general and not a transcendental term. A sign that we are presuming a context is our ability to recognize unusual uses and to notice how they initiate a process of active comparison. Hence to speak of Providence as a game, in which we would be pawns of the Almighty, is a very deliberate sort of predication obviously in-

4. At this point, Wittgenstein and W. V. O. Quine are not far removed; cf. Quine, *Methods of Logic* (New York, 1950), p. xv.

tended to cast light into obscure regions. It is a forced assimilation of something whose ways are unknown—God's providence —to a context more hospitable, with hopes of leading one on to some understanding of it. This is the unique and irreplaceable role of metaphor.

At this point we need only note that this proper role presumes a more settled generic usage. If one objects that an assimilation of contexts so abrupt as this can also be misleading, we must count that among the unavoidable risks of inquiry. We can also point out the remarkable affinities between this contemporary account of the role of metaphor and Aquinas' insistence that certain terms may be predicated of God because they are able "to lead us on (by the hand) to some understanding of things divine." [5]

"Transcendentals"

Transcendental terms like one, being. and true, however, manifest an established transcategorical usage. So there is nothing forced in their application and no hint that they are "playing away from home" or being employed in an unusual manner that would call for an active comparison with their normal employ. Indeed attempts to establish criteria for their *proper* employ inevitably elicit counterexamples: 'unity' is notoriously elusive; 'being' (or 'exists') cannot be interpreted as spatiotemporal location without eliminating most of the established grammar of our talk about thoughts and intentional activity generally; 'true' suggests all the difficulties surrounding a definition for 'verified.'

Our inability to provide an account for terms like these cer-

5. Max Black's treatment in *Models and Metaphors* (Ithaca, N.Y., 1962) may well be considered a locus of contemporary philosophical treatment, although one should read it with the background of earlier treatments by I. A. Richards, *Philosophy of Rhetoric* (Oxford, 1936), Middleton Murry, *Countries of the Mind* (Oxford, 1931), and W. Bedell Stanford, *Greek Metaphor* (Oxford, 1936). A quite complete bibliography can be found in Douglas Berggren, "Use and Abuse of Metaphor," *Rev. Meta.* 16 (1923–63) 237–58, 450–72. Of these, the most useful to me have been the studies by Owen Barfield, Cleanth Brooks, C. S. Lewis, and Philip Wheelwright.

tainly helps give them an air of excessive abstractness. And we
have seen that an irreducibly schematic account is one of the
most effective signs of transcendental usage, if not its constitutive feature. It is no wonder then that our established transcategorical usage is especially vulnerable to charges of abstractness, since the very structure of these expressions prohibits their
being used descriptively. So the only fruitful tack remaining is to
inquire into the why and wherefore of such an established usage,
and search out the reasons why we insist upon using terms whose
meaning continues to resist straightforward formulation.

Appraisal Terms

Now appraisal or evaluation terms such as just, fruitful, and
genuine combine something of the bite of a general term with the
established, unforced usage of transcendentals. Like common
nouns, they have reasonably clear uses in the context of ordinary
life and, like transcendental terms, they possess a natural affinity
for extended usage beyond categorical lines. Appraisal terms
seem to own an inner "differentiability" which, for example,
allows us to appeal to a justice that mocks our conceptions of
justice. No specific conception of justice can claim to be adequate to the promise of the concept, and this "fact" expresses
one of the formal features of the concept *justice* which enables
it to do the job it does.[6]

The classic way of calling attention to this affinity with transcendentals is to show that any general formula offered to cover
our use of ethical or appraisal terms is inadequate. Inaugurated
by Plato in the earliest dialogues, this tactic has been employed
more recently to criticize Kant's moral maxim and Bentham's
ethical calculus. Yet the absence of adequate definition has

6. It belongs to literature to manifest the inherent dialectic of these
terms. Professor L. C. Knights, wishing to summon the force of *King
Lear,* can only say (with apologies for the paraphrase) that "all the
forms of self-protective legalistic justice are shown in their utter inadequacy when contrasted with the reconciling and transforming justice of
Cordelia's free forgiveness of her father" (in *Theology and the University,* ed. J. Coulson, Baltimore, 1964, p. 215).

never succeeded in banning or even in undermining our use of these terms. So I have suggested that some affinity with the language-user must be operating here as well as in the hold which transendental terms have upon us.

One affinity between appraisal and transcendental expressions came to light in Aquinas. For the working notion in his theory of theological discourse is *perfection,* where the expression designates a set of terms which stand in for multiple and even unlimited realizations. Yet perfection appeals all the while to a dimension of aspiration and fulfillment which apparently guides us in using these terms.

A DISTINCTION PROPOSED AND WEIGHED

The suggestion, then, is to associate the transcendentals with those regulative principles that mark the horizon of any inquiry, and to link appraisal or evaluative usage with the inquirer's aspirations to personal fulfillment. And since inquiry is not so independent of inquirers as some methodologists would have us think, the two usages are complementary and often interpenetrate. Thus Peirce's insistence that logic presupposes an ethics represents a position more and more tenable today.[7] But on this hypothesis what becomes of common nouns and their metaphorical uses?

Language as Inherently Metaphorical

In a measure, the answer depends upon a theory of metaphor. But relying on my earlier remarks and the wealth of studies recently made of metaphorical usage, we may regard certain claims established.[8] The more we are led to recognize the ubiquity of metaphor in ordinary speech, the less plausible is the Renaissance account of its role as decorating a skeleton of expository prose or rational argument. In fact, the contrary seems to be the case: metaphor plays a unique and irreplacable

7. C. S. Peirce, *Collected Papers* (Cambridge, Mass., 1931) 2.773, 4.440, 5.108, 5.130.
8. See the studies mentioned in n. 5.

part in human discourse, from poetry to ordinary conversation to scientific models. Nor is this merely a thesis about language. For as the decorative theory reflected a world view—that of the Age of Reason—so does the contrary inherent theory.[9]

And the implications of the contrasting world views are extraordinarily far-reaching. The nub of the Renaissance theory about metaphor was an assumption about the nature of the universe, and one shared in many ways by later-day positivism. Counting metaphor as a replaceable rhetorical device presumes that we must always be able, sooner or later, to hit upon a proper and unambiguous description. But this presumption reaches to the very structure of the world. It assumes that the world is of such a piece with our language that (in principle) nothing prohibits our giving a complete description of it. The uncertainties of our ordinary language may have to be corrected, and much ingenuity shown in constructing a language equal to the task, but an unambiguous picture of the world is renderable in principle. Hence it is but a matter of time and effort. On this view, philosophical problems do indeed become puzzles, kinks in our language to be unraveled by a more logically perspicuous mode of expression.

And if the implications of this theory about metaphor display a remarkable affinity with the aspirations of Wittgenstein in the *Tractatus,* it should not be surprising to find the contrary inherent theory supported by the *Investigations.* Wittgenstein's fundamental contention that the function of philosophy is to show and not to state may link both periods, but the manner of manifesting is radically different in the *Tractatus* and the *Investigations.* That difference is marked by an increased attention to ordinary usage, replete with analogies and metaphors. Note how similar is Wittgenstein's notion of language games to the account an apologist of the inherent theory gives of the function of metaphor: "to produce a shift in the whole structure

9. Colin Turbayne in *Myth of Metaphor* (New Haven, 1962) traces the influence of metaphor on the world views of Newton and Berkeley; Elizabeth Sewell traces the interaction of metaphor and world view in countless ways in *Human Metaphor* (Notre Dame, 1964).

of language and in this way to enable us to look once again at what we see *through* language." [10]

The fact and the centrality of metaphorical usage, then, bespeak a tendency inherent to language-users. It reflects a need to extend the categories embodied in generic terms the better to assimilate new domains or to cast fresh light on familiar ones by illuminating yet other similarities and differences. This very demand highlights dimensions of language-users obscured by the decorative theory. These dimensions are summed up in what I have called the dramatic character of language.

We force associations in metaphors because we intend to illuminate. We are quite conscious that these associations may be misleading; yet sometimes we employ them *because* of their propensity to mislead. A conscious strategy like this one bespeaks our awareness of the importance stage-setting plays in human exchange. Certain misconceptions, by now fairly sedimented in our usage, must be exposed and shown for what they are. And the only probe we possess is a still more accurate employ of language.

But how can we master—control, correct, and criticize—this use of language? How do we decide which metaphor is more appropriate? Literary critics sometimes invoke canons for this sort of thing, but the canons as well as their application vary from one critic to another. And if literary criticism remains more an art than a science, so does the more general testing of ordinary usage. Moreover, the inherent theory of metaphor that I have adopted eschews an ideal of correct usage. No metaphor can claim to be the right one because this very claim would render all the others superfluous and merely decorative.

Yet within limits we can recognize certain "sort-crossings" as more appropriate—at least to a given context—than others. Again within limits this kind of appropriateness can be argued for and so gradually learned. But what cannot be acquired and must be presupposed is the original reflective and critical ability which issues in *recognitions* like these: that a metaphor fits the

10. J. M. Cameron, "Words and Meaning in Poetry and Philosophy," *Downside Rev.* 69 (1951) 302.

occasion.[11] Metaphorical usage is certainly not alone in witnessing to the presence of this autocritical power in rational discourse and inquiry, but it offers a particularly dramatic instance of that power in action.

Analogy Distinguished from Metaphor

What then can we say to our original question: Is the tradition justified in singling out properly analogous usage from metaphor? Is there warrant for differentiating, for example, theological from biblical usage? To the extent that transcendental and appraisal terms seem to contain, through the sanction of usage, "an inner differentiability" opening them to a progressive and unlimited refinement, the answer would seem to be yes, the traditional distinction is justified. But the process of refinement will progress and reveal its limitless character only if the schematic structure of these expressions is clearly recognized. Beyond a series of inadequate descriptions, we can say only what they do not mean, and point to an affinity they reflect with some basic human aspirations to fulfillment.

Thomas Gilby supplies a useful illustration of this process in an attempt to understand what classical political philosophy means by the "common good." He is forced into a negative shift which deftly exhibits the point I have been insisting upon. While it is the purpose of community and society alike to secure a common good, the term common, he reminds us,

> has a double meaning, for it can be read either collectively, to mean the sum total of all the parts, or distributively, to mean what all share in whether they be taken singly or all together. . . . Collectively, the common good stands for a heap-value, the integrity of a whole body, the majority benefit according to individualistic utilitarianism, the racial or proletarian lump according to totalitarianism. To the collective good all partial and particular goods are, rightly and naturally subservient: the hand goes up to protect the

11. Eugene Gendlin has examined this peculiar quality of necessity in my use of expressions in "Expressive Meaning," in James M. Edie (ed.) *An Invitation to Phenomenology* (Chicago, 1965), pp. 240–51.

body, private interest gives way before public benefit, a minister surrenders his own opinion in the corporate decision of the Cabinet. Distributively, the common good is a freer value, more versatile, and *not so easily imagined.* It is *not* an accumulation of particulars, but a whole that can be repeated again and again. As in the logic of predication so in the philosophy of society, a whole is formed which suffers *no* dimunition or subtraction from the presence or absence of particular subjects.[12]

What makes a society unique—the distributively common good—can be conveyed to us only metaphorically ("freer, more versatile") or negatively ("not . . . imagined, not an accumulation"). Yet baffling as they are to the powers of straightforward discourse to formulate, expressions like common good remain part of our working vocabulary. There is something about the relationship of person to society which cannot be formulated. We do not know what it is, this unimaginable relationship, but we are compelled to admit that it exists, and give it a psuedodescriptive label like common good. Any attempt to translate into alternative descriptive phrases what we mean when we use "common good" slides off into disavowals, as Gilby's prose illustrates.

More generally, to speak of common good as an analogous expression is accurate. But it should be clear by now that we are not licensed thereby to speak of arriving at its meaning *analogously* while other terms would be regarded as delivering their meaning straightforwardly. To acknowledge that the expression is analogous admits that we have no straightforward way of finding out what it means, though we do use it and use it for certain definite purposes.

Evaluating the Distinction

The traditional distinction between proper and improperly analogous language, then, can be gravely misleading if it suggests that a privileged set of terms is available that is exempt from the

12. Thomas Gilby, *Between Community and Society* (London, 1953, p. 89; emphasis added).

ongoing activity of criticizing and correcting metaphorical associations which we have seen to be so characteristic of human discourse. On our account, whatever force properly analogous terms enjoy derives from the special role they play in normal human exchange.

At this level the descriptive accounts we can offer, say, of a just social order, are both necessary and relevant. If 'just' is to be classed as "properly analogous," that is because any descriptive formulation of it can be tested against evaluative uses of the same term, and the description will be granted kinship yet denied equivalence. So in the measure that a descriptive formulation is laden with metaphors—metaphors which indeed suggest and give leads to evaluative usage—terms with established trancendental or appraisal uses are dependent on a background and texture of usage I have characterized as metaphorical.

Metaphorical language, then, is a sign of the capacity for reflective discrimination which is bodied forth so explicitly in our use of analogous terms. Learning how to use metaphor with ever greater precision exercises that capacity. One may or may not become reflectively articulate about one's discrimination; a poet need not become a critic. Philosophers are critics, however, as are most critics philosophers. And the sign of their kinship is recourse to those expressions designed to recall the various discriminating capacities of language as we use it: analogous expressions. The sign of a critic's (or a philosopher's) power, furthermore, lies in the way in which he uses these expressions. For the manner in which he uses them betrays his grasp of their formal features. A master craftsman knows tools and treasures his own.

We have no new name for the person who judges how effectively a philosopher or critic is employing his tools. The only name we have for such a task is *critical* and the only canons are philosophical. There is no issue from this apparent impasse; to fabricate a meta-level inquiry only postpones the question. If we recall that analogous expressions belong among a philosopher's indispensable tools, then we can appreciate the situation rather than deplore it. The fact that a philosopher must be philosophy's critic is one of the distinguishing features of that activity. Since analogous expressions are set apart as a group of terms that play a role within a language as well as make reference to that language's functioning, it is no wonder that a philosopher finds them so useful.

The "facts" of philosophic inquiry reflect the formal features of those expressions which we need to execute that inquiry, as the contours of a craft reflect the possibilities latent in its tools. Not that just anyone can read a plane in the smooth features of a tabletop, but a perceptive woodworker can. The sensitivity to formal features and hence to the multiple ways in which a craft reflects its tools is one fruit of that discipline called philosophy. A primary aim of this inquiry—and one evidenced in its organization and prosecution—was to remind us that such a sensitivity cannot be expected short of engaging in that discipline. We cannot expect a general theory of analogy for the same reasons that philosophy shatters the general theoretical impulse. The possibilities of a craft are latent in the formal features of its tools.

11. Conclusion: Analogies in Use

The multiple uses of analogies have been illustrated and I have tried to distinguish them along lines separating models shaped to specific inquiries from more pervasive expressions tailored to transcategorical roles. In any case, analogies draw attention both to similarities and to dissimilarities, and only a selected part of these will prove relevant. So something more must be operative if analogies are to function usefully.

It belongs to an ongoing inquiry to separate the useful from the spurious. Subsequent inquiry plays a more evident role in the case of analogies functioning as models, but transcategorical and evaluative terms are subject to criticism as well. These, too, all carry vestiges of descriptive use. In fact, it is difficult if not impossible to find any expression that will not lead in directions which may prove misleading—as 'immutable' used of God connotes 'immoble' and 'fixed'. A simple caveat or disclaimer, however explicit, will not suffice to correct the wrong lead. The shape of the inquiry itself must serve to modify the influence of the original analogy.[1]

The procedures for correcting analogies differ from one subject matter to another. Scientific models can count on a number of converging techniques for testing their merits. By following out various sets of implications, we may gradually become clearer as to which implications remain in force and which must be cut. On this basis we can weigh the model's capacity to point up relevant dimensions of the object against its propensity to mislead. In the kinetic theory of gases, for example, questions such as whether the postulated particles possess elastic properties or not were asked only when they arose in handling different properties like viscosity of the fluids in question. It is useful to recall that there is still weighing to be done here, though the nature of the evidence renders one's reasons more commu-

1. I have tried to show this in a few instances in "Kant and Philosophical Knowledge" (*New Scholasticism* 38, 1964, 189–213).

nicable. While a single counterexample *logically* demolishes a theory, practicing researchers are more conservative than reflective methodologists.

Judging the relative merits of metaphorical or figurative usage in literature is of course not nearly so sure a thing. We can certainly grow in sensitivity, develop skills of literary criticism, and even become increasingly articulate and persuasive in guiding others to a similar appraisal. But the judgments of a literary critic remain open to dispute in a much greater measure than the appraisals a scientist renders on a current model. Yet the fact that one's judgment is disputed does not threaten the enterprise of criticism. In fact, critics do not consider failing to resolve an issue as incapacitating. Quite the contrary: the proposal that they could find a resolution of a scientific sort would constitute a serious threat to their style of inquiry.[2]

Philosophical autocriticism looks to where the pervasive images lead us, and musters every salient example to help us achieve a sense for the resulting projected trajectory: whether it enhances or distorts the inquiry which it proposes to unfold. Time becomes an aggravating factor here, for philosophical analogies are so intimately bound up with every form of discourse that their import can gradually make itself known. By that time these very images have had a hand in shaping our feeling for appropriate expression. So we are, it seems, inherently incapable of "getting a perfectly clear picture" of where it is we are being led. Add to this the inevitable shift in cultural concerns and context of interpretation from one period of history to another, and we have a picture of the nearly insuperable obstacles to critical philosophical inquiry.

We must rely on ways of posing the question in times past, for

2. In a clear and provocative paper that highlights many of the issues of this inquiry, W. B. Gallie argues that certain key expressions we must needs employ are *essentially contested,* such that no general method is available for monitoring their proper use, yet ongoing inquiry can discriminate among uses by helping us recognize one as more appropriate than another ("Essentially Contested Concepts," *Pro. Aris. Soc.* 56, (1955–56, reprinted in Max Black, ed., *Importance of Language,* Englewood Cliffs, N.J., 1962, pp. 121–46).

some of the virtues and the flaws of a problematic will come to
light only over a period of time and in confrontation with issues.
Yet we can never be sure of accurately reflecting the significance
of these past expressions; the charge of misinterpretation can
never completely be downed. Instead of directly confronting
these thorny objections, however, the inquirer can attempt to
turn them to his advantage. This is what I have tried to do by
tracing threads of similarity from one thinker to another, and
from earlier to later epochs. By proposing and discovering a
common theme, we may establish a kind of continuity and base
of interpretation; by accenting variations upon it, we can guard
against a rendering too artificially uniform.

Theology, finally, seems to demand another analogy with
opposing connotations to complement the one in use. Paradox
has been welcomed in theology since the earliest attempts at
expressing the inexpressible, the so-called negative theology. It
is usually conceded, however, that this is not enough. While the
air of mystery generated by the paradoxical affirmation of oppositions may help create an atmosphere, it could never lead to
knowledge, for the simple reason that the statements taken together are not coherent. Something more is needed. And this
we have seen consists of terms sufficiently empirical to be germane
to our experience, yet sufficiently resilient to be said of God.
These expressions comprise what Aquinas called perfections.
In the present account they have been found to include both
transcategorical and evaluative terms. Finding their foothold
more in human aspiration than achievement, no formula can
limit the range of application of these terms. They both allow
the demand that one's appreciation of their range and depth
grow indefinitely.

That is as close as we can come to a logical structure for these
expressions which fits them for use of God. But here too, when
the proper type of expression is settled on, correction may well
be called for, at least in the form of an extended commentary.
For any term will be freighted with cultural connotations and
descriptive affinities (like perfect itself, or magnanimous, wise,
and loving) which may lead us to confine God within certain

culture-bound, even idiosyncratic, features of experience. It is necessary then, that a properly theological predicate belong to the class of perfections. But this fact alone will not assure its propriety. For not all perfections will prove equally appropriate to the task. Nothing short of actually using them to do theology can show which predicates are to be preferred. So there is corroboration from the most difficult quarter for our recurring theme of this final survey: in no case does a procedure exist allowing us to pick out the right analogy before the actual inquiry has begun.

Hence while we have no right to speak of analogy as a device guaranteeing results in *any* quarter, we can speak of it as a family of techniques useful in leading us on to understanding in *every* quarter. And we must speak of analogy in this vein, if only to call attention to the openness and flexibility of inquiry wherever it is carried out. That there are different procedures for appraising, criticizing, and correcting analogies in different sorts of inquiry parallels a similar pluralism in methods of verification. That analogies are nonetheless useful to every sort of inquiry testifies to something about the world and about the language-user.

Furthermore, the ways in which we find ourselves employing analogous expressions exhibit something of the manner in which we participate in our language and in the world which that language lays open to us. The "fact" that the structural features of these expressions will not allow them to be taken in straightforward assertive fashion forces us to realize that something other than describing a relationship is going on when we use them. I have spoken of this other posture as participating, for that term has often been used to try to characterize those formal features of our situation which we cannot be said to be *related to,* since they constitute the very manner in which we can relate at all. As we might expect, 'participating' is an analogous term. So the only way in which we can elucidate its meaning is to put it to use. I use it here as a name for whatever it is that we stand to learn about ourselves as language-users as we try to understand what *this* fact tells us about ourselves and our world.

Index

Abstractive theorist: Scotus, not Aquinas, 115

Account: an analogous expression, in Aristotle, 46; reflective quality of, 134*n;* "criteria" for appraising, 157–60; always inadequate, 162; never quite clear about, 175

Act: of existing, 147–51; in context of persons, 151–53; not regularity, 152. *See also* Being

Agnosticism, 126, 127; Aquinas' excessive, 96; of definition, 128

Ana-logical: as supra-logical, 121, 242

Analogous concept, 191; foreign to Aquinas, 154; relative novelty of, 208

Analogous discourse: crucial maneuver in, 48; central issue of, 65; in Anderson, 200–02

Analogous expressions: and "common univocal core," 21; characteristics of, 23; distinguished from generic usage, 23; as a subject for "grammatical" analysis, 32; not restricted to intrasystematic function, 224; ubiquity of, 235; structural feature of, 236

"Analogously speaking": Aquinas' idiom, 121

Analogous terms: set off from univocal, 13; and primary analogate, 14; properly, as schematic, 16; adaptability to diverse contexts, 20; as the so-called transcendentals, 22; "explains" as an analogous term, 174; in Simon,

204; ubiquity of, 209; and appraisal terms, 212; and language user, 223; unique role of, in discourse, 223; and metaphorical language, 262. *See also* Analogous expressions

Analogous usage: formal explanations self-defeating, 19–20; Greek and medieval traditions, 22; distinguish from generic usage, 23; queer, 24; privileged instance in, 90*n*20; in Scotus, 109; justification of, 132, 244; question of, wrong-headed for Aquinas, 172; no unified theory of, in Aquinas, 198; and metaphor, in Simon, 204–05; different accounting of, and role, 208; demands judgment, 208; and decision, 244; and metaphor, 260–61

Analogous use: proper, no method of assuring, 242

Analogue(s): and common intention, 144; prime, man as locus of aspirations, 145

Analogy: won't work, 9; no theory of, in Aquinas, 170; no need for, 180; a family of techniques, 267. *See also* Analogous expression; Analogous usage

Anderson, James F., 12, 198; requirements for properly analogous discourse, 200–02; analogy proper, 253–54

Angels, 165–68; knowledge of, tricky, 165; not bodies, not God, 165; irrelevant to Aquinas' ontology, 167

Apostel, Leo: models in science, 20
Appraisal terms: 153, 216, 226–30,
    241, 256–57; and analogous
    terms, 212; presuppose a stan-
    dard 217; "inner differentiabil-
    ity" of, 256, 260
Attribution, analogy of, 13, 190
Austin, John, 133n29, 216; on
    traditional logic, 22; similarity
    as criterion of generic use, 23
Avicenna, 97; and being, 100, 105;
    and common nature, 179
Awareness: as knowing that, 152;
    as presence, 152; and judgment,
    160–61; not knowledge, not in-
    tuition, 161

Barth, Karl, 126
Being: not a common concept, 14;
    ways of, 14; in Aristotle, 83–
    86, 87; univocity of, 96; in
    Scotus, 99, 109–10, 179, 182,
    199; in Avicenna, 100; proper
    object of intellect, 100; intrinsic
    modes of, 101; not susceptible
    of definition, 104; primary ob-
    ject of understanding, 104; anal-
    ogy of, Thomistic idiom, 121;
    ground of, 129, 169; order in,
    130; regularities of, 130; a mere
    fact, 131; never appears, 131;
    not a feature, 131; analogy of,
    foreign to Aquinas, 154; com-
    munality of, 179; first and most
    common object of intellect, 181;
    said in many ways, 182; most
    certain notion, 184; part of every
    concept, 184; and concept, 191;
    as a perfection, 192; analogous
    usage of, and analogy of, 195–
    96; not an ordinary predicate,
    195; and "realistic metaphysics,"
    199; beyond genus and differ-
    ence, 216; in Heidegger, 237n;

"a thing" (= a "fact"), 238; as
    a superproperty, 239
Belief: and order, 39
Blanche, F. A., 12
Bochenski, I. M., 15–19
Boehner, Philotheus, 189n
Boethius, 136, 175n4
Bonhoeffer, Thomas, 142n40
Braithwaite, R. B., 212n
Brumbaugh, Robert, 42, 46n10

Cajetan, 21; on analogous predica-
    tion, 9–11; his plausability ques-
    tioned, 11–15; thrust of his
    work, 14; two recent salvage
    attempts, 15–20; target of recent
    critics, 120; case against, 122;
    and analogy of attribution, 190;
    inspiration of Thomists, 203;
    and analogy proper, 253
Carnap, Rudolph, 154–55, 158n,
    230
Certitude: demand for, in Scotus,
    180, 183
Chomsky, Noam, 209n11
Common formal properties: se-
    mantical and syntactical, 16–17
"Common intention": a metalin-
    guistic expression, 144
Common nature, 180, 188; and
    problem of universals, 173
Common notions, 69
Concept(s): common, 14, 110;
    formation (building), 103, 104,
    106, 107, 114, 181, 184, 188;
    simple, 103, 107, 110, 114, 181;
    composite, 103, 110, 114; as
    similitude, 109, 110; and 'term,'
    189; and word, 189; must be
    univocal, 191
Conscious activity, 151–53
Consciousness: reflective moment
    of, 134; Augustinian approach
    to God, 152

Context: decides appropriate use, 168; of language, 243
Contingencies, future: Aristotle and Aquinas, 137
Cornford, F. M., 42n7
Creation, 201; beyond human comprehension, 150; hidden element in Aquinas' philosophy, 150
Creator: one-who-explains-existence, 149
Crowe, Frederick, 80n, 162n

Decision(s): new usage introduced by, 148; according to W. Sellars, 155; and causal modalities, 155; and choice, 158n, 245-46; and values operative in discourse, 158; and statements about God, 164; and the status of analogy, 201; and linguistic role, 210; or option, 211-12; describing a, 212; using language analogously, 241; sufficient reason for analogous language, 241; and judgment, 241-51; must be responsible, 244, 247
Definition(s): perspicuity essential in, 72; real and nominal, 231-35
DeLubac, Henri, 134n
Descartes, René, 152, 181
Description, 219n9
Designation: and signification, 189n
Dialectic, 42, 248n; as dialogue, in Plato, 27; propaedeutic, how necessary, 49; double focus of, 52; beyond axiomatic accounts, 59; dispense with images, 59; moves in "pure thought," 59; not intuition, 65; uniqueness of, 65-66
Dialogic style, 68
Dianoia, 69; distinct from episteme, 44

"Dimension internal": and degree of analogy, 18
Discourse: unique role of analogous terms in, 223; inadequate, 239-40
Discovery, paradox of, 156
Doig, James, 174n
Doing, 155
Dunne, John S., 151n

Eikasia, 60n33
Emmet, Dorothy, 27-28, 209
Entity, as a self, 84
Episteme, 69; and dianoia, 44; an intuition of "the good," 45; irreducibly pluralistic, 70
Epistemology, of Scotus, 116-18
Equivocal terms, 218-22
Equivocity, 9; and metaphor, 71
Error, watchdog for, 178
Evaluative term: reflects a decision, 249
Execution: determined by self-awareness, not logic, 169
Existence: its brute "thereness," 129; and regularities, 130; a perfection, 147. See also Being; Existing
"Existential question," 167
"Existential turn": in Aquinas and contemporary Thomists, 147
'Explains': an analogous term, 174
Explanation, difficulties of, 413
Existing, act of, 147-51; demands to be explained, 148; not something we do, 148; what a man does—refuted, 148n54; said properly only of creator, 149; reflects need for intelligibility, 150; and analogy, 201. See also Being

Fact, linguistic, 218

Facticity: a mystification, 129; in Heidegger, 129*n*22

Falsehood, necessity of, 25

Feuling, D.: the mean, 78*n*8

"Flat constative," 216

Focal meaning, 83, 86, 87, 98, 99, 202; principle of, in Aristotle, 75; ambiguity in 88; precedence over analogy, 90; reference to one, 122; and proportionality, 126*n*18

Form: dramatic and literary, of the dialogues, 46–47; literary, and method, 48

"Form of laws," 158

Fulfillment: proper subject of, 140; demands for, and language, 163; personal, and "negative judgment," 163; anthropomorphic notion, 226, 227

Gendlin, Eugene, 260*n*

General terms: distinct from analogous, 22; as "problem of universals," 22; designate individuals, 188

Gilby, Thomas: "common good," metaphorically and negatively, 260–61

Gilson, Etienne, 99, 134, 179, 204, 244; analogy and judgment, 153–54; "vehemence for the abstract" in Scotus, 180

God: utterly transcendent, 95, 239; knowledge of, 104, 126–28; names of, 115, 197; unknown to us, 116; talk about, 125; "naming," peculiarities in, 125–34; improperly knowable, 126; outside of any genus, 126; total ignorance about, 127–28; being itself (*ipsum esse*), 128; ground of being, 128; to "describe," by causality, 132; as first principle, 132; meaning of term, undetermined, 132; fulfills demand for intelligibility, 134; problem of revealing himself in human speech, 136; problem of term used, 137; names of attributes of, significance, 138; terms of, denote perfections, 139; a move to, 145–46; what-explains-existence, 149; discourse about, 149*n*56; Augustinian approach, 152; concept of, inadequate, 164; speaking about, a decision, 164, 249; terms used of, negated, 164; unique among separables, 165; not a thing, 169, 237, 239; unique case of transcendent predication, 169; ways of speaking about, 178, 237, 238; attributes of, explanation of, 179; exists, problem of, 179*n*1; predicates used of, 206; and perfection, 231; and transcendentals and appraisal terms, 231; uncharacterizable, 231; and "the universe," 231–37; language about, ontological interpretation, 231–37; and everything, 235; and a pantheist, 236; transcendent cause, 236; cause of the world, 236, 237; language about, semantic interpretation, 237–41; to be, 239; "necessary existence" of, 239*n;* and fractured syntax, 240

Good: the peculiar pitfalls of, 38; better term than "order," 54; connotes affinity and attraction, 54; as ordering principle, 60; no account of, possible, 64; as analogous, 67

Grammar: defined, 32; "depth," of key expressions, 32

Hamelyn, D. W.: *eikasia*, 60*n*33
Hare, R. H., 156
Havelock, A. E., 54*n*
Hayen, Andre, 149*n*56
Hegel, 237
Heidegger, 237
Henry of Ghent, 96, 97, 191; self-defeating form of analogy, 104; theory of analogy, 117
Hesse, Mary, 18–19
Homōnuma, 69

Identity: a restricted similarity, 178
Illumination: in Albert and Alexander, 138
"Imitation" and "participation," 84
Induction, 87
Inquirer: affinity of and order, 41
Inquiry: Socrates' method of, 37–42; and intuition, 58; method of, 58–60; search for goal of, 65; manners that shape, 111; into reason for existing, 133; never ends, 135; role of perfections in, 147; into the *good*, 194
Insight: no schema can provide, 9; subjects analogies to discernment, 28
Intellect/will: breaks down in Aquinas, 141
Intelligibility: demand for, 147; requirements of, 153; of the whole, 167
Intendit significare, 139
Intent: and linguistic role, 210
Intentionality (*nous*), 178
Intuition: not Plato's answer, 45; as epistemological *deus ex machina*, 46; conflicts with method, 49; in Plato, 49–51; and inquiry, 58; knowledge by acquaintance, 114, 115; of value, and aspiration, 143
Isomorphy: Bochenski's criterion,

18; Apostel on, 20; approximate, 177

Jaeger, Werner, 71
John of St. Thomas, 97
Judgment: as composition, 107–08; true, in Scotus, 108; intellect and will engaged in, 153; appraisal and decision, 153; to recognize one account over another, 160; link between contemporary and classical, 160; and awareness, 160–61; negative, need of, 165; and order, 208; and analogous usage, 208, 251; and decision, 241–51
Justice, 61–63, 162–63

Kant, Immanuel, 121, 130, 256; critic of first-cause formulation, 132; critique of cause in Aquinas, 133; inspires an interpretation of Aquinas, 134; "regulative principles," 158, 235
Kierkegaard, Soren A., 78, 134*n*
Klubertanz, George, 119
Knights, L. C., 256*n*
Knowledge: scientific, irreducibly pluralistic, 70; distinct and indistinct, 105–06, 107; by abstraction, 114; by acquaintance (intuition), 114; relation to faith, 126
Knower, affinity between, and known, 174

Lessing, Gotthold E., 135*n*
Life: language, a form of, 121*n*5; 244
Logic: formal properties of, 16; formal function of, 20; limitations of, 20; fails with *one* and *unity*, 43; in Aristotle, 66; broad sense, 111; and grammar, for

Logic (*continued*)
  medievals, 136; execution not
  determined by, 169; and person,
  170; of genus with difference,
  182; life and language beyond,
  242; and language user, 242–52;
  presupposes ethics, 257
Logos: and language, 154
Lonergan, Bernard, J., 161*n;* concept formation, 123; judgment,
  153; "theorem of universal instrumentality," 236*n*
Lyttkens, Hampus, 119; appraisal
  of analogy, 164

MacDonald, Margaret: dangers of
  analogies, 24; different conception of language from Wisdom's,
  25–26
McInerny, Ralph, 119, 144, 203,
  208
Maimonides, 132
Man: as locus of aspirations,
  prime analogue, 145; originality
  to, and value, 145; to be, never
  merely being there, 151
Manuductio ("lead on to"), 122,
  134, 139, 206; and induction,
  89; key to naming God, 115
Maritain, Jacques, 12, 161*n,* 202*n6*
Mathematical proportion: not useful, also misleading, 10
Mathematical ratio: merely equality, 185
Mathematician: as inadequate, 42
Mathematics: as ordering prin-
  ciple, 78
Maurer, Armand, 187*n*
Meaning: and use, 162–65; and
  use in community, 211; and ac-
  tion, 211
Menges, M. C., 193*n;* univocity in
  Ockham, 191*n35*
Mens: in Augustine, 142*n40*

Metaphor, 185; metaphor and
  analogy, 27; selecting an appropriate, 28; and categories, 30;
  and myth, 59–60; in Aristotle,
  71–75; Aristotle's views, ambivalent, 71; master of metaphor,
  sign of genius, 72; no place for
  in dialectical disputation, 72;
  perspicuity in use of, 72–73;
  and simile, 74; ubiquity of, 178;
  distinct from analogy proper,
  201; live and dead, 204; and
  analogous usage, 205; most
  prominent of figures of speech,
  215; and "crossing sorts," 220–
  21; domesticated and sedimented, 221; unique and irreplaceable role of, 254–55, 257–
  58; and world views, 258; and
  correct usage, 259
Metaphorical analogy: distinct
  from analogy proper, 253
Metaphysician: not an answer-man
  for Aquinas, 173
Metaphysics: ways of speaking
  peculiarly apt for, 15; and analogy, 27; and essential natures,
  175; and structure of language,
  175; adequate pursuit of, impossible, 175; and certain knowledge, 184; analogy, key to, 200
Method: of dialectic and of hypothesis distinct, 44–45; or intuition, 45–46, 49–51; in Plato,
  45–46, 49, 59; and literary form,
  48; of inquiry, 58–60; metaphysical, and form of question,
  176
Mill, John Stuart, 87
Model(s): in scientific theory, 18;
  scientific, purpose-oriented, 20;
  role in language, 216: indispensability of, 242; challenges
  accounts of scientific theory,

252; prevalent in scientific discourse, 253; analogies functioning as, 264; points up relevant dimensions of object, 264
Modes, intrinsic, 101, 181–82, 193n
Modes of speech, 197–99
Mondin, Battista, 119
Move: to inquiring about God, 134, 145–46
Muskens, G. L.: classifications of analogy, 79
Myth, 28, 87; and metaphor, 59–60

Name, 108–09; analogous, 110; representation of elements of reality, 113; designates in a certain manner, 138
"Negative judgment": rejects formulation, 164
Neo-Platonism, 167
Nettleship, R. L., 52n20
Nominalism and hyperrealism, 186
Noun(s): common, and metaphorical use, 257
Nous (intentionality), 178
Novak, Michael, 242n33
Nowell-Smith, P. H., 217n5

Object: affinity of inquirer and, 41
Objections, relevance of, 160
Ockham, William of, 185–93
"One": "The One," as "unity," 40; in Aristotle, 85
"One formula," 191n34
"One word, one meaning," 102
Ontologists, easy way of, 130
Order: and belief, 39; as the good, 39; burden of all the dialogues, 39; consistency, manifestation of, 39; found in reason, 39; in mathematics, 39; avoids narrow moral connotations, 54; demands for, and language, 163; and usage, 206; and judgment, 208

Ordering principle, 55–56
Owen, G. E. L., 71, 90; "focal meaning," 83, 85
Owens, Joseph, 83–84

Paradox, 24–27; of discovery, 156; and negative theology, 266
Paronyms: and modes, 110
"Participation", 267; and "imitation," 84
Penido, Maurillo Teixera-Leite, 12, 203n6
Perfection(s): senses of, 139–40; resists an accounting, 140; tied to fulfillment, 140; undeveloped in Aquinas, 142; inner dialectic of notion of, 145; Scotus and Aquinas on, 180; and being, 192; absolute, 207; working notion in Aquinas, 257; used to do theology, 266–67
Person: as paradigm for nature, 144; and conscious activity, 151–52
Phelan, G. B., 148n54, 202n6
Philosopher: "true nature" of, 64
Philosophical anthropology, 141–44; and epistemology, 127; and Wittgenstein and J. L. Austin, 127n; and ontological formula, 145
Pieper, Josef, 150
Pierce, C. S., 47, 143, 155, 161n; secondness, 129; limits of discourse, 231; Doing, death of pragmatism, 245n35; on volition and decison in inquiry, 247–48; logic presupposes and ethics, 257
"Playing a role": more than doing, 155–56
Poet: master of metaphor, 72
Predication: analogous, as mathematical proportion, 9; divine,

Predication (*continued*)
98; analogical, 124; analogous, and structure of predicate terms, 137; God, unique case of transcendent, 169
Preller, Victor, 223*n*11; real and nominal definitions, 235*n;* decision, 242*n*33
Presence: and awareness, 151–52
"Principle of order" (or "order"): translation of *ton agathon,* 39
Proper proportionality, 12, 205, 208; and ana-logic, 121; difficulties encountered in, 122; as paradigmatic for analogy, 124; and metaphorical analogy, 253
Proportion: = *analogia,* 52; and metaphor, 74; and simile, 74; in Aristotle, 74–75; in Aquinas, 75; in Plato, 76; schema of, 82; and attributing perfections to God, 117
Proportionality, 99; device for normalizing ambiguous usage, 10; improper, 11; a bag of tricks, 13; analogy of, and univocity, 200; in Simon, 203

Quality: not relevant in mathematics, 44
Question: Aquinas on form of, 111; manner of asking and answering, 111; difference in style of, 130; "which will not down," 211, 223
Questioning: limits of, 135
Quine, W. V. O.: role of logical schemata, 224*n*12
Quod nomen designat: and *modus quo,* 138

Ratio communis, 225
Recognition, 89*n,* 230; of needs, and language, 163

Reference: and sense, 188
Reflection, 134
Regularities: and existence, 130
Relevance, 18, 177; judging, and "seeing," 59; of objections, 160; and similarity, 176–77; and evaluative language, 210; and propositions and internal properties, 226*n*
Res/modus, 136–39, 162, 164, 178–80; in Boethius, 136; in Scotus, 136, 199; in Alexander, 138; Aquinas rejects or curtails, 139, 163, 198, 251*n;* in Ockham, 186; in Anselm, 234
Resemblance, 131*n;* proportional, 203
Ross, James, 15–19, 89*n*
Ryle, Gilbert, 42; "the One" as "unity," 40

Sayre, Kenneth M., 158*n;* decision and choice, 245
Say/shown, 197–99
Schema: designedly "empty of content," 16
Schemes: priveleged set of expressions, 224–25
Science: unifying multiplicity, 70
Scripture: metaphorical expressions of, 167
Self-awareness: determines execution, 169
Sellars, Wilfrid, 154–55, 242*n*33; linguistic role, 210–11; dot-quotes, 224*n;* empirical knowledge as rational, 248*n*
Sense: and reference, 188
Separables: and language, 165; unique status of God among, 165
Separation: as against abstraction, 164
Sewell, Elizabeth, 258*n*

Show/state: function of philosophy in Wittgenstein, 258

Signification: primarily designation, 189n

Similarity: and common formal properties, 17; vacuous criterion of generic usage, 23; in dissimilarity, 72, 177, 185, 242, 243; relevant, 75; or analogy, 108–10; proportional, 124, 200–02; many kinds of, in ordinary talk, 125; need to look for, 134; structural, insufficiency of, 144; formulae of, between God and creation denied, 164; weak form of sameness, 176; in Ockham, 186–88; and reference, 192n; proportional, 200–02; and irreducibly analogous, 210

"Similar to", 176; irremediable circularity of, 14; weak form of "equal to," 75; entire spectrum of uses of, 125

Simile: distinct from metaphor, 73

Similitude: single, not proportional, 14; utterly gratuitous at times, 15

Simon, Yves, 12; ordered usage, 202–08

Skepticism: "knowledge that" leads to, 131n

Smith, John E.: "knowledge that," 131n; "Dialectic gone mad," 148n54

"Something": manner of talking about any object, 113; a mere index, 113; no conceptual content to, 113

"Something common": and analogy, 19

"Sort-crossings," 220, 259

Standard: presupposed in appraisal terms, 217; denominated from its role, 219n9; and elucidation,

226n; and appraisal term, 227; and evaluative language, 250; and unambiguous formulation, 250

Statement: and proposition, 194

Structures, linguistic: and personal awareness, 174

Sunōnuma, 69

Surprise: distinguishes metaphor from simile, 73

Sylvester of Ferrara, 12, 203

Taylor, A. E., 43n

Term(s): transcategorical, 95, 222–26; aspects of the world, 108, 110; meaning of a, 115; systematically ambiguous, 133; "used analogously," 154; how related, 172; of evaluation, analogous, 209; chance-equivocal, 218; equivocal-by-design, 218; defining, 220; division of, inadequate, but favorable, 254

Tillich, Paul, 132; similarities with Aquinas, 129

Ton agathon: as "principle of order," 39

Transcendental (terms), 95, 243; do not specify being, 182; loses definite meaning, 222–23; meaning relative to inquiry, 223; not restricted to intrasystematic function, 224; and metaphysical inquiry, 226; inability to account for, 255–56; "inner differentiability" of, 260

Truth: in Scotus, 108; Ockham's criterion for, 188n33

Turbayne, Colin, 258n

Understanding: as seeing in Scotus, 122; of recognition, 158

Unity: in Parmenides, 42; scheme of, 225

Universals: problem of, 172; and *common nature*, 173; and metaphysical reflection, 174

Univocal terms, 70, 144, 218; division of, and equivocal, 71

Univocity, 129, 191n35; of being, 96, 104, 179; betray analogy, 110; and analogy, 182; three degrees of, 186; and analogy of proportionality, 201; distinguishing features of, 218

Usage: new, introduced by decision, 148; a demand for order, 165; as a drive to know, 165; ordered, 202–08; Aquinas' working concern for, 208; nonevaluative, possible, 209; univocal and analogous, 218–22; univocal and ordinary, 218–22; generic, 254–55

Use: and meaning, 162–65; and mention, 197; versus formulation, 197–98; and meaning, 211

Value: inner affinity with man, 140; enters the world with man, 141; measure of man's fulfillment, 141; and man, 144

Verbs, "consignification" of, 136

Vision: Plato's model of, objected to, 45

Wahl, Jean, 43n

Wells, Rulon, 210n

William of Ockham, 185–93

Willing, and question of intelligibility of existence, 141

Wisdom, John, 209, 244; *Philosophy and Psychoanalysis,* 24–27; and MacDonald's conception of language, 25; and Plato's view dialectic is dialogue, 27; objection to, 27; utility of paradox, 27

Wit: and metaphor, in Aristotle, 220

Wittgenstein, Ludwig, 28, 122, 133, 134, 177, 185, 209, 220, 222, 238; and philosopher's statements, 26; selecting and appropriate metaphor, 28; effect of *Investigations,* 29; use of 'kind,' 114n54; and analogous usage, 123; selecting an idiom, 143; language idling, 149n54; "playing a role," 155, 157; laws and forms of laws, 158; wary guide on general terms, 218; diverse usage of language, 219; propositions, properties and relevance, 226n; subtleties in general terms, 230; formation of general terms, 254; *Tractatus* contra *Investigations,* 258

Wolfson, H. A., 71n

Wolter, A., 102, 103

Word(s): unit of meaning, 102, 104; denote things, 179; and concept, 189; name things, 199

Zemach, Edy, 218n